Published by Ockley Books Limited

First published December 2020

ISBN 978-1-910906-23-1

Layout & design by Michael Kinlan, front cover by Steve Leard

Printed & bound by:
Biddles Printing, King's Lynn

WALL OF SPORT

STEVE HILL

OCKLEY BOOKS
.com

"Reaches levels of interesting I could only dream of."

STEVE DAVIS

"Steve Hill conclusively proves there isn't
more to life than watching sport on TV."

NIGEL ADDERLEY, TALKSPORT

"A true multiscreen experience - have device, will watch,
any sport, any time, any place. A marathon run at a sprinter's
pace sustained by wry humour and infectious enthusiasm."

JONATHAN LEGARD, BBC

"If anyone can convey the humour in the utter futility that is our
obsession with watching sport at every possible opportunity, it is
Steve Hill. A read more entertaining than much of what he spent
his time watching. First class."

DAVE POWELL, LIVERPOOL ECHO

"The tone of voice is matter of fact, but the sarcastic
acceptance of his fate is very funny."

JAMES BROWN, LOADED FOUNDER

ABOUT THE AUTHOR

Steve Hill is a widely published journalist who lives in North West London and watches a lot of sport. His previous book, The Card, was nominated for the William Hill Sports Book of the Year 2018. He rarely mentions it.

TWITTER: @HILLYTHEFISH

FOR HER INDOORS AND THE BOY

2018

MONDAY JANUARY 1ST

Wake up. Time to drive. Destination Guiseley aka Gizlee. Towelling myself off, a cursory perusal of BT Sport on the iPad reveals that Western Sydney Wanderers are 2-1 up against Melbourne City in the A-League, Australia's 2018 sporting calendar already under way. Sport never sleeps.

Melbourne scorer and former Leeds United player Ross McCormack is substituted, and I vaguely remember him lobbing the Watford keeper at a game that I attended with the owner of the house I have just woken up in. McCormack does't know it yet, but before the year is out he will briefly play alongside the fastest man on earth.

Leaving Watford Gap in my rear-view mirror, I drive alone, wearing a garish Chester FC smock, the car eating the M1 on the first day of the year. I successfully navigate Leeds, the chunky satnav of yore now replaced by the vastly superior Google Maps, which had been sitting on my phone all along, silently awaiting activation.

The car radio is enthused with the prospect of a fresh year of sport sprawling ahead, filled with limitless possibilities. It begins with live commentary of the Premier League early kickoff, Brighton versus Bournemouth, the South Coast non-derby. Transferring the commentary to headphones, I optimistically wander round Gizlee looking for a chippy, on New Year's Day. As I cross the road, I hear a goal, which means I've missed a goal. Abandoning my fanciful quest for chips, I continue following the match on the pub TV, a full-blooded 2-2 draw between the South Coast non-rivals providing a tasty start to the year.

It's the usual pub, the usual away faces, except one. But for the second season running I am joined by Leeds fan Seffers, a sympathetic Chester supporter for the day. And we really need sympathy. Mired in a National League relegation dogfight, anything less than a win today will see us staring into the abyss with little chance of salvation.

Sheltering in a rudimentary stand from the mandatory rain, remarkably a victory seems within the realms of possibility when we take a first half lead. It's a lead that we maintain until ten seconds before the end of the game, conceding an equaliser deep into injury time, a proverbial kick in the balls and punch in the face, the entire day ruined for the sake of ten bastard seconds.

Back in the car, I emit frequent and vociferous bursts of foul and abusive language. Mild distraction is provided by driving past signs for Pudsey, former home of the late, great darts commentator Sid Waddell. I wistfully recall the time that I played pool with him in Las Vegas and how he punctuated every story by punching me hard on the upper arm. Drew 2-2.

With pleasing symmetry, I make it back to Watford Gap in time for a prime seat in front of the PDC World Championship Darts Final, aka the Sid Waddell Trophy, live from Alexandra Palace. Watching it in the kitchen in eye-watering Sky Sports HD, I also treat myself to a National League side dish of Bromley 4-2 Ebbsfleet on BT Sport on my phone, pondering the horrific possibility that had Chester been selected for live coverage, I may have had to miss the darts.

As usual, I have watched pretty much every dart of the tournament, remaining in thrall to the sport ever since 100-1 Ipswich farmhand Keith Deller memorably vanquished the peerless Eric Bristow in the 1983 final, with Waddell in overdrive on commentary. I once enthusiastically shook Deller's hand at Ally Pally and told him that he was the reason I was here today (at the darts, not on the Earth).

Bristow begat Taylor, the master eventually vanquished by his pupil, who went on to become the greatest of all time, an unrivalled reign that finally ends today. Astonishingly, despite announcing his retirement earlier in the year, Phil 'The Power' Taylor has hauled himself into the final for one last hurrah, looking for a staggering 17th World Championship title. In his way stands debutant Rob 'Voltage' Cross, a former electrician who has undergone a meteoric rise in the last year. Upstairs, The Boy is crying for me to put him to bed, but this is the World Darts Final. This boy can wait.

There are no scripts in sport, and there is no dream ending for Taylor. Cross elevates his game to almost supernatural levels, unerringly finding trebles and doubles, with The Power visibly reeling from the onslaught. An old warrior's last stand, the aging behemoth is felled by the young buck amid emotional scenes. It's the end of an era, if not necessarily a changing of the guard. Time will tell, but Cross appears to be the real deal, and his fairytale victory is arguably on a par with Deller in '83. Whatever happens, we will never see the likes of Taylor again. And with any luck, I'll never have to interview him again either.

TUESDAY JANUARY 2ND

Following an extended festive tour, we are finally back home in time to watch Swansea v Spurs on my big bastard telly. Despite a proper upbringing, The Boy has been got at by a cousin and now thinks that he supports Spurs. If I attempt to quell this aberration it might make it worse. Instead, I am playing the long game in the hope that he will eventually see the light at the end of Bumper's Lane.

A shrewd observer of the game even at this young age, The Boy proffers the opinion that Swansea play in white because swans are white. He may have a point. It's a foul evening in South Wales and Spurs take the lead with a clearly offside goal, thus rendering the result and the entire Premier League redundant. If only there were some way that the referee could be assisted, perhaps by video. Spurs score a fortuitous second near the end of the game and The Swans' goose is cooked.

WEDNESDAY JANUARY 3RD

The relentless daily onslaught of televised football continues. What now? Arsenal v Chelsea? IN. The festive period is traditionally berated for the abnormal workload that it puts on the players. Never mind the players, what about the viewers? I'm going blind here. In the event, it's a ding-dong-do, a thrilling 2-2 draw with all the goals coming in the last half hour.

There's a change of pace later on as we go to from North London to South Australia for the Sydney test, the fifth and final instalment of another dismal Ashes tour. As I do whenever I see him on screen, I recall the time that Alastair Cook shook my hand, a great moment in a great batsman's life.

I have previously watched entire away Ashes series live (on TV), but the timings are crippling, even for nocturnal me. Instead, I retreat to bed to follow the action live on Test Match Special – headphones in, missives from the colonies, a secret world unfolding under the covers.

THURSDAY JANUARY 4TH

Anyway, Happy New Year. A World Cup year, the best kind of year. Several of the future squad are on show tonight in the Premier League as Spurs take on West Ham in this never-ending festive feast of football. Didn't we just watch Spurs? Due to their new stadium being under construction, the game is being played at Tottenham's temporary Wembley home. We can see the Wembley arch from our house, an impossibly thrilling spectacle, like a Bat Signal summoning us to the television. The game is less exciting, a torpid first half consigning The Boy to the land of nod. As such he misses a pair of stunning long-range, second-half goals, the only highlights of an inconsequential 1-1 draw.

At 3:50am I find myself watching a cricket ball being measured in Australia, which doesn't seem a particularly good use of my time. I have been intermittently watching test cricket since the 1980s without really having the first idea of what's going on. Having never played the game to any kind of standard, I don't even really know the field positions and refuse to take the couple of minutes required to familiarise myself with them. This may explain why I often prefer listening to cricket than watching it, an abstract experience vaguely comparable to the shipping forecast: Dogger, Fisher, German Bight, Cow Corner, Point, Silly Mid-off...

FRIDAY JANUARY 5TH

A quick check on Perth v Adelaide in the A-League then we're into the Ashes highlights plus a touch of the South Africa v India test. The BBC is peddling winter sports on the Red Button ahead of the Winter Olympics, so I dip into a bit of live bobsleigh and skeleton World Cup. Sliding down a chute headfirst on a tea tray is patently not a sport. The wonder is not that it is done well, but that it is done at all. That said, apparently Latvia's Martins Dukurs is the man to beat.

With five hours until kickoff, this will have to do. To increase the excitement, I watch it in splitscreen with the cricket as India begin their innings. I've got tickets for two days of England v India at Trent Bridge in July. They've been forced upon me and I don't really want them, primarily because there's nothing I like less than spending my own money. It also seems too far away to comprehend, a fantastical dream of short sleeves and cold lagers, a world away from sitting indoors in bleak midwinter seeking sporting titbits.

Meanwhile, the BBC continues to groom me for the godforsaken Winter Olympics. Despite the early favouritism, Dukurs comes a disappointing fifth, with Korean Yun Sung-bin victorious by four tenths of a second. What a time to be alive.

Mercifully, the main event finally ticks over as the FA Cup third round begins in earnest, with Liverpool v Everton live from Anfield in crystal clear BBC One HD on Freeview. There's late drama as Liverpool new boy van Dijk heads a dramatic winner to dispatch the Toffees 2-1 and crush the blue half of Merseyside, a cruel throwback to when they used to meet in the final.

SATURDAY JANUARY 6TH

Ebbsfleet United away finally lures me out of the house, a long-distance fixture for The Mighty Chester, but vaguely local for me, albeit via a ludicrously expensive train with the added jeopardy that if you fall asleep you wake up in France. I've seen us play here before, although I believe the home team were then known as Gravesend & Northfleet.

With no pubs within reasonable walking distance of the ground, the clubhouse it is, where we watch the early FA Cup third round game on what appears to be a re-purposed office monitor, while sat on swivel chairs, presumably a job lot in some kind of fire sale. Fleetwood draw 0-0 with Leicester, Jamie Vardy unable to play against his former club in a wretched game. The Evertonian turns up with his son, sadness in his eyes when I mention the previous night's result. Offering a sliver of hope, Chester sneak an unexpected 1-0 win, prompting a hint of trouble after the game.

Heading back to London, I met up with Ipswich fan Bealesy, fresh from reporting on Millwall v Barnsley for Soccer Saturday. We head to the preposterous Café Football in Westfield Stratford, where I count 16 TV screens, all showing Norwich v Chelsea, another tiresome FA Cup goalless draw to sandwich the 1-0 National League win. Goals, goals, goals...

Following a bout of unnecessary speed drinking – "it's not a cup of tea" – I make it home for Match Of The Day's FA Cup highlights. First up is Premier League Stoke's 2-1 defeat at League Two Coventry. Technically a shock, if an unmemorable one, it signals the end of Stoke boss Mark Hughes's reign, the first managerial casualty of the year. The football segues into the cricket, which in turn segues into blackness as Morpheus takes me into his gentle arms (I fall asleep stinking of ale).

SUNDAY JANUARY 7TH

The FA Cup weekend continues apace, in my case in the bath on the iPad. While the hallowed third round is traditionally fêted for throwing up shocks, these days a shock would constitute a Premier League club fielding a full-strength team and actually attempting to win the game, and indeed the competition. Unless there's a particularly cavernous gap between the two clubs, nowadays if a team is knocked out by a side from a lower division it's generally downgraded to an 'upset' rather than a bona fide shock.

I also check in on the BDO World Darts Championship, a slew of familiar faces returning for their annual shot at the big time, presumably preserved in aspic for the remainder of the year. Meanwhile, in a non-shock, Lionel Messi scores for Barcelona. At one point I have three screens on the go. I briefly look out of the window at the local gym, for which I have been sent a free pass as part of the annual treadmill of guilt and shame.

The BDO finishes early so I watch a repeat of Big Cliff Lazarenko v Eric Bristow from 1986 on my phone during Match Of The Day's FA Cup highlights while waiting for the cricket. The road to the Superbowl is shortening by the day and I attempt to watch an NFL Wild Card game, but can't get my head round it.

Thousands of miles away, the England cricket captain has shat himself. Joe Root is apparently suffering 'stomach trouble' as the team attempt to bat all day in order to secure a 3-0 defeat. Mindless. Sleep.

MONDAY JANUARY 8TH

I gaze wistfully out of the bedroom window at the gym and then make the careful and considered decision to watch the BDO darts in the bath. Canada's David 'Excalibur' Cameron is taking on the wiry young German, Michael Unterbuchner, in the preliminary round. Hilariously, some of the crowd are wearing David Cameron masks – the failed Prime Minister, not the darts player, or indeed the former Chester City striker.

The clatter of dart on board sounds so much cheaper than the exquisite thud of the PDC counterpart. Nevertheless, it's an absolute thriller, the German taking it in the final set, signalling my cue to get out of the bath and rejoin the human race. Or at least watch the next match downstairs.

Apropos of nothing, The Boy announces that he wants to be a You-Tuber and a footballer so he can make a trillion pounds. With one eye on the latter, he's signed up to Charlie Merson's Soccer School, which in winter takes place in the sports hall of a nearby school. Taking a stint in goal, at one point The Boy pulls off a double save worthy of Jim Montgomery in the 1973 FA Cup Final.

Sat on a gym bench watching the action with the other parents, Chelsea Dad fills me in on the latest in the Mourinho/Conte tabloid spat, of which I have little or no knowledge or indeed interest. A battle of words between the current and previous Stamford Bridge incumbents; apparently one of them has been criticising the other's hair. The game's gone.

I'm back home in time to watch the FA Cup draw live on the BBC, forgetting to bemoan the fact that it was better on the wireless at Monday lunchtime. The reward of a trip to Middlesbrough awaits the winners of improbable rivals Brighton and Crystal Palace in the Monday night game, in which VAR is available. In the event it's not used as Brighton nick it 2-1, with a late Glenn Murray goal securing a trip to his native North East.

I inadvertently sleep through the darts, waking to see Darryl 'The Dazzler' Fitton win with a 170 checkout and then announce that he needs a hip replacement. What a sport. Shifting continents and time zones, I toy with the New Zealand v Pakistan One Day International before briefly watching Johanna Konta lose in Sydney. And so to bed. To listen to the Ashes.

TUESDAY JANUARY 9TH

As tradition dictates, I wake up in time to watch the darts in bed on the ancient portable TV, now incongruously on Channel 4 following decades at the Beeb. After the Lord Mayor's Show that is the PDC, the BDO is considered a poor relation these days. But it used to be the only game in town, Lakeside providing a Mecca to the beer-swilling greats still associated with this most noble of sports. Traditionally the first major sporting event of the year, it has been scorched onto the nascent calendar for decades, as representative of early January as bitter cold, discarded Christmas trees and intense paralysing depression.

Martin Phillips of Wales is playing today, or as he's known in our house, my dad's bin man. It's a particularly literal soubriquet, earned due to the fact that my dad has a house in Wales for which Phillips is the bin man (as well as other houses, it's not a bespoke service). When he's not throwing arrows, he's throwing rubbish, presumably with a long-standing arrangement that he'll need a few days off every January.

Meanwhile, the National League continues apace, but sadly Fylde away is out of my radius of attendance on a Tuesday night. Instead, I am glued to the club's free radio commentary while keeping an eye on Manchester City v Bristol City in the first leg of the Carabao Cup semi-final.

In the big game, Fylde predictably take the lead, but a Chester equaliser sends me into a frenzy, a physical sensation triggered by someone in Lancashire kicking a ball into a net. Everything else is a blur and I catch sight of myself in the mirror, a feral mess, virtually in spasm in response to this slice of minuscule good fortune.

The Man City score is a mere footnote, although for what it's worth they snatch a late winner to save face, 2-1. Meanwhile at Lakeside, Unterbuchner makes it through to the next round, dumping out third seed Jamie 'Yozza' Hughes in a dramatic fifth set tiebreak. On the other side of the world, Heather Watson wins a tennis match at 2:20am our time.

WEDNESDAY JANUARY 10TH

Groundhog Day. The Unterbuchner shock continues to reverberate throughout the world of darts, and my bubble bath. He will now face the bin man Phillips in round two, but who will be taking out the trash? Elsewhere, former champion and Dorset farmer Scott 'Scotty Dog' Mitchell is gone. He's not dead, he's just been knocked out of the Worlds, free to concentrate on chasing livestock instead of doubles.

Football never stops, but I manage to sleep through Chelsea 0-0 Arsenal in the first leg of their Carabao Cup semi-final. I also miss reigning Lakeside champion Glen Durrant beating Darryl Fitton, as former champion Scott 'Scotty 2 Hotty' Waites also makes it through. In further darts-based action, I flick on Bullseye to see the non-darts player throw exactly 101 to win a car, one of the most extraordinary things I've ever seen.

Stumbling across Carabao Cup highlights on Channel 5+1, the action – or lack of – confirms that sleep was a better option. Meanwhile the VAR arguments continue apace as host Colin Murray compares it to Brexit.

THURSDAY JANUARY 11TH

11:47am: darts in bed. "You're obsessed", hisses Her Indoors, somewhat prophetically. What else am I going to watch? The Boy is claiming illness and has commandeered the iPad. As such I have to resort to watching the darts on my phone in the bath. It's not ideal, but it's a sacrifice that I am prepared to make for this sport and this championship.

Anyway, it's only the Youth Final. They are children, but already imbued with the countenance and build of seasoned darters, the Dutch lad van Tergouw resembling the Augustus Gloop of the oche. Astonishingly he picks off a 170 – ten times his age – on the way to steamrollering his opponent. Like all great drama there's a back-story, and it transpires that he lost his dad at the age of six. The sight of his mother weeping sets me off. Quarter past one in the afternoon and I'm blinking back tears over a fat lad from Utrecht. What a sport.

The action continues apace, with Lakeside fixture Deta 'The Dark Destroyer' Hedman making progress in the women's tournament. In the men's, Jim 'The Quiff' Williams conquers Conan 'The Barbarian' Whitehead, a game that The Boy discovers me watching from the safety of the day bed. I also watch a repeat of England's final Ashes demise, which confirms that Jimmy Anderson was given out despite not hitting the ball, thus invalidating the entire series, and the sport.

Resuming the darts downstairs, The Boy says that Trina Gulliver looks like Arsène Wenger. Nevertheless, she generates a victory against Dutch temptress Aileen de Graaf. Come on Aileen. And finally, the Bin Man is gone, banished back to Wales by the devastating Unterbuchner.

Daddy's been watching darts all day. Not left the house, not even to put the bins out.

FRIDAY JANUARY 12TH

Welcome back to Lakeside. The Boy is downstairs watching a blue-haired YouTuber playing video games for money. I make him a second cereal and inform him that I'm going back to bed to watch darts. He calls me lazy. Anything but - it's the best of nine sets.

And all nine are contested as Scott Waites finally overcomes Andy Baetens in what is described as "one of the greatest comebacks we've ever seen at Lakeside". The Belgian, who missed match darts, is almost in tears.

And in a clash of the titans, multiple champion Trina Gulliver MBE is dispatched by glamorous Ellesmere Port-based Russian, Anastasia Dobromyslova. Arguably the perfect woman, Dobromyslova is personable, attractive, good at darts and lives near Chester.

In the final match of the afternoon session, Middlesbrough fan Glen 'Duzza' Durrant comes from behind to beat The Quiff and promptly pledges his future to the BDO. Meanwhile, I pledge my immediate future to foraging for food, taking advantage of the break in play to do a quick Sainsbury's run. I return in time to see Lisa Ashton take down The Dark Destroyer to set up a final with the Russian Princess.

Some football finally breaks out, of sorts, with the Sheffield derby reaching half time without a shot on target. Unlike the darts, where an epic battle ensues between Unterbuchner and Richard Veenstra, the Bavarian stick insect versus the wet-permed Lowlander. On the cusp of victory, Unterbuchner undergoes some kind of meltdown that is cruel to watch, enabling the Dutchman to force a decider. But seemingly re-animated, the German takes the final set for victory, later revealing that he has a mental coach. As the Steel City derby finishes goalless at Bramall Lane, the next quarter-final is arguably even more epic, with Mark McGeeney beating Welsh roofer Wayne Warren in a tiebreaker amid talk of fatigue.

I should coco. Apart from the Sainsbury's run, I have now been watching darts for 12 hours. When I close my eyes, I see a board. I must sleep, for Essex awaits.

SATURDAY JANUARY 13TH

East Thurrock United away in the FA Trophy. This is how I live. Originally intending to drive to deepest, darkest Essex alone, I somehow manage to convince Her Indoors and The Boy to join me. As well as the pleasure of their company, crucially this means that I can get driven home after the game – win or lose, we'll have some booze; if we draw, we'll have some more. Skirting the top of the capital, the scenery goes from residential to industrial and eventually rural.

Parking near the ground, we traverse an ancient churchyard to the nearby village pub. The usual faces are in, except for one, a massive away day prompted by the chance of taking a step closer to Wembley. In the event, debutant Gary Roberts is sent off, we lose 1-0, and striker Ross Hannah swears at a kid, an incident that I extrapolate into a newspaper column that pays for my day out. I'd still rather be in the FA Trophy.

We get back home to find the second men's darts semi-final locked at 2-2, Mark McGeeney leaning back at the oche to counteract his burgeoning gut. It's a technique that pays off as he finally ends the run of the brave Bavarian. Remember the name: Michael Unterbuchner. The German Pob.

With McGeeney securing his place in tomorrow's final, I accidentally see the score of the previous semi, a brutal reminder that sport should always be watched live. Durrant has beaten Waites and will contest the title. I manage to salvage something with unseen footage of the afternoon's women's final, with Lancashire's Lisa Ashton downing the Russian Princess. Fuck it all.

It's been a long day, and I sleep through Channel 5's EFL Goals before rallying for Match Of The Day, then the NFL, then the cricket as England's ODI series gets under way at the Melbourne Cricket Ground. Been there. Twice.

SUNDAY JANUARY 14TH

Two weeks after Phil Taylor threw his last competitive dart, we're back at Ally Pally. This is the day in the sporting calendar that darts segues seamlessly into snooker as the historic Masters kicks off at its relatively new home following years at Wembley Conference Centre. In front of a packed palace, Mark Williams and Mark Selby open proceedings with a frame that is so shit it results in a re-rack. Elsewhere, England have astonishingly won some cricket overnight and Sanchez hasn't travelled to Bournemouth.

It's a perfect storm of sport including a gripping BDO final that sees Glen Durrant retain his title. Meanwhile in the Premier League, Bournemouth beat Arsenal and in a mesmerising match Liverpool overcome Manchester City 4-3.

There's barely time to breath and we're into more snooker. Keeping an eye on Nantes v Paris Saint Germain on my phone; sensationally the ref kicks a player: Man Bites Dog. The NFL playoffs are under way, with one game described as among the greatest in history. I won't remember it. There's also the small matter of the U-19 Cricket World Cup as England take on Namibia. More NFL: The Vikings are moving on. And of course, at midnight the Australian Open Tennis begins, bookending a 24-hour sporting day. I can't cope.

MONDAY JANUARY 15TH

For marketing purposes, this is apparently the most depressing day of the year. As it transpires, it's fairly grim – news breaks of the untimely passing of Cyrille Regis, pioneering footballer and erstwhile Chester City legend. RIP Big Cyrille.

Following Saturday's debacle, I torture myself further by listening to the FA Trophy draw on talkSPORT, with our dismal exit in East Thurrock described as a shock. Not to anyone who was there. In the event we dodge a trip to Spennymoor, famously the home of former referee George Courtney, when such information was mandatory.

Ding v Day in the snooker signals bath time. Then we're back to Charlie Merson's Soccer School, where Chelsea Dad peruses the England fixtures with only 149 days to go until the World Cup. Saints Dad reveals that he was at Vicarage Road at the weekend, where he and his young son were thrown out of the Watford end for celebrating a Southampton goal, then generously relocated in the away end.

Back home for the snooker, Day dicks Ding and Trump trumps Wenbo. Meanwhile, Man United maul Stoke. I can't commit to the Australian tennis at this early stage. Spotting Sharapova, I recall the time I refused to have my photo taken with her as she was taller than me. Presumably still is.

TUESDAY JANUARY 16TH

Time for a bit of Ronnie O'Sullivan in the bath (me not him). Multiple world champions Stephen Hendry and Steve Davis discuss his appeal. Inevitably someone in the crowd shouts, "Go on Ronnie!". Perversely, I haven't always been a fan, but as the greats have dropped out of the game I have come round to Ronnie as he is simply the best and most watchable player, often on a different plane to the indistinguishable automatons on the circuit. In a sea of beige, he is the man in black, the Picasso of the baize. And a colossal moaner.

Within minutes he secures the first frame with an effortless century. And another! Dennis Taylor correctly observes that "we're watching a genius at work". Davis goes one further, describing him as "shamanic", "unnatural" and even "upsetting".

With a lot of snooker you occasionally look up at the action. When Ronnie is playing you can't look away. Marco Fu may as well have sent a body double. Still in full flow, Davis compares him with Tiger Woods, Roger Federer, even Tommy the Pinball Wizard in so much as he is at one with the table. As for the man himself, following a rapid and comprehensive victory, Ronnie says he had a virus and feels dizzy and doesn't care if he wins.

The manner of victory is so swift that it's all over before I can get in front of the big telly, and I almost feel short-changed. I'm not exactly shy of sport, however. India v South Africa rumbles on allied to an evening session of further snooker, FA Cup replays and even a touch of French football. At one point I find myself watching five different screens, like a sporting version of The Man Who Fell To Earth.

Ten days after their turgid draw, Leicester dispatch Fleetwood in a game that will enter the history books for featuring the first goal in England to be awarded by VAR, following a borderline offside decision. Remember the name: Kelechi Iheanacho. It's a deferred celebration, but a celebration nonetheless. A goal is a goal is a goal.

With the FA Cup games wrapping up, I listen to extra time commentary of West Ham v Shrewsbury, the Premier League side squeezing out a 1-0 win to avoid potential penalty embarrassment. In the midst of this, back at Ally Pally, Kyren Wilson turns over Barry 'The Hawk' Hawkins 6-4 in a thriller that regretfully I am unable to give my full attention. Likewise the Australian Open, where Great Britain's Kyle Edmund is in action. No Murray, no hurry.

WEDNESDAY JANUARY 17TH

Settling into the routine of 1pm snooker, it's Sean Murphy versus Ali 'The Captain' Carter, so named due to carrying a pilot's licence. With the afternoon school run cruelly interrupting the action, I simply press pause on the iPad and continue from where I left off, a world away from the VHS 80s of snooker's prime.

Following their stultifyingly dull goalless draw, Chelsea and Norwich are at Stamford Bridge to settle it, with kickoff delayed by 15 minutes. With time to fill, talk turns to the late Cyrille Regis. It makes for difficult viewing as Dion Dublin breaks down in tears at the loss of his friend and mentor. He is consoled by Alan Shearer of all people, in a rare show of humanity. It may be the first time I've ever had any respect for him, apart from when he made me a cup of tea.

It's a dismal first half, and I dip into Higgins v McGill, locked in a Caledonian tussle at the palace. Meanwhile, PSG are scoring at will, notching eight without reply against Dijon – couldn't cut the m-m-m-mustard...

Chelsea appear to be going through, but a last-minute Norwich equaliser condemns me to extra time, including two red cards. Penalties now, with the Premier League side finally victorious and Norwich fans running for their train.

On the other side of the world, Johanna Konta is out of the Australian Open. England turn over Bangladesh. All is quiet, not even a mouse. Fuck mice.

THURSDAY JANUARY 18TH

It's Ronnie day. Gusts blow outside, but all is still inside the palace where the king continues his reign. He's up against the fiery Northern Irishman, Mark 'The Pistol' Allen. For the second match running, Ronnie owns up to a foul. What a sport. Imagine that happening in football. At 3-1 down Ronnie starts missing easy shots, plummeting helplessly to the ground in the turn-based tightrope walk that is professional snooker. It's all over before the school run. Ronnie: gone! As ever, it's a huge loss to the tournament and crucially, my entertainment.

I bump into Chelsea Dad, who tells me that he left Stamford Bridge in the 93rd minute at 1-0 up, thus missing the Norwich equaliser and the subsequent extra time and penalties. Amateur night. Never leave early.

In a rare break from sport, I venture to Shepherd's Bush to watch comedy duo, The Scummy Mummies, who I know. One of their dads is Jossy out of 80s kids TV show, Jossy's Giants, and he immediately asks me if I can name 16 players to represent both Chelsea and Arsenal. I get a few of them, as he continues to canvas all-comers.

Back home, I attempt to watch a recording of Wilson v Williams in the Masters. Asleep within seconds.

FRIDAY JANUARY 19TH

7:30am, not at my best, I listen to cricket amid fitful sleep until the snooker. I have to leave Trump and Murphy to it as I pick up The Boy from school and drive to Birmingham, where Her Indoors is on Strictly business and has a hotel room. I take The Boy to Pizza Express, where the astonishingly slow service enables me to watch Higgins v Day to a conclusion on my phone. I still don't know the Trump v Murphy result and am looking forward to holing up in the hotel and watching it on catch-up. Strolling past BBC Birmingham, a news ticker informs me that Trump fought off a comeback, referring to the flamboyant Bristolian cuesmith, not the beleaguered American President. Thanks, that's my evening ruined. I watch it anyway, chased down with a repeat of a goalless draw between Derby County and Bristol City. These are the good times.

SATURDAY JANUARY 20TH

I drive to Chester with hope in my heart and have it summarily rammed down my throat by a desultory 3-1 defeat to Gateshead. Fuck Gateshead. I manage to get back for Football On 5 presented by Caroline Barker, who I once briefly met at The Non-League Paper Awards. Pure showbiz.

I fall asleep during Match Of The Day and head to bed for the snooker semi between Trump and Wilson, passing out during the deciding frame. I sleep-listen to the entire 3rd ODI, a series for which I still have no visual cue, although I imagine it involves men hitting a ball with a bat. BT Sport offers a replay service in which they clearly display the score thus rendering it entirely redundant. Mindless.

SUNDAY JANUARY 21ST

I attempt to catch up with the snooker as Trump capitulates, leaving me to squeeze in the Higgins v Allen semi with the final almost upon us. I speed-watch it on iPlayer at double-speed. I don't need commentary as I'm listening to The Fall. It's an imperfect method as unless it goes to a decider you can generally gauge who is going to win by how long is left.

Kyren Wilson speeds through to face The Pistol in the final. A tense affair, at one point Wilson is distracted by an audience member's phone. The referee orders the offender to be thrown out, and is greeted by cheers from the baying crowd. Wilson then asks for him not to be thrown out, and is greeted by cheers from the sympathetic crowd.

It's a solitary Super Sunday game: Southampton 1-1 Spurs. Who cares? Me, presumably, as I dutifully watch it.

I'm losing touch with the Australian Open – almost an invisible tournament due to the time difference – although I manage to catch a glimpse of Nadal pulling pink shorts out of his arse crack. He had his photo taken with me once, and as such I consider him a close personal friend.

The snooker wraps up with a first Masters win for Mark 'The Pistol' Allen, no doubt celebrated long into the night. Not here, as Match Of The Day 2 sends me to sleep meaning that I miss the end of the Patriots win. Hauling myself to bed, the final Superbowl place is contested by Vikings and Eagles. It could happen.

MONDAY JANUARY 22ND

On the school run The Boy helpfully points out: "You're getting grey hair. Can you do some exercise to give you stamina?". Seems unlikely, although with his words ringing in my ears I force myself to do a hugely unpleasant 20 lengths at the nearby dipper.

Despite the risible pseudo-science of the marketing skunks, this is arguably the real Blue Monday, the first of the year without the safety net of snooker or darts. Instead, thoughts turn to the azure courts of Melbourne where Djokovic – The Terminator – is struggling in a first set tiebreak with Chung. Jon McEnroe on commentary brings back memories of the 1980 Wimbledon Final versus Bjorn Borg, the first tennis match I have any genuine recollection of watching, in so much as I know where I was geographically, in what room and where the TV was.

Today's fare is less memorable, and indeed largely unwatchable due to a kit clash. How hard is it for tennis players to wear a different coloured shirt? It's soon all over as Djokovic limps out of the tournament 3-0, citing injury.

As if to exacerbate the vacuum left by the lack of snooker and darts, this is the day that the BBC broadcasts Indoor Bowls. Not for me, Jeff – that is where I draw the line. Obviously if I watched it, I would almost certainly get into it, but there have to be standards.

Sad news filters through from the world of football, which is mourning the loss of legendary player and broadcaster Jimmy Armfield. Out of respect, the Wembley Arch is poignantly lit up in the tangerine of Blackpool, where Armfield played his entire Football League career.

Live on Sky Sports, Swansea beat Liverpool and the earth continues to turn. Seeking late night thrills, I turn to New Zealand where England are taking on Australia in the U-19 Cricket World Cup. It's a thankless task as we as we collapse at the hands of a flaxen-haired leg spinner called Lloyd Pope, who is already drawing inevitable comparisons with Shane Warne, another close personal friend, and the only person I've ever interviewed who later remembered me, or at least pretended to.

There is further English interest down under in Melbourne where Kyle Edmund is taking on the Bulgarian, Grigor Dimitrov. Sadly they're both dressed in pink so I can't tell who is who and hence refuse to watch it. And so to bed. At least I managed to not watch the bowls.

TUESDAY JANUARY 23RD

Edmund has done it, victorious overnight. But it's bad news for my buddy Nadal, who retires injured. They're dropping like flies in what is technically a non-contact sport. Despite my best intentions, I have a quick look at the Indoor Bowls mixed doubles final, but find it too confusing.

The evening revolves around multimedia coverage of Chester's 1-1 draw with Hartlepool, which garners less coverage than Manchester City squeaking past Bristol City to secure a place in the Carabao Cup Final. Some kind of energy drink, apparently.

WEDNESDAY JANUARY 24TH

South Africa are trouncing India in the bath – not literally, of course. Transfer deadline day is approaching and with a week to go, Sky Sports are already working themselves into a frenzy at the prospect of some employee administration.

By way of respite I watch Wrexham 2-3 Arsenal on my phone in HD, taking a minuscule slice of deferred pleasure from a 40-year-old FA Cup tie. Back to the future, and in Australia Federer rips through Berdych 3-0. If anyone can stake a claim to be a GOAT, it's Federer.

Settling in to watch the second Carabao Cup semi, my phone chirrups with six letters that change everything: RIP MES. Mark E Smith, the iconic leader of The Fall, the only group that matters, has died. It's not unexpected, but it's a blow that overshadows all sport. Arsenal beat Chelsea 2-1, but I watch it on splitscreen with 6Music, which plays all Fall all night, out of respect. As midnight approaches, Gideon Coe reads out my email.

THURSDAY JANUARY 25TH

Edmund loses early doors down under. Who cares? I couldn't even tell you what he looks like. I'm only really arsed about Murray and he's not there. He was there in Melbourne 2011 when I attended my only professional tennis tournament, having to sit through the previous match in order to ensure a seat to watch Murray knock some Bulgar about. It wasn't even the first time I'd hung around for him. A few years prior to that, I waited for three hours in a freezing multi-storey car park in Soho in midwinter for a monosyllabic unused interview with the then teenage star. Showbiz.

Back to this evening and there's no proper football on, although I do manage to find a bit of Club Brugge v KV Oostende in the Belgian Pro League on a new self-explanatory channel called FreeSports.

As for my own club, news breaks that due to gross financial mismanagement, Chester need to raise £100,000 simply to stay in business. Not again...

I've lost interest in the U-19 cricket, plus the big boys are in action in the 4th ODI. It's not a great start as they are soon 4 for 3 (or 3 for 4) and then 8 for 5. I continue the carnage in bed on TMS, lapsing into unconsciousness in seconds. It's Australia's day on Australia Day.

FRIDAY JANUARY 26TH

In a very watered-down Likely Lads scenario, I attempt to avoid the ODI result by watching India v South Africa in the bath. I finally track down ODI highlights on BT Sport. Unsurprisingly, England have lost, but only just.

It's a more clear-cut affair in the FA Cup, live on the BBC, with Yeovil succumbing 0-4 to Manchester United as I spend the entire match pissing about on my phone. Improbably, my back still hurts from my impromptu 20 lengths on Monday. Fuck swimming.

A BBC trailer for the forthcoming Winter Olympics claims "the fearless are here". Good for them. I'm straight into the Darts Masters on ITV4, live from Milton Keynes. World Champion Rob Cross is safely through, 25 days after his historic victory. Next up: Alan 'Chuck' Norris v Peter 'Snakebite' Wright. Here comes the weekend, the weekend is here...

SATURDAY JANUARY 27TH

The Australian Open Tennis women's final is under way so I listen under the covers before grabbing a screen for the final few points as Wozniacki squeaks past Halep. Not a clue. Whatever happened to that lovely Martina Navratilova? Where is Chris Evert Lloyd? Is Jo Durie still playing? Who's afraid of Virginia Wade?

More pressing matters are afoot. The beleaguered Chester FC have a tricky away fixture at relatively nearby Maidenhead. It's a full family outing, with Her Indoors and The Boy along for the ride. Due to the club's desperate financial situation there's a whip-round in the pub. I begrudgingly donate a fiver. I don't see why I should bail them out having spunked thousands of pounds travelling thousands of miles to watch them over the years.

As well as the usual faces, we are also joined by a friend of Her Indoors plus young son, neither of whom have ever been to a football match. It's a rude awakening as the Chester Zombie unleashes an eye-watering torrent of arse gas, interspersed with foul and abusive language largely directed at the home goalkeeper and his mother.

It's arguably worse on the pitch where we have a man sent off early doors and succumb to a 3-0 pasting. Tired and emotional, I let Her Indoors drive me home and awake at midnight for a bit of England U-19 v Bangladesh U-19. Presumably due to a technical issue there is no score on the screen, thus rendering the action largely abstract.

I take solace in a recording of the FA Cup Match Of The Day. It ends with footage of the famous occasion when Mark E Smith read the football scores. It breaks my fucking heart.

Test Match Special in bed for the 5th ODI. The blackness comes swiftly.

SUNDAY JANUARY 28TH

The ODI is still going, and I savour the last knockings of a thrilling England win largely orchestrated by young Tom Curran. The Guardian app ruins the tennis by blatantly informing me that Federer has won the Australian Open, thus securing an astonishing 20th Grand Slam. What a GOAT.

Spread over the entire weekend, the FA Cup trundles on, now unofficially a reserve team competition. In darts terms it's like the BDO compared to the PDC of The Premier League. A real shame.

There is of course actual darts on ITV4, and World Champion Rob Cross – who watched the tournament last year – is knocked out by the Serbian-born Austrian Mensur Suljović. A tricky customer, I once saw Mensur give James Wade a decent game at the palace on the same night that England secured the Ashes in Australia. True story.

This cavalcade of sport means that I don't make it downstairs until 3:30 pm, only hunger driving me out of my horizontal reverie. I actually toy with the idea of going to Milton Keynes to watch the darts, but rapidly come to my senses. In the event it's an all-Dutch final, as Michael van Gerwen overcomes Raymond van Barneveld in a thriller to trouser 60 grand. No Blue Monday for MvG.

The darts pleasingly segues into Match Of The Day, which in turn yields to the U-19 Cricket World Cup. England lose to Bangladesh, and Australia clinch victory over Afghanistan at 3:44am.

MONDAY JANUARY 29TH

Another Monday in January. Fuck this life. I would go swimming again, but I need a haircut. It's actually a fairly barren sporting schedule, although amazingly England U-19s have a 7th-place playoff to contest.

In an attempt to fill the sporting void, I watch the darts-themed episode of Minder, titled Broken Arrow. Arthur Daley claims that darts is respectable now as "it's on BBC Two". Mainly set in the back rooms of dodgy pubs, the episode features some astonishingly poor special effects, with the darts simply appearing in the board as presumably this was easier than getting someone to throw a 180.

In the evening, we're back at Charlie Merson's Soccer School. Merse Junior is staunchly anti-VAR, berating another Salah dive with the suggestion that if it was a penalty, you would have to give a hundred per game. To punctuate his point, he rips a shot into the net with some venom.

Shockingly, there's no football on the box tonight so no structure to the evening. What am I supposed to do? Play online poker, I suppose. I win $31.44 while succumbing to the U-19 cricket as India beat Pakistan, again at 3:44am. I'm absolutely fine, thanks.

TUESDAY JANUARY 30TH

Finally, the Premier League is back on the box. This is more like it, a bank of screens, my happy place. Huddersfield take on Liverpool on BT Sport while in the Championship, Sheffield United are up against Aston Villa on Sky. As is often the case with multiscreening, I don't really watch any of it, but it's nice to know it's there. And to further prove that I am in control, I don't even watch the U-19 cricket 5th-place playoff. Shove it.

WEDNESDAY JANUARY 31ST

It's finally Deadline Day and Jim White is already going off his napper on talkSPORT, at one point appropriating MC Hammer in an ill-advised rap. The German Masters snooker is also under way, live from the Tempodrom, already reduced to a background sport.

A number of so-called chain transfers are hanging in the balance, like buying a house. Sky Sports News attempts to enliven proceedings with a barely-clad female presenter. Live from the make-up room, Jim

White appears, eating a sandwich in his trademark yellow tie. It's a tiresome charade, the novelty of which has long since worn off, essentially basic admin elevated to the status of high drama. Nothing really exciting has happened since Peter Odemwingie drove to QPR and they left him in his car. And of course the time at Everton when a Sky Sports reporter was accosted by a massive purple dildo.

No such entertainment is proffered this year, and besides there is an actual match on the box, Tottenham v Manchester United at Wembley, which prompts The Boy to check the veracity of the arch from the kitchen window. I watch the second half in bed on my phone and promptly fall asleep, briefly aware of Harry Redknapp banging on about something or nothing. I awake to the minute for the start of a midweek Match Of The Day, one of the more illicit thrills of the sporting calendar.

January is over: stick it in the books. I think about leaving the house.

THURSDAY FEBRUARY 1ST

Pro Bull Riding on FreeSports is a step too far, not least for the bull. Furthermore, somewhat snookered, I have yet to get a handle on the German Masters, another made-up event shoehorned into the relentless cue sport calendar.

Back in England, it's a big day in the North as tonight sees the first game of Super League XXIII, a beast-based affair between Warrington Wolves and Leeds Rhinos. Neither creature is indigenous to the respective towns, and this is little more than a crass Americanisation of a traditional sport. They might as well be playing Seattle Jellyfish.

Anyway, fuck rugby league. Tonight's main event is the return of Premier League Darts, a hugely successful addition to the traditional tungsten tour. Contrary to popular belief, darts isn't just for Christmas. The greatest trick that Sky ever pulled was taking the arrows to the provinces, filling vast arenas with pissed-up locals, gleefully pouring gallons of fizzy muck into their heads while bellowing at a couple of blokes slinging darts on a distant stage.

Without the darts, it's basically a televised beer festival, and tonight's opener comes from Dublin's fair city. It's introduced by the venerable Dave Clarke, who accurately describes the Premier League as "16 weeks of darting mayhem".

Clarke was in the off-strip Vegas bar – BJ's – where I played pool with Sid Waddell, but I didn't speak to him. When we landed back at Gatwick, he bade farewell to Sid as he retrieved his baggage. Referring to The Circus Tavern, Purfleet, then home of the pending World Darts Championship, Clarke uttered the immortal line, "I'll see you at the upholstered sewer". Naturally I made a mental note of this description and successfully recycled it in print.

Darts has long since crawled out of the sewer, and tonight's opening fixtures are played in a 13,000-capacity arena. But we are now living in the post-Taylor era. An ever-present since the inception of the Premier League, and multiple winner of the event (him not me), I was there when Taylor beat James Wade in the 2010 final at Wembley Arena. In an extraordinary sequence of events, finals night actually took place a day later than intended due to a power cut in the Wembley area that left thousands of darts fans stranded outside the venue.

I was among the diminished crowd that returned the following night, but I had to nip out to watch England play Mexico at nearby Wembley Stadium before they headed to the South Africa World Cup. Sprinting back to the darts on the final whistle, the final was underway and I was devastated to learn that Taylor had thrown a nine-darter. In a remarkable night that saw darts fan Stephen Fry join Sid in the commentary booth, astonishingly The Power threw another nine-darter to make darting history. As Sid said: "I cannot believe my goggling bins."

Back in Dublin, it's not just The Power that is missing. Tonight, for the first time there are no walk-on girls, a massive blow for those who prefer their hairy-arsed darters to be accompanied by glamorous assistants. Formula One may have garnered the headlines for its equivalent purge, but political correctness has also struck at the heart of the rarefied world of darts, despite no perceptible protests. Reader, James Wade married one of them.

As well as providing incongruous eye candy, there is a suggestion that the glamorous assistants were also there in case any player was too drunk to find the stage, a role now taken by a pair of comedy bouncers. Either way, the ban is rendered largely pointless by the appearance of scantily-clad dancing girls on the stage, who greet the players with a rudimentary cheerleader routine.

As for the darts, presumably still seething, Michael van Gerwen steamrollers bewildered debutant Rob Cross 7-2 to exact a modicum of revenge for his World Championship defeat; MvG a memorable scalp en route to the title for the former electrician.

It's a long night of darts, but there's still time for a touch of the German Masters, where I find Mark Selby in trouble against Xiao Guodong. On the stroke of midnight, the Jester from Leicester is gone. As am I. Up the stairs, mister.

FRIDAY FEBRUARY 2ND

No warning, we're straight into the Davis Cup, some kind of ancient international tennis competition that Great Britain recently won for the first time in centuries. On the portable, in bed, it's not going so well today, and allied to the GB defeat is unfamiliar sunlight that burns my retinas through the tiny screen.

In search of respite, I talk to my Google Home Mini and make a brief foray into the netherworld of talkSPORT2 to discover highlights of last night's Premier League Darts. It's finally happened - darts on the radio.

The evening's entertainment is Bolton Wanderers v Bristol City, but I struggle to care. Briefly flicking over to rugby league, it seems to consist of squat northern men bellowing "Move!".

The German Masters snooker is more suited to the late-night vibe, and in a marquee match, Trump overcomes Ding. Still seeking thrills, I delve into the U-19 Cricket World Cup match between Australia and India. To really ramp up the tension, I put a free £2 bet on Australia, which is a waste of free money, and my life. Under the covers, I attempt to watch India's innings on the Betfair app. Rain stops play.

SATURDAY FEBRUARY 3RD

Some kind of T20 tri-series is underway, and TMS broadcasts Australia beating New Zealand as cricket overlaps the various time zones, a permanent summer for those involved. Looking out of the bedroom window, it's a vile day here, yet people are still doing sport as far as the eye can see. There is no Chester game today so no real structure to the proceedings, just an ad hoc dribble of relentless sport. I retire to bed for Football Focus where Spurs boss Pochettino reveals that he is a big Game of Thrones fan, and that his favourite book is Aldous Huxley's Brave New World. What access.

Meanwhile, it is revealed that Man City have spent more on their defence than 52 countries have spent on their military defence. And following the week's sad news, there is a tearful tribute to Big Cyrille.

I begrudgingly watch Burnley v Man City in the bath then back in bed, but foolishly miss the Burnley equaliser by watching U-19 cricket, Australia's Pope being sprayed all over the infield.

The Davis Cup goes up against rugby union on Freeview, whereas in the snooker Dott v Murphy is moving on apace, with the reedy-voiced Scot 3-2 up as Kilmarnock beat Celtic 1-0 on my phone. By the time Final Score comes around, Dott is through and we're into Arsenal v Everton versus France v Ireland in splitscreen. Briefly surveying the egg-based action, The Boy surmises that "in rugby you basically get a headache every second". Ireland score a drop-goal after phase 38, sparking feral scenes.

Match Of The Day segues into a Superbowl preview, where it is a chilly minus 20 degrees in Minneapolis.

SUNDAY FEBRUARY 4TH

Cricket's Big Bash is finally over, for both the men and the women. Good – no interest. I manage ten minutes of the A-League match between Brisbane and Melbourne City then sleep until the dying throes of the Davis Cup. I struggle with Palace v Newcastle as I have to source a child's birthday present, so am forced to listen to the match on my phone, returning for the last knockings of a 1-1 draw including an unseen Jonjo Shelvey shirt pull, thus rendering the game void.

In the egg world, ITV show Italy 10-17 England at the Olympic Stadium, Rome. Any footage of the Olympic Stadium always brings back memories of when I sprinted onto the pitch in an orange bib to buff Ian Wright's head following England's qualification for World Cup '98. Similarly, a touch of Caen v Nantes on the iPad reminds me of standing in the away end with the Bordeaux fans mainlining industrial strength weed through an impromptu bog roll bong.

For once, Super Sunday is actually fairly super, and Liverpool v Spurs takes the big screen, relegating rugby to the iPad and French football to the phone. Salah immediately makes it 1-0, the Egyptian currently being commemorated in a Soccer AM-endorsed song that has all the longevity of The Wealdstone Raider non-phenomenon. For the record, it goes a little bit like this: "Salah/Ba-ba-ba-ba-ba/Mane Mane/ We've got Firmino/But we sold Coutinho."

The last ten minutes of the match is bedlam, and when the dust settles it's a 2-2 draw. I've lost track of the godforsaken German Masters, but as tradition dictates, Sunday night is final night, and Mark Williams is all over Graeme Dott like a soup sandwich, 6-1 then 7-1 up. As The Boy shrewdly points out: "snooker is cruel because you just need to watch your opponent smash you until they miss. At least in football you can get the ball off them." It finishes 9-1, with The Pocket Dynamo failing to live up to his secondary nickname: 'Pot The Lot' Dott. It might only be the German Masters, but it's a rare title for the genial Welshman.

The road to the Superbowl is long and ultimately pointless if you think about it. But first, Match Of The Day 2, minus Mark Chapman who is in Minneapolis for the big one. I join them in the dead of night for what is an extraordinary game between the New England Patriots and the Philadelphia Eagles. At one point, Patriots quarterback and poster boy Tom Brady, is sacked, providing a defining image of him throwing air, incredulous that the ball is no longer in his grip.

My associate, The Watford Gap, phones during the half-time Timberlake show, safe in the knowledge that I'll be up, deep into the early hours of Monday morning. Eagles overcome the odds to triumph 41-33 in an event for which a 30-second commercial costs $5m. But I had two quid on The Eagles at 7/4, so who's the real winner?

MONDAY FEBRUARY 5TH

The Boy is skiving school, but makes a miraculous recovery in time for Charlie Merson's Soccer School. Chelsea Dad relates the tale of his mate leaving his house ten minutes before the end of Liverpool v Spurs, thus missing three goals and a penalty save. Tit.

I make it home for Monday Night Football, Watford v Chelsea. I barely watch it, but manage to catch the goals plus a cheeky winner for Genoa at Lazio in the Olympic Stadium, scene of probably my greatest pitch invasion.

It's now only four days until the Winter Olympics, as Eurosport has been reminding us for a month. I watch the Superbowl highlights. Some game.

TUESDAY FEBRUARY 6TH

A relatively barren schedule sees Bayern Munich 4-0 up at Paderborn in the cup. Closer to home, Swansea are at home to Notts County in an FA Cup replay on BBC One in a half-empty stadium. I'm almost tempted by Lincoln City v Chelsea U-21 in the previously unacknowledged Checkatrade Trophy. In the more established FA Cup, The Swans are 4-1 up at half time and eventually crush their lower league opponents 8-1. Eight bloody one!

Lincoln win their tie via the short-lived and much-derided ABBA penalty shootout system, securing a Wembley final and prompting a pitch invasion. In the Checkatrade. The game's gone.

WEDNESDAY FEBRUARY 7TH

In the T20 highlights, England suffer what is described as "a collapse of epic proportions".

In the evening I attend a local pub quiz with other school parents. One of the rounds requires us to name Football League clubs beginning with W. One of my team-mates suggests Wycombe Abbey. Another has a stab at Westfield. Unsurprisingly, we don't win. I get back for FA Cup replay highlights of Tottenham Hotspur 2-0 Newport County at Wembley.

THURSDAY FEBRUARY 8TH

This is a low. The Snooker Shoot Out on ITV4, live from the Watford Colosseum. Played under a disco ball in short sleeves, it's a like a youth club has been given a new snooker table. The crowd are even encouraged to chant during play. Ray Reardon must be spinning in his grave.

"Beep beep beep", goes the shot clock. "That's annoying", says The Boy, speaking for all of us. "It's getting on my nerves."

With ten-minute matches, it makes for good betting, although you may as well have a punt on the toss of a coin. Despite the madness, Jimmy White goes through: Go on Jimmy! Another close personal friend, I have interviewed The Whirlwind multiple times. He even turned up for a few of them, most memorably having to be prised out of Spearmint Rhino to a pub over the road, insisting on taking a brace of strippers with him and disappearing into a cubicle to "speak to my solicitor" before the photoshoot.

Thursday night means Premier League Darts, and the circus has come to the Cardiff Motorpoint. Still struggling to come to terms with his newfound status, World Champion Rob Cross is on the wrong end of a 7-1 pasting from Simon 'The Wizard' Whitlock.

In the early hours, the Winter Olympics jumps the gun with a touch of pre-ceremony curling and figure skating: not a sport.

FRIDAY FEBRUARY 9TH

Despite the relentless publicity campaign, I have somehow conspired to miss the opening ceremony of the Winter Olympics. Good. Opening ceremonies are tiresome, as indeed are closing ceremonies. Most ceremonies, basically.

Back in Watford, the Shoot Out continues apace, like a macabre scientific experiment. Presumably the audience are shipped in from somewhere, or perhaps guarded overnight. It turns out that the Winter Olympics opening ceremony is still going; I rewind to the money shot of the lighting of the torch, an extraordinary flaming protuberance rising from the depths to consummate its icy recipient. A remarkable political moment, it dramatically captures the power of sport, even eclipsing the disco ball at the Watford Colosseum.

Millwall 1-1 Cardiff in the Championship provides a pre-cursor to the curling, although the skiing is delayed due to snow. There's also some impressive snowboarding, an activity I have actually attempted in four separate global venues, with little success.

I take an early night for the cricket. On talkSPORT, a man is attempting to identify cat food, dog food, and a Fray Bentos pie. We are through the looking glass.

SATURDAY FEBRUARY 10TH

Hurrah! Team GB has its first gold medal, in some kind of skiing event. Go Team GB, you big-toothed Home Counties whoppers. In actual sport, England have suffered a cursory T20 defeat.

Leaving the televisual safety blanket behind, I step blinking into the daylight and find myself on a train full of Barbour jackets bellowing about Twickenham. I won't be joining them. Me and my Barbour are heading for Woking to see Chester endure an inevitable defeat in another shit sandwich of a season.

As usual, I meet some faces in Sovereigns. In an absolute travesty of a decision, Spurs v Arsenal is jettisoned in favour of the rugby match between Ireland and Italy at the behest of a ruddy Celt in industrial orange legwear.

Chester inevitably lose, 1-0. Back in Sovereigns for England v Wales in the rugby, I switch to O'Neill's with some lads to see England win, although I find myself drawn towards Dagenham & Redbridge v Aldershot in the National League on another screen. Stumbling to the station, I catch a glimpse of Man City 3-1 Leicester in a pub window. I couldn't help myself.

Piling onto the sofa for Channel 5 Goals, the last thing I remember is Bristol City 3-3 Sunderland, described as 'The Miracle of

Bristanbul'. Awaking at 11:45pm, this gives me five minutes to restart Match Of The Day on iPlayer then pause for snacks. These are more or less virgin matches, results unknown, and I drink them in.

Figure skating is still not a sport, yet still I watch.

SUNDAY FEBRUARY 11TH

I manage the second half of Huddersfield 4-1 Bournemouth on my phone. Still the Snooker Shoot Out continues. The Winter Olympics whiteout hurts my eyes. Propping up two iPads at the end of the bath, I sink into Newcastle v Man United plus the Snooker Shoot Out.

Back on dry land still goalless, and we're straight into the Six Nations, Scotland v France, with a choice of three European football matches on my phone. When am I supposed to eat? Her Indoors demands that I put the Winter Olympics on. She hates all sport, yet will happily watch someone slide down a snowy mountain on a pair of planks.

It's one of those bewildering Sundays with three Premier league games, kickoff times uncertain. Somewhere in the midst of this, Scotland beat France at rugby. The audience at Watford Colosseum are almost ready to be released back into society. In a thrilling final, Michael Georgiou fights off a late surge from 'Pot The Lot' Dott to claim an unlikely victory as I keep an eye on the National League highlights. It's a busy Match Of The Day 2, and we're back into the curling.

MONDAY FEBRUARY 12TH

Half term? Sake. For reasons unknown I find myself at a museum looking at a fatberg – quite disappointing, not very big. Repairing to the nearest pub, I instinctively face the TV where Federer is winning something or other, then Sky Sports News keeps me abreast of matters while I am out of the house.

I mercifully rectify this abnormality, and return home to sleep through the second half of Chelsea 3-0 West Brom. With the T20 to come, I bide my time with curling and snowboarding, giggling childishly at the Slovenian boarder, Tit Štante. Bed.

TUESDAY FEBRUARY 13TH

I catch a tiny snippet of the T20 on TMS, the mere tone of voice enough to suggest that it's bad news.

In an unprecedented second consecutive sojourn out of the house, I attend a pop concert by the beat combo British Sea Power in Camden with my Watford-supporting associate, The Watford Gap, who has travelled down from Watford Gap.

It's fucking great, and we get back in time for highlights of the Champions League first leg, result unknown: Juventus 2-2 Spurs, an absolute ding-dong-do. We also have a look at Basel 0-4 Manchester City in splitscreen with men's curling, as GB beat the Swiss in an extra end. Scenes. I retire to bed to listen to this morning's cricket. The skating can figure itself out.

WEDNESDAY FEBRUARY 14TH

Winter Olympics all afternoon. Cold outside, cold inside. The Champions League comes thick and fast, and Porto v Liverpool takes pride of place on the big TV, with Real Madrid v Paris Saint Germain on the laptop, where a BT Sport pop-up ruins the score. And again. I switch to the non-enhanced player in an attempt to stem the ruinous score flashes. A quick look at the two-man luge: idiotic.

I wolf down a Valentine's meal in open play, reduced to listening on 5live as The Boy kicks a ball against the kitchen wall in his new boots. Once he's in bed, I head upstairs to watch highlights of the games I've just watched, with ITV fielding a strong front three of Pougatch, Keane and Dixon.

This delivers me almost seamlessly to my midnight appointment with the women's curling, bewitched by captain Eve Muirhead: those eyes, that mouth, barking unintelligible instructions at her Caledonian charges. Four years is long enough to forget the rules, and I pass the time entertaining elaborate fantasies.

"Stone's in the house."

"Drop the hammer."

It's basically Scottish women with mops, shouting at each other. What's not to like? At one point, Muirhead drops a clearly visible "Fuck sake!". In a big shock, USA win the game. Fuck sake.

With the clatter of sticks in my ears, I lapse into unconsciousness listening to commentary of Canada v USA in the women's ice hockey, while providing Her Indoors with unwanted score updates: 2-0 Canada, latest. Happy Valentine's Day.

THURSDAY FEBRUARY 15TH

For reasons unfathomable, Her Indoors is off work and is spending her precious leisure time watching figure skating and skiing. Skiing is not a sport, it's a type of holiday. You might as well watch someone sunbathing.

Thankfully there's an early Europa League game, but unfortunately I end up following it in a Tesco car park as Arsenal rack up three goals without reply at Östersunds, wherever that is. Due to the unscheduled excursion, I am forced to spend the entire night on catch-up, with ITV+1 coming to the rescue. And with Her Indoors insisting on watching scripted drama, I even have to watch a repeat of the Premier League Darts, starting at 1am.

Over in PyeongChang, Martins Dukurs is back on the skeleton. Team GB's Dom Parsons misses out by 2/100 of a second, but then takes bronze as Dukurs errs. Medal is not a verb. I hang around for a bit of hockey, then T20 in bed. Could do with Australia winning this.

FRIDAY FEBRUARY 16TH

Phil Taylor appears to be enjoying his retirement, tweeting about the best cricket match he has ever seen. I spend an hour leathering a ball round the backfield, managing to twist my ankle while stretching, also caking my trainers in mud. The Boy openly laughs at my lack of control.

Fuck this, I'm off to Camden to see The Damned with Bealesy, sacrificing two FA Cup games. Bealesy doesn't get involved in any afters as he has to stay sharp for Southend v Portsmouth in case Jeff Stelling needs a score update from Roots Hall, home of The Lord Mayor's Buffet.

I fall asleep during the curling, but rewind it at 5am to see us stick it up Denmark. Go on Eve!

SATURDAY FEBRUARY 17TH

Sleeping well past Football Focus, I manage the last knockings of Sheffield Wednesday 0-0 Swansea. Immersing myself in warm water, I listen to commentary of Chester v Eastleigh, bucking at a Ross Hannah goal for The Seals. The waves have barely subsided when Beastly Eastleigh equalise, but Hannah strikes again minutes before half time. This gives me time to fashion a rudimentary breakfast, which I enjoy in the garden with the commentary, performing laps of the mini-goal as Chester secure a 3-1 win on 90 minutes. Should have gone.

Huddersfield v Man United degenerates into another VAR shambles and I begrudgingly find myself agreeing with Robbie Savage. I don't really consider him a friend as he supports Wrexham, but he was once on my table at the darts, and I briefly acted as his impromptu secretary as punters threw items at me in order for him to sign them.

I don't really care about the Winter Olympics, but I'm a sucker for a medal ceremony, and inadvertently find myself becoming mildly tearful at a replay of Lizzy Yarnold receiving gold. Match Of The Day is safely recorded and features Gabby Logan in a fetching pair of red flares. A story breaks about West Brom players stealing a taxi in Barcelona and I don't know what's real anymore.

I spend the following hours not watching skiing. At about 6am, England lose a couple of wickets so I crawl into bed for TMS, minutes before Her Indoors gets up.

SUNDAY FEBRUARY 18TH

I manage to hear England win their match, but somehow not qualify on net run rate. Forget it, it's out of my life. This takes me straight into the Championship derby between Norwich and Ipswich, one half in bed, one in the bath. A late Ipswich goal is celebrated by their manager Mick McCarthy, who patently roars, "FUCK OFF!". Astonishingly, Norwich equalise with seven seconds of injury time left.

I wolf down a bit of egg on toast while keeping an eye on Hamilton v Rangers on the iPad, a game that absurdly finishes 3-5. Meanwhile Celtic and St Johnstone grind out a goalless draw in the same sport.

The Boy drags me onto the backfield for a kickabout, but I maintain radio contact with sport via 5live, who are building up to the big FA Cup game as Spurs travel to Spotland to take on Rochdale.

Paid contrarian Chris Sutton is the guest, and the presenter attempts to bait him into saying something controversial about the about the FA Cup draw time. Surprisingly, the former Norwich striker remains largely unfazed, which is not in his contract.

BBC One broadcasts the game and it's an absolute humdinger that puts The Boy through the full gamut of emotions, with the home side equalising late on to secure a replay at Wembley, counter-intuitively. Over on Sky, Real Madrid are winning 5-3 at Betis, whereas in France, Marseille are beating despised rivals Bordeaux 1-0, no doubt watched by my Bordeaux-supporting emigrant associate, The Driver. Meanwhile, in PyeongChang, there's a repeat of a controversial curling incident in which Eve Muirhead is deemed to have fouled. It's all about Eve.

MONDAY FEBRUARY 19TH

I have been in a nocturnal pit of despair since The Ashes, but now face the horror of the Monday morning school run. But first, men's curling, and we watch GB's final victorious end on the kitchen table over breakfast.

I drop The Boy off and return immediately to the repair tank, awaking for a replay of Eve and the team against the Swiss. This makes me late for the school pick-up, forcing me to drive.

Monday night is Merson soccer night, and The Boy is resplendent in his new boots. He claims that they're better than Nike, as we have somehow convinced him that Asda is short for Adidas. In fairness, he almost christens them with a goal.

On the bench, Chelsea Dad has secured tickets for Barcelona. I also have chat with Ipswich Mum, who advises me of a hitherto unknown terrace song that goes a little bit like this: "Delia Smith is a fucking cunt, Norwich are going down!"

As is the modern way, FA Cup weekend stretches into Monday evening, and we get back for Wigan v Man City, a repeat of the 2013 final that Wigan improbably won. Astonishingly, history repeats itself, and Wigan sneak a 1-0 win, a genuine giant-killing that I watch on the ancient portable, thus giving it an added retro feel, almost as if the FA Cup still matters. With the cup shock on The Beeb, Sky ambitiously pitch Blackburn v Bury against it, an iPad side dish for a perfunctory 2-0 home win.

There's more snooker on ITV4, but I'm too late for Ronnie who has already cruised through 4-0. Ryan Day v Jack Lisowski drifts past midnight in a deserted Preston Guild Hall, segueing into men's curling. Apart from the Prince William look-a-like, I am yet to get the measure of Team GB's men, but they overcome Norway 10-3. Credit to Norway for their comedy leggings.

TUESDAY FEBRUARY 20TH

I show The Boy the Wigan game over breakfast with a touch of women's curling. We cycle to school and I resume the curling in bed as we beat Japan. News breaks of a third failed drugs test, a risible skier. And a skater is crying about being disqualified.

I am awake but in limbo, only the white glare of the interminable Winter Olympics stretching ahead of me. Seeking respite, I fall asleep during a repeat of game five of last year's baseball World Series. This takes me into the snooker, where Masters winner Mark 'The Pistol' Allen already has a frame on the board. He swaggers into a 3-0 lead, but is clawed back to 3-3, at which point I spot a doppelganger of myself in the crowd. What's happening? Am I there? Bristling with impotent rage, Allen loses 4-3, falling at the first hurdle in this most unforgiving of sports.

Some kind of UEFA Youth League has sprung up on BT Sport, and Man City beat Inter on pens. As for the big boys in the Champions League, Chelsea v Barca and Bayern v Beşiktaş is little more than a footnote to live commentary of Chester's home defeat to Leyton Orient. Now back from her travels, Her Indoors requests a lift. No chance.

As is becoming routine, I am up all night with four Scottish scrubbers. Lovely Eve with her beguiling eyes, the one with the underbite, the Frozen princess, the other one. Canada have their own Eve 2.0 in the shape of the shapely Rachel Homan. What a sport. On the ice, GB triumph to dump the favourites and secure a semi-final place. The ice hockey segues into cricket's tri-series final as we approach a full 24 hours of sport. Not bad for a Tuesday.

WEDNESDAY FEBRUARY 21ST

The snooker plods on in Preston, and I catch a glimpse of the vampiric Mark Selby. Despite being dubbed 'The Jester from Leicester'

– presumably purely because it rhymes – the man looks like a walking
blood transfusion, natural light but a rumour. He should relocate to
East Yorkshire and restyle himself as the Ghoul from Goole.

This UEFA Youth thing keeps popping up in early afternoon,
and I manage to see Spurs beat Monaco on penalties. Sadly, I have to
leave the house before Liverpool v Man United, live from Tranmere's
Prenton Park with the respective teams managed by retired midfield
powerhouses Steven Gerrard and Nicky Butt.

I bed in for the evening behind a wall of European football, plus
a touch of Ronnie and Derby 2-2 Leeds on the big screen. Fuck the
Winter Olympics, where a curler has been sent home for taking
drugs. What drugs, exactly? Manchester United grind out a tedious
goalless draw in Seville, where they manage a total of one shot on
target. Paul Scholes berates them, a dour man talking about a dour
game, some kind of meta-misery. Mildly more entertaining, Shakhtar
beat Roma 2-1 on my phone.

It's too cold downstairs, so I repair to my office bed for ITV
highlights. Former Chester defender Lee Dixon mispronounces the
word lackadaisical as "lacksadaisical", which is a real shame. There's
snooker on the iPad, and John Higgins v Xiao Guodong goes all the
way in the World Grand Prix, with the Scotsman dispatched 4-3 on
the cusp of midnight.

In PyeongChang, Team GB's men are in a curling playoff against
Switzerland, with Steve Cram, a genuine Olympian, on commen-
tary. He's clearly done his homework and reveals that one of the
Swiss team's favourite players is Paul Scholes. As Cram says, Team
GB are "prolonging the dying embers of their Olympic campaign",
but they go from 4-1 up to 9-5 down, and summarily shit the ice.

It's a piss-poor effort and a waste of my valuable time. Mildly
furious, I ice hockey myself to sleep. Not a euphemism.

THURSDAY FEBRUARY 22ND

More curling, a semi-final between USA and Canada, something of a
local derby. USA win, and I watch the final end in the garden in rare
sunshine. Will this winter ever end?

I have a look at a random early Europa League tie and then head
into town to drink fizzy muck with horrible blokes. On the tube back

there is a gaggle of Östersunds fans, fresh from their match at The Emirates. I can't get a read on them – surely if they'd gone through they'd be swinging off the handrails. It turns out they did actually beat Arsenal 2-1, but lost 4-2 on aggregate. I catch the highlights on ITV+1 then wake up for a repeat of the women's ice hockey shootout between the USA and Canada.

FRIDAY FEBRUARY 23RD

I wake up with four Scottish scrubbers and a semi, but sadly Eve and the girls lose to Sweden and the dream of gold is over. Having missed it live due to drinking lager in a pub, I watch a repeat of the Premier League Darts from Berlin, where the atmosphere is surprisingly subdued.

Snooker takes a back seat as I find myself sucked into Germany improbably beating Canada at men's ice hockey, an historic result that makes me late for the school run. Despite there being plenty of live sport on offer, there's unwelcome talk of a family movie. As such, I am forced to endure Yogi Bear on the big TV, while multiscreening Hull 1-0 Sheffield United, Warrington 16-10 Wigan, plus France v Italy. In the snooker, Ronnie goes 4-2 down to Stephen Maguire, but effortlessly reels off four consecutive frames to clinch victory. Go on Ronnie!

SATURDAY FEBRUARY 24TH

Dagenham & Redbridge away. I'm still scarred from last season, when Chester threw away a 2-1 lead in the final minutes to lose 3-2. Nevertheless, I meet the same fellow Chester fan, known as The Hack, in the same London Bridge pub for a pre-match tincture. It's teeming with Shrewsbury fans, some of whom are falling down drunk. They're on their way to Charlton Athletic, where they will win 2-0.

We also get chatting to a couple of middle-aged Guiseley fans, fellow National League relegation certainties, on their way to Sutton United. One of them is referred to as Cilla, due to an extraordinary hairstyle last sported by the late Cilla Black. The other refers to himself as a "glass half full kind of guy" and talks us through various outlandish permutations that will see Gizlee survive, beginning with a win at Sutton today. They will lose 4-0.

The pub is showing Leicester v Stoke, but unusually I stand with my back to it. The women's curling takes pride of place, with a bronze medal up for grabs in the third-place playoff. It begins to slip away from Team GB, and Eve gambles the lot on an aggressively launched stone. It goes horribly wrong and the bronze is trickling through our fingers. So farewell, fair ice maidens, we shared many a thrilling night. But now you must return to your box for another four years.

And we'd better get our arses to Daggers in an attempt to salvage something from this sporting day. At 2-1 up I declare out loud that I've resigned myself to defeat, perhaps in attempt to cushion the blow. It can't possibly happen again. Of course it can, with Dagenham equalising in the 85th minute and then winning courtesy of a comedy own-goal in the 88th. Fuck this life.

Numbing the pain in the Daggers bar, Scotland beat England at rugby, and Watford beat Everton at football. I get home and there's no Match Of The Day, which throws everything off-kilter. England take on New Zealand in an ODI. They lose. Make it stop.

SUNDAY FEBRUARY 25TH

Spurs beat Palace 1-0 with an 88th-minute Harry Kane winner. To paraphrase something I once read by a soccer-phobic American, two teams ran around for 90 minutes then some guy scored a touchdown with his head. What a sport. Ronnie versus Ding is the snooker final, but I lapse into unconsciousness during Man United 2-1 Chelsea.

Proof if proof were needed that Olympics is sport for people who don't like sport: yet again I find Her Indoors watching figure skating. Sake. I have a bit of Olympic business to tie up, and watch Germany come within 56 seconds of ice hockey gold before losing to Russia in overtime.

The women's curling final in PyeongChang clashes with the Carabao Cup final at Wembley. Sweden beat Korea, and Manchester City trounce Arsenal 3-0. On the green baize in Preston, Ronnie cursorily swats Ding aside to stick another trophy in the cabinet. Go on Ronnie!

MONDAY FEBRUARY 26TH

What? The applause has barely died down in Preston, and we're straight into snooker's Welsh Open. Preposterous. It at least tides me over until Charlie Merson's Soccer School. The man himself performs a decent lob, less than 24 hours after his dad handed over The League

Cup to Manchester City at Wembley. He also shows us a meme on his phone of an Arsenal kid crying that is doing the rounds for the next ten minutes until some other shit comes up.

As for my kid, The Boy slots home his American-style penalty, and also saves the efforts of the sons of the dads flanking me. I don't say anything, but simply revel in the reflected glory.

There is no televised English football tonight, an absolute disgrace. Instead, The Boy watches urban mountain biking from Santiago on YouTube, scant replacement.

Most of it was shit, but the Winter Olympics has left something of a void in the schedule. In a rare foray into scripted drama, we watch the Golden Gordon episode of Ripping Yarns: "Useless, useless bastards!"

It's too close to home, it's too near the bone.

TUESDAY FEBRUARY 27TH

It's hard to get too excited, but I half-heartedly watch the Welsh Open snooker. So cold. Apparently, Mark Williams has had a spat with pro-turned-pundit Darren Morgan, and there's some mild entertainment when they are forced to sit next to each other, with Williams refusing to make eye contact with his fellow Welshman.

Ken Doherty v Matthew Stevens is the showpiece game, bringing back memories of when I briefly met Doherty while interviewing Steve Davis. I was also at The Crucible to see Stevens contest the 2005 World Championship. As such, whenever he's on screen I can't help but shout "Go on, Matthew!" in a Welsh accent, as his supporters did on the night, albeit in vain.

Finally, some football, an FA Cup replay between Swansea and Sheffield Wednesday, the latter managed by a man with an extremely handsome moustache. It's a joyless 2-0 home victory with all the magic of a reserve game. Mercifully, there's no extra time.

Meanwhile, England are taking on New Zealand in the second ODI, with violent criminal Ben Stokes welcomed back into the fold having missed The Ashes for beating some people senseless with his bare fists outside a Bristol nightclub. The temperature is sub-zero here while those bastards are basking in endless summer. England are skittling them, and I listen to TMS in bed, tactically setting my phone to sleep in order to maintain the mystery.

WEDNESDAY FEBRUARY 28TH

Ronnie v Graeme Dott in the bath. Not literally. I've still got the cricket hanging over me. Did we win? Did we lose? Can you have a draw? All will be revealed, when I get round to it.

Meanwhile in Cardiff, Ding is gone, slamming the cue ball down the table by hand in rage, beaten 4-1 by the unknown Liam Highfield. Ronnie is of course mercurial, and I sit up and watch an effortless century, of which he has made the best part of a thousand in his career. As is his wont, he seamlessly switches from his left to his right hand, something that was once deemed disrespectful by the French-Canadian Alain Robidoux.

Old Willie Thorne is in the studio and is rightly dazzled by The Rocket's brilliance. As for the pending World Championship, Ronnie concedes, "I probably will have a go." Of course he will.

Trump is gone, a headline writer's dream: man with same name as other man has different job. Surely nobody can stop Ronnie now, except himself. Or maybe Selby.

There's a bit of early Coppa Italia as Juventus beat Atalanta. Then we're into the main event, the FA Cup replay between Spurs and Rochdale at Wembley with VAR in the snow, as the so-called 'Beast from the East' has the country in its icy grip. To describe the game as a farce is to do a disservice to the noble art form. It's an absolute shambles, with baffling decisions poorly executed and overcomplicated by the introduction of unreliable technology. And it goes on for ages, players and supporters simply hanging around while the officials pontificate. At one point a handful of players are almost offside from a penalty, which is then disallowed for a shimmy. Rochdale have their moment in the snow, equalising Tottenham's opener, before eventually succumbing to a 6-1 defeat on a night that does very little to advance the cause of this new technology.

Following a cursory visit to the Olympic Stadium to see Milan beat Lazio on penalties, I finally catch up with the ODI, an easy win for England. In the snooker, Selby is still playing past midnight and the TV coverage simply stops, leaving him to it. If a tree falls in a forest and nobody is there to hear it, does it make a sound?

THURSDAY MARCH 1ST

I have a quick look at South Africa v Australia in the cricket, but sensibly opt for the snooker instead. Improbably, today's sporting feast is weather-affected as the Beast from the East has shat its load, making this a designated Snow Day. No school today.

It's the coldest spring day on record, and PyeongChang has come to North West London, with numerous kids hurtling down a nearby slope on a variety of makeshift sledges. I am even interviewed by an ITV news crew about how I have managed to juggle work with the impromptu childcare. I mumble some hollow platitudes, but what I don't tell them is that I am now forced to watch Ronnie on a slight delay. It's a swift business, however, as he dispatches the unknown David Grace 4-0 inside 45 minutes, knocking in hundred breaks like shelling peas, inexorably approaching a thousand professional centuries. It's simply an honour to share the planet with him, and I will always treasure that magical afternoon when he indulged me in a brief and unremarkable conference call phone interview.

For reasons unknown, Arsenal are playing Man City again, and Man City are winning 3-0 again, in front of a slew of empty seats at The Emirates. I spend half time up to my elbow in human excrement attempting to unblock the upstairs bog. As such, I miss a second half Arsenal penalty, as do they, again failing to register a consolation goal.

My sewage hell is mildly alleviated by balancing the iPad on the towel rail for the Premier League Darts. Having finally cleared the blockage, I retire to the day bed to dual-screen football and darts. It takes me until the end of the third darts match to realise that this is a repeat of the opening night in Dublin. What's happening? Astonishingly, tonight's scheduled event in Exeter has been cancelled due to the adverse weather, despite being an indoor sport. Snow stops play. You couldn't make it up.

Of course this throws tomorrow's UK Open in nearby Minehead into doubt. I am always impressed by the elegance of this scheduling, with the entire darting fraternity decamping to Devon; the cream of the Premier League doing battle in Exeter on the Thursday before they jam themselves into Butlin's Minehead for the weekend to join the bottom-feeders on ITV4. Presumably some punters do both events, quite literally living the darting dream.

Denied the basic human right of live darts, I half-watch women's football, with recently-installed England manager Phil Neville making his debut in the improbably named SheBelieves Cup, live from Columbus, Ohio. Impressively, England turn over France 4-1. What a time to be alive.

After a touch of cricket highlights and a trawl of the snooker, I retire to bed. Fuck it all.

FRIDAY MARCH 2ND

The UK Open is going ahead, but in another landmark ruling for darts it will take place with no audience due to weather-related safety concerns in and around the venue. Wow. Darts without a baying crowd is basically just a game of darts, two blokes slinging arrows to win outrageous fortunes. It'll never catch on.

Undeterred, I watch the opener in the bath, Paul 'The Asset' Nicholson v Terry 'The Bull' Jenkins. I have to do a double take at a completely bald Jenkins – the years have not been kind to the veteran Hereford slinger. Back when he was more hirsute, I saw him lose to Barney in the final of the 2006 Desert Classic in a sweltering Las Vegas. Taking place in a vast conference room in the bowels of the Mandalay Bay Hotel, despite being a televised extravaganza back in Britain, the only suggestion that a major sporting event was happening was a piece of landscape A4 paper pinned to a closed door, simply bearing the word 'DARTS'.

It's decidedly chillier in Butlin's Minehead, and Nicholson has turned up in a long-sleeved, skin-tight undergarment replete with electronic gadget on his throwing arm. It seems to do the trick as he hits the break 5-0 up in a race to six. Astonishingly, The Bull rallies and somehow pulls it back to 5-5 to force a decider. Tragically he misses four match darts, confirming his long-held reputation as a choker. Nicholson finally picks him off for his first televised win since 2014. What drama.

With Minehead now resembling Narnia, players are racing through the snow to get there for the 4pm cut-off. The presenters have at least made it, the odd couple of Jacqui Oatley and Chris Mason, respectively a head girl in a leather blouson and an aggravated burglar in a floral shirt. Ground support is provided by a bobble-hatted Ned Boulting, who reveals that the heating has stopped working in the multi-board room, which now resembles the tundra. At one point he finds a player chucking darts in a hoodie.

Next up is Richie Burnett versus the young Ryan Harrington, son of former pro turned commentator Rod. A previous Lakeside Champion, Burnett, the self-styled Prince of Wales, has had a chequered career, including an extended spell clearing railway sidings. Having been lured back to the sport, he then faced a further setback in the shape of an 18-month ban for testing positive for cocaine. He's certainly got the nose for it.

But he's back, up against an opponent whose father he used to play pairs with when Harrington junior was only seven. It's a scrappy affair, the fresh-faced Harrington trading legs with the Welsh Begbie, perennially scowling and gurning, and still employing an awkward leg-oriented throwing action. The match goes the distance and at 5-5, Burnett implausibly busts 99. Harrington cleans up to leave the Welshman absolutely seething. Meanwhile, in warmer climes, the cricket continues. In Durban, the cameraman picks out a pair of bikini-clad spectators. Lovely stuff.

Even for me, this is a lot of darts. There's progress for Margate's Kirk Shepherd, still the biggest outsider ever to have made a PDC World Championship Final when he lost to John Part in 2008. I am reminded of the time that Shepherd urinated next to me at Birmingham Arena on a Premier League night. Heavily refreshed, cock in hand, he assured me that it was only a matter of time before he retook his place among the elite, something that is yet to materialise. Ever the sage, Waddell did not concur.

The next game is actively boring, Lee Evans versus former youth champion Dimitri Van den Bergh, aka The Dream Maker, in a deserted Minehead Butlin's, in the snow. With Chris Mason commentating in a snorkel parka, the Belgian's dreams come tumbling down as he is duly dispatched 6-3. Raymond van Barneveld survives multiple match darts to squeeze past the unheralded Mike Norton, then we're into the live third round draw.

Football interrupts play as Middlesbrough beat Leeds 3-0, and Monaco beat Bordeaux 2-1. I tell The Boy that I've been to both grounds, but he's not interested.

Back at the darts, the giants are tumbling. Barney gone, Lewis gone, Wright gone, Chisnall gone. It's almost like they want to get out of there. The UK Open has been described as the FA Cup of darts and the big names are perhaps mirroring the indifference of football's Premier League counterparts. Or perhaps it's harder to play with the adverse conditions and tiny crowd, the equivalent of going to a non-league ground.

The biggest shock is yet to come. Astonishingly, the world's greatest player, Michael van Gerwen, is beaten by unfancied Jeffrey de Zwaan, the darting equivalent of Wigan beating Man City. "I think I'm dreaming", says the gobsmacked de Zwaan.

A further giant of indoor sport is felled when Ronnie is rolled over 5-1 by John Higgins. Sake. Numb with sport, I watch 25 overs of the 3rd ODI before TMS takes me under.

SATURDAY MARCH 3RD

Without ever leaving my bed, I travel across the sporting universe to Brisbane for a bit of A-league soccer, then to South Africa for a bit of cricket. Football Focus brings me back to earth, then Burnley v Everton in the bath bleeds into darts and snooker for a triple-screen breakfast.

I stick on some old boots and have a kickabout with The Boy in the snow. I accidentally see a partial cricket headline: "England Hold". Hold what? Their plums? An inquest after defeat? A party to celebrate victory?

All these thought are racing through my fevered mind as I watch the highlights of the third ODI in New Zealand. As it turns out, the hosts need six from the final ball, and England hold their nerve. The so-called teatime game sees Liverpool beat Newcastle 2-0 on BT Sport, and in Spain Ronaldo scores his 300th league goal.

There's barely any respite, with an onslaught of darts, snooker, and Goals On 5, featuring Colin Murray, Chris Iwelumo and Caroline Barker, two-thirds of whom I have met. Absolute showbiz.

Match Of The Day is slightly delayed, but I manage to cope. In America, it's the opening day of Major League Soccer, and I try not to get sucked in by Orlando v Washington DC. I don't want it in my life. It finishes 1-1.

SUNDAY MARCH 4TH

Mid-morning, there's nightmarish talk of a family day out. Mercifully I awake to an empty house, and find Blackburn already 2-0 up against Wigan. Tragically, an Italian footballer has died in his sleep, and the entire country's fixtures are postponed out of respect. Roger Bannister has also died, 64 years after running the first four-minute mile.

There's an overlap with Brighton v Arsenal, and I controversially opt for League One on the iPad plus the Premier League on 5live, where I hear Brighton take the lead just as Wigan pull it back to 2-2. Obviously I keep an eye on the snooker and darts as well. I'm not an animal.

Arsenal turn it round to win 2-1 as the family return with food in time for Man City 1-0 Chelsea, as turgid a match as I have ever seen. And I have seen hundreds of Chester matches. At half time, I momentarily look at the Motocross World Championship, improbably a sport that I briefly competed in as a child.

Weird scenes inside Butlin's Minehead as the UK Open continues, a tawdry event overseen by only a handful of friends and family, the general public locked out due to health and safety political correctness gone mad. I happily dual-screen it with the concluding session of the snooker as Higgins takes on Barry 'The Hawk' Hawkins in the final of whatever fucking tournament it is this week. For reasons unknown, a rowdy element of the crowd sporadically sings "Barry's off to Nando's", an accusation that the Kent potter later denies.

Suddenly the SheBelieves Cup looms into view, with England taking on Germany. Sake, can't miss that. The Germans take an early lead, but we immediately equalise, much to Phil Neville's delight. Yeah well done, but I've never forgiven him for conceding that penalty against Romania in Euro 2000 in Charleroi, right in front of me (although I was secretly glad I could go home the next day).

I pass out and wake to find England beating Germany, Higgins beating Hawkins, and somebody called Cadby beating Gary Anderson in the darts. England eventually draw 2-2, and I catch the last knockings of Marseille 1-1 Nantes, an injury-time equaliser for the home team almost 20 years since I was there for the opening game of England's ill-fated World Cup '98 campaign.

In Minehead and Cardiff respectively, Gary Anderson and John Higgins simultaneously clinch victory in the darts and the snooker, celebrating on either side of a stretch of sea. Meanwhile, half a world away in Seattle, the newly-formed Los Angeles FC are preparing to play their first ever MLS game. Maybe they can be my US team. After all, I've been to LA more than any other American city. Veteran manager Bob Bradley is at the helm, and I stick the game on the big telly for this auspicious occasion. Sadly, I miss the historic kickoff while making a sandwich. I just about catch their first ever goal while pissing about with Match Of The Day 2 on the laptop. On Oscar night, Los Angeles have their Hollywood ending, winning 1-0 as a bemused Ron Burgundy looks on.

There's barely time for a brew and more food before Sporting Kansas City v New York City. Trailing 2-0, the home side have a penalty overturned by VAR. What a time to be alive. NYC then have a man sent off on VAR. Like it or not, VAR is coming.

MONDAY MARCH 5TH

Feast to famine. There is no discernible sport to be found, so I pace around like a caged animal. I'm assuming South Africa didn't overturn a 100-run deficit with one wicket left. In further cricket news, the England team has again covered itself in glory with reports of an altercation in a bar in Durban. Dickheads.

Trawling the schedules, there is some kind of school rugby on FreeSports. Not interested. Meanwhile, Olympic mod Bradley Wiggins has denied taking drugs, which presumably puts him in a tiny minority in the cycling fraternity. Not so much a sport as a narcotic mode of transport.

At Monday Night Soccer School, The Boy scores a cracker, drilling it into the far corner. We watch the first half of Crystal Palace v Man United, The Boy still basking in the glory of his goal, talking me through it ad nauseum. In an attempt to change the subject, I tell him about the time Eric Cantona karate-kicked some Palace whopper in the chest, and he seems mildly impressed.

I take in the second half upstairs, actually watching it, vicariously feeling the pain and elation as Palace squander a two-goal lead to lose 3-2 in injury time. There's a close-up of Roy Hodgson as he dispatches a pellet of sputum, bested in the cruellest fashion by miserable, moaning Mourinho, as he's known in our house.

TUESDAY MARCH 6TH

Boris Johnson has claimed that England could pull out of the World Cup because a Russian spy was poisoned in Salisbury. That will definitely happen then.

Out of nowhere, the World Junior Curling Championship has sprung up, Korea v Scotland. Sadly, we have to leave for school with it poised after nine ends. As The Boy says: "What is wrong with their minds? It's spring, not winter." Korea win 8-5.

It's big-time knockout Champions League night. PSG v Real Madrid takes pride of place on the big bastard telly, a 2-1 win for the Spanish club seeing them comfortably through on aggregate. By virtue of being 5-0 up from the away leg, Liverpool are relegated to the iPad, a shrewd decision as they grind out a goalless draw against Porto. Former Real Madrid stopper Iker Casillas is in nets for the Portuguese outfit, a player against whom I once took a penalty, hopelessly floating it into his midriff.

The Champions League is of course a footnote compared to phone commentary of Chester v Dover, which has me in its grip. Dover's first goal physically knocks the wind out of me and I have to lie down, horizontally absorbing an own goal minutes later for a desultory 2-0 defeat. In all the excitement, I've swerved Shrewsbury 1-0 Yeovil in the Checkatrade Trophy, with The Shrews securing a Wembley final with Lincoln. An absolute disgrace. Still, only 100 days to the World Cup.

I'm straight into the 4th ODI, driven upstairs by the cold. Records tumble as England embark on a ludicrous innings, with talk of reaching 400. This is rapidly silenced by a total collapse that sees them just about survive the requisite 50 overs. New Zealand lose their openers within minutes before bedding in for the long haul. TMS swiftly takes me under ahead of my high noon appointment with highlights.

WEDNESDAY MARCH 7TH

Cricket highlights in the bath, having successfully managed to avoid the score this time. It's a ridiculous run chase and New Zealand clinch it with three balls to spare to level the series at 2-2, with the decider on Friday night. Scenes.

News breaks of a player called Sanchez Watt being sent off for repeatedly telling the ref his surname, which tickles The Boy. He's less impressed by Spurs, who conspire to lose 2-1 to Juventus at Wembley and so tumble out of the Champions League. What a Spurs-up. Man City even lose at home to Basel by the same score, albeit with a comfortable aggregate buffer. Toss in a bit of Leeds 0-3 Wolves in the Championship and it's been an eventful night of football.

But it's not over yet, as the Champions League ITV highlights segue seamlessly into the SheBelieves Cup where England are taking on the USA. We lose 1-0 to a hapless own goal, and Phil Neville is not happy, although he does reveal that they're all off to Disneyland.

THURSDAY MARCH 8TH

Once the last bastion of football-free existence, Thursday night is now Europa League night. As such, Arsenal are away to AC Milan. Foregone conclusion, Arsenal without a chance. Fuck me, they've only gone and scored. I actually miss the early goal as I am pissing about, but manage to see their second on my phone at the dinner table as they secure a famous victory.

It's all too much, and I remember that Premier League Darts is back, live in Leeds. I'm so discombobulated that I miss the first two games. We're into the second phase of Europa games, so I make the considered decision to watch darts in bed with a side dish of Marseille v Athletic Bilbao. At some point a headline pops up: Dani Alves Denies Wiping Nose On Ronaldo. What a world we live in today.

I take it down a notch with ITV Europa League highlights. Mark Pougatch is corralling guests Kevin Campbell and Glenn Hoddle, only one of whom once lost his job for saying something weird about disabled people.

FRIDAY MARCH 9TH

Cricket in bed, South Africa v Australia. Pointless. I have a look at the repeat of the Premier League Darts, but there's no explanation proffered as to what they're going to do about the postponed Exeter fixtures. Fuming, I flick on to Eurosport where I am offered "a one-frame playoff for a place in the second round of the Gibraltar Open".

I'll take it. Matthew Stevens and Mike Dunn are locked at 3-3 in the opening day of yet another snooker tournament. Go on Matthew! The Welshman sneaks through, as according to the commentary, Dunn "couldn't quite deliver the killing thrust". What a sport. I flip back to the darts where MvG is giving a big-tongued interview, then settle on the cricket.

Following a cursory viewing of Golden Gordon – "Eight bloody one!" – we watch the second half of Hibs 2-0 Hearts, the Edinburgh derby kicking off Sky's so-called Rivalry Weekend.

In the Gibraltar Open, Dominic 'The Spaceman' Dale loses 4-3 to veteran Ken Doherty.

"Is he really a spaceman?" inquires The Boy.

"No, he's a liar", I confirm.

In the Olympic Stadium, Roma beat Torino 3-0, but Italian football is still reeling from the tragic death of Fiorentina's Davide Astori.

In the big ODI decider, England win the toss and choose to bowl. They say that magic doesn't exist, but we have travelled from Scotland to Gibraltar to Italy to New Zealand without ever leaving the house. What a Friday night. The dream scenario is that we skittle them out and knock off the total in time for bed, as with highlights not until 3:30 pm tomorrow it's a perilous business. Set a modest total, our batsmen do the business and it's a comfortable win. I feel almost nothing, but am at least in bed by 5am.

SATURDAY MARCH 10TH

Manchester United versus Liverpool. Now that is a rivalry, and one that is subjected to a 90-minute radio build-up: blah blah history, blah blah bragging rights. Meanwhile, a pair of unknowns are going cue-to-cue in Gibraltar, and the cricket is ticking over in South Africa. There's further cricket in the shape of some kind of World Cup qualifier between the Windies and Ireland. Apparently Ireland have a cricket team now, and the West Indies are officially called 'the Windies'. I can't get involved in that.

The big game kicks off and there is a clearly audible chant of "Your support is fucking shit", with no apology from Sky. I take a side match of Eibar v Real Madrid, with a Ronaldo brace either side of an Eibar equaliser securing victory.

Old Trafford is the place to be though, and it's an incredibly tense encounter, even for a so-called lunchtime game, with an absurd 12:30pm kickoff. An early Rashford brace puts United in charge, but Liverpool halve the deficit. It's an absolute onslaught, but the Mancs hold firm.

I decompress in the garden with a bit of Final Score, raising an eyebrow at two 7-1 scorelines in The National League.

"Is swingball a sport?" asks The Boy. I think we all know the answer, but I indulge him in a game anyway, with talkSPORT on my headphones informing me of trouble at West Ham.

Ireland beat Scotland at rugby, then France beat England to hand Ireland the Six Nations. I watch Chelsea 2-1 Palace with The Boy and briefly pass out. Still they pot on in Gibraltar, presumably oblivious to a pitch invasion at Lille. As a rare treat I watch Match Of The Day in the conjugal bed. The blackness comes swiftly.

SUNDAY MARCH 11TH

Up at 8:30am, nervous as a kitten. Sky may not acknowledge it, but this is the true rivalry of the weekend, the spicy cross-border derby encounter between Wrexham and Chester. It's the first one I've missed at The Racecourse for years, but my attendance is made untenable by virtue of it being 200 miles away with a noon kickoff on Mothering Sunday. Mainly though, it's because its live on BT Sport, thus enabling me to become an armchair supporter for the day.

The Boy is downstairs singing the Match Of The Day theme tune, so I kill time with cricket in the bath, South Africa taking charge. The big game finally comes around. We lose 2-0. Fuck that.

We don't watch it, but there's a lesser derby in Scotland, Rangers 2-3 Celtic. We catch a bit of Arsenal v Watford including a Deeney penalty miss, but are ripped away from the screen at Her Indoors' behest for a Mother's Day outing. Unbelievable. The car radio provides a lifeline and we don't get out until we've heard the conclusion of John Motson's last-ever radio commentary. Not one for a fuss, he simply signs off from a 48-year shift without fanfare.

I manage a bit of Bournemouth v Spurs on headphones, but have to endure a total sporting blackout during a Chinese meal. I don't like it, but I've got to go along with it. Piling back in the car, Spurs are scoring at will as The Boy bucks in the back, and we get home to see them clinch a 4-1 win, albeit with the loss of Harry Kane to injury, live on Sky. Let's never leave the house again.

The evening is a mess of Spanish football, Major League Soccer, tennis, and the Gibraltar Open final, contestants unknown. There are even rumours of my close personal friend Tiger Woods putting in a shift in some golf tournament.

Disturbing news come from Greece, where the owner of a football club has apparently taken to the pitch wielding a gun. And finally, footage emerges of Jamie Carragher unleashing an enormous volley of phlegm from and at a moving vehicle. Lovely stuff.

MONDAY MARCH 12TH

Oh Monday, I'm dreaming about you. South Africa need four to win and level the series. None of it matters, we're all going to die. Meanwhile, there's another ICC World Cup Qualifier between the Netherlands and the Windies. The Dutch are weeping, in four languages at least. Rain stops play.

In Greece, gun stops play, as all Greek football is suspended after what appears to be open warfare. With the changing of the seasons, The Boy's Monday night football takes place outside tonight, yet another American penalties contest, whereby the taker runs from the halfway line before taking his shot. I believe the late Jimmy Hill was a big advocate of the system. Chat among the dads is about Carragher's phlegm, and he is notably absent from Sky's Monday Night Football, Stoke v Man City.

Breaking news: Southampton sack Pellegrino. Hughes, Allardyce, Pardew, Pulis: assemble.

TUESDAY MARCH 13TH

As clear a signifier of the advent of spring as daffodils and lambs, the Cheltenham festival is under way on ITV, the whitest event in all sport. Presented by Ed Chamberlin, the old Etonian is in his natural environment after years of dodging Jamie Carragher's spittle of a Monday night. Nevertheless, it's something of an idiot's guide to racing, with the level of chat scarcely any less inane than in football: "How much pressure are you under?"

What a fucking stupid question. Unless you're a deep-sea diver there is no empirical answer. See also momentum and confidence.

I lose my first two bets and hence any subsequent interest. Without a bet it's simply some animals running in a field, patently not a sport. It is however a decent day out, essentially a drinking orgy interrupted by some horse races. I've been a couple of times, and toy with the idea of going again. Of course I won't.

Looking to recoup my losses, I have a cheeky bet in-running on La Bague Au Roi, my heart pounding at the prospect of free money. Sadly, the nag is a bag of shit, clipping the last fence to finish his chances and my bet.

Real sport ensues in the evening in the shape of the Champions League second legs, where Manchester United need to beat Sevilla in order to progress. Alan Green on 5live says they have been "set up pathetically by Jose Mourinho" and it's a turgid goalless first half. On BT Sport at half time Paul Scholes says "they haven't got a goal in them". He's wrong, but it only comes late on after Sevilla have scored twice. Remember the name: Wissam Ben Yedder, the Frenchman sending the Northern powerhouse tumbling out in some disgrace.

There's a bit of other business, with Cardiff winning at Brentford and Roma squeezing past Shakhtar on away goals, which Gary Lineker hates. I've always found them rather exotic.

I leave BT Sport on after the highlights and inadvertently get sucked into an ESPN 30 For 30 film called Unguarded, about Chris Herren, the professional basketball player who spent most of his career in the grip of a crippling drug addiction. It's absolutely gut wrenching and I sit wrought on the sofa, something in my eye, sir.

It's almost enough to finish me off, but I am snagged by live Paralympic curling, Team GB versus Germany. We stick it up them 8-3. Bring on the USA.

WEDNESDAY MARCH 14TH

Chancing my arm at Cheltenham again, I pick up an each-way winner in the bath. I'm already up on the day and I haven't even washed my hair yet. And another! The school run interrupts the gambling spree, but I return to bag another winner, with The Boy riding along on my knee as the valiant nag crosses the line. Good parenting.

There's a swathe of early football, with all manner of UEFA Youth League games before the real thing. It's a packed house at Beşiktaş despite the home team being 5-0 down to Bayern from the first leg. With play briefly interrupted by a cat on the pitch, the Germans cruise to an 8-1 aggregate victory. Eight bloody one! Barcelona tear Chelsea a new arsehole 3-0 for a 4-1 aggregate victory, and English interest in the Champions League is rapidly diminishing.

Jim Bowen has died, as indeed has Stephen Hawking, with the non-darts player going first, as tradition dictates. Out of respect, I watch four episodes of Bullseye back-to-back.

At the Paralympic curling, Team GB go down to a narrow 5-4 defeat by Korea. As the final stone slides past its target I let out a primal "No!".

THURSDAY MARCH 15TH

Up early, slim pickings. The Windies post 197 against Afghanistan in an ICC Word Cup qualifier. When is this so-called World Cup anyway? In the wake of the Salisbury poisonings, there is further talk of the England team being withdrawn from the actual World Cup. The Royal Family have already confirmed that they won't be going, which will be a massive loss to the competition. Surely the only reason to tune into the World Cup is to see a horse-faced parasite in a Doctor Who scarf pretending to care.

I watch the last knockings of the Paralympic curling, a dead rubber against China on Channel 4+1. Team GB are so far behind that they simply stop broadcasting it. Home before the post-cards. An absolute disgrace.

In the first race at Cheltenham, my horse skulks at the back then pulls up. I give up in disgust and turn it off. Afghanistan chase down the Windies, bringing us closer to the main event, Arsenal v AC Milan, the Italians apparently managed by Ray Winstone. It's preceded by a swathe of support matches in this never-ending feast of football. Arsenal swat AC Milan aside 3-1, a hugely confusing result for the anti-Wenger brigade.

Again, I forget about the Premier League Darts – in Nottingham - missing the first two matches and any explanation of the cancelled fixtures, if indeed there ever was one. There's a lot of love for the late Bullseye host Jim Bowen in the room, and the ever-colourful

Peter 'Snakebite' Wright turns up with a temporary Bully tattoo on his shaven head. At least I hope it's temporary. Ever on point, Dave Clarke signs off with a poignant "You can't beat a bit of Bully".

This just leaves Europa League highlights, with Mark Pougatch overseeing the battle of knitwear between a manspreading Glenn Hoddle and a glowering cross-legged Roy Keane. As is traditional in the run-up to a World Cup, England's best player has knackered a foot. Like Beckham and Rooney before him, Harry Kane is on footwatch, but is 'expected to return to first team training next month'.

FRIDAY MARCH 16TH

En route to Bournemouth to see my old dear, Champions League and Europa League draw in the car. Liverpool will play... Manchester City. Scenes. Arsenal will play... CSKA Moscow. A footnote.

I drive past the Bournemouth International Centre and show The Boy where I once saw Phil Taylor score a total of seven with three darts.

In a sport-free household, options are limited and we are forced to watch some shit about dogs. Thankfully I have travelled with screens, and manage to catch Lille taking an early lead atop the Monaco car park. Elsewhere, FIFA confirm VAR for the World Cup, and miserable moaning Mourinho embarks on a deranged rant about "football 'eritage".

Six dead horses at Cheltenham.

SATURDAY MARCH 17TH

Kevin Pietersen announces his retirement. Fuck KP. I once endured a painstaking interview with him in the media room at Lord's. He said nothing of note and seemingly had no interest in being there other than to trouser thousands of pounds for endorsing a product that he had little or no concept of.

I start the day with a touch of Sydney 1-2 Brisbane in the A-League. Sydney have a goal disallowed by VAR because somebody's arm is offside. But you can't score with your arm. Pathetic, although proceedings are enlivened when the ref does a couple of neat nutmegs.

I have kickabout with The Boy in the snow on a Bournemouth clifftop, a clear and obvious error. We head back indoors for the Swansea v Spurs FA Cup quarter-final, with side dishes of Fulham v QPR and Football Focus. Despite being away from my control centre, I manage a solid 12 hours of sport, tracing the mini-Beast from the East across the various screens. Bolton v Villa is almost a total whiteout, little more than a screensaver. Reduced to two screens for dinner, I have to position Liverpool v Watford on the floor, which is very disrespectful to Salah and his four goals.

Forced to watch Gogglebox, there's a clip of Mourinho, and someone says "his ambition exceeds his language". I fuck it all off and watch Match Of The Day in bed.

SUNDAY MARCH 18TH

More FA Cup quarter-finals. With military timing, we watch the first half of Wigan v Southampton with my dad, then take in the second half in the car. Showing a lack of respect for the FA Cup, The Boy falls asleep before the denouement, a perfunctory 2-0 win for the away side. Back in London, a frozen house awaits for Freeview HD coverage of Leicester v Chelsea, the first half of which The Boy wisely sleeps through. Deadlocked at 1-1, for the first time in an original quarter-final tie, there is extra time. What a time to be alive. Chelsea nick it.

MONDAY MARCH 19TH

Last two overs of Zimbabwe v West Indies - basically all you need - as the Windies complete the run chase with an over in hand. Monday night football has mercifully been moved back indoors, and The Boy saves a penalty from mini-Ronaldo. Charlie Merson is increasingly absent and the fat lad taking the session commends his young charges for "operating under pressure". There is talk of a dad's five-a-side game – I simply won't be there.

It's international week so Sky stick on any old shit. Doncaster v Bradford in League One, managed by Darren Ferguson and Simon Grayson respectively, these tragic men clinging onto the third tier of the managerial merry-go-round. Meanwhile, even lower down, Martin Allen starts his fifth spell at Barnet.

The Donny match is almost unwatchable, only enlivened by a flare in the home end early in the second half.

Meanwhile, having held its breath for over a week, snooker is back, a quick return to Wales for the Players Championship. Ding and Allen are locked into a best of 11. Viva Llandudno!

Back in Donny, two late goals from 80s-haired John Marquis secures victory for the hosts, "as they chase Bradford City out of their town". Strong.

TUESDAY MARCH 20TH

A picture emerges of former Aston Villa boss John Gregory in a sari having won the Indian Super League with Chennaiyin FC. I don't know what's real anymore.

Back in Wales, ubiquitous MC John McDonald - a man who makes a living by shouting the names of darts and snooker players – manages a passable stab at "Llandudno". Selby is felled by Ryan Day, resurgent since lifting the Gibraltar Open. The evening sees Ronnie take on Dott, the squeaky Scot just about avoiding a whitewash in a 6-1 drubbing.

Meanwhile in the National League, relegation rivals Solihull turn over Bromley to hammer a nail in the coffin of Chester FC.

WEDNESDAY MARCH 21ST

Burnley goalkeeper Nick Pope claims that "I've played in some cold, dark leagues", somehow suggesting that lower division football operates in its own microclimate. In golf, Rory McIlroy admits that his putting is inspired by Wayne Rooney's pre-penalty or free-kick ritual of tapping his toe on the ground before his run-up. As Shaun Ryder claimed in his autobiography, all footballers basically have OCD. Repetition, repetition, repetition. That said, Rooney has missed a few pens recently.

Apropos of nothing, The Boy asks "why are West Ham so bad when they used to be good?". It's hard to say. Perhaps they're struggling to adapt to the London Stadium after leaving their beloved Upton Park. A lack of investment from a self-serving board? Maybe they were never that good.

Less than three weeks after it was transformed into Ice Planet Hoth, I take a perch in the garden for Scotland v the Windies on the iPad. Rain stops play and Scotland are out – what a waste of their time and mine. Jip Jaap Stam has been sacked by Reading, increasingly proving a better player than manager. Nevertheless, he will always have my utmost respect for describing the Neville brothers as a pair of "busy cunts".

I leave the snooker at Trump 3-3 Maguire for the school run, an extraordinary sacrifice. A kickabout breaks out and I am pressganged into goal, where I make a decent save from The Boy. No favours. Still harbouring hopes of turning pro, on the walk home he says he'll probably play for Chelsea for practice before joining Spurs. That's the spirit.

Ronnie v Ding is the big one, but Her Indoors FaceTimes from Los Angeles just as Barrow v Hartlepool gets underway on BT Sport. I flip the camera round so she can see it, but she doesn't seem that interested. Unfortunately, The Boy has to go to bed, thus missing a spectacular long-range effort from Hartlepool. I consider waking him.

Back at Venue Cymru, Llandudno, Ronnie dispatches Ding with his third century of the evening. In some cricket, England find themselves at an historic low of 23-8 v New Zealand, eventually all out for 58. Bring 'em home.

THURSDAY MARCH 22ND

Upon waking, The Boy's first words are "What was the score between Barrow and Hartlepool?". Well young man, let me tell you, it was a hard-fought 2-1 win for Hartlepool, the Monkey Hangers coming from behind to take all three points in Cumbria. He seems satisfied with this, and launches into the Match Of The Day theme tune.

England are struggling at the breakfast table, but we have to leave them to it for the school run. Plodding home, on talkSPORT Alan Brazil is taking your calls on Jack Wilshere. Meanwhile, South Africa are 33 for 1, losing wickets at a more respectable rate.

What the fuck is this? China versus Wales? As host Jason Mohammed says, "live football on a Thursday morning, what a treat!". I don't know why, I don't know how, but I am all over it like a soup sandwich. In a new dawn for Welsh football, it's Ryan 'Giggsy' Giggs's first game as manager, having played no friendlies for Wales between 1991 and 2000. Opting for the tracksuit approach, he uses he his pre-match interview to claim "Gareth Bale is welcomed like a God".

China, for their part, are managed by Italian legend Marcello Lippi, or as John Hartson maintains, "Lippo". Hartson also reveals that Gareth Bale has come 7,500 miles on two different flights, basically describing how international travel works. It doesn't seem to have adversely affected him as he opens the scoring on exactly two minutes, the first of a hat-trick in a 6-0 win.

"Shouldn't you be in work?" asks the commentator. What a time to be housebound, although the edge is slightly taken off by a glimpse of a Wrexham flag. Fuck Wrexham.

South Africa are ticking over, Trump is getting a grip of Robertson, and Zlatan Ibrahimović has quit Manchester United to join LA Galaxy. Closer to home, John McDonald has impressively got himself from Llandudno to Glasgow to bellow the names of the Premier League Darts players. With the league taking shape, the cream is rising to the top, and I splitscreen it as Mark Williams holds off a spirited Ryan Day comeback in Wales.

At 1am I am back in New Zealand at a virtually empty ground, a handful of Barmy Army numpties bellowing an echo-afflicted rendition of Jerusalem. I've been around the world of sport, whereas Her Indoors has been around the actual world, returning from LA, oblivious to the Zlatan news, or indeed who he is or what he does. At the cricket, rain stops play and the last thing I see is the Cookie Monster running for cover.

FRIDAY MARCH 23RD

"Dad, I did a pee for 38 seconds."

Well done son, although the world record currently stands at 508 seconds.

I endure four hours of Test Match Special chat before the game is eventually rained off, taking mild solace in South Africa v Australia and the crucial Ireland v Afghanistan qualifier.

In something of a departure, I catch the last knockings of AFL Essendon v Adelaide Crows in Australian Rules Football. It's definitely Australian, not sure about the rules. Either way, the home team grabs victory in front of a raucous crowd of 43,016.

Still chasing my tail from the previous weekend, I finally immerse myself in suds and catch up with Channel 5's EFL Goals. I think I preferred it when it was called The Endsleigh League. The EFL sound like they should be marching round Luton in a yellow bib hurling abuse at minorities.

Impressively, John McDonald is back in Llandudno for 1pm to introduce Murphy v McGill, fighting for the last semi-final place alongside a strong field of Ronnie, Trump and Williams. I once saw McDonald having a meal in the hospitality area at Ally Pally. What a story.

I find myself increasingly drawn to the Afghan run chase. They get there with five balls to spare, and so will head to the Cricket World Cup in England and Wales in 2019, unlike Ireland and Scotland, who will stay at home.

School interrupts snooker and I leave it at 2-3, returning at 4-4 and 42 points each before Murphy eventually triumphs in a decider.

There's talk of going up the road for a curry, but it's almost time for the Netherlands v England. I like both things so embark on a dangerous strategy of watching the football on +1. Stuffed to the gills, Her Indoors sorts out the telly while we stand in the hall with fingers in our ears. Mission accomplished, and as the mascots line up, a sweet young girl performs an impressive double V-sign.

The real action is to be found at Venue Cymru, where the tension is palpable. Locked at 5-5, Ronnie and Trump face a final-frame shootout. Snooker is such a psychological sport, and Ronnie sits brooding, playing with his hands, seemingly oblivious to his opponent. As the balls are racked, Trump nervously glances in his direction and in that instant you feel the game is lost. It is.

Meanwhile, in the country formerly known as Holland, England have recorded their first win over the Dutch since Euro '96, courtesy of a Jesse Lingard goal. We're probably going to win the World Cup.

SATURDAY MARCH 24TH

We travel more in hope than expectation. Like visiting a terminally ill patient, I'm off to Sutton United to see the death throes of Chester FC's wretched season. I miss my train by ten seconds, so miss the next one by two minutes. I wander round West Hampstead for 25 minutes, inadvertently finding myself in a bookshop listening to The Smiths. Not a good look. Coming to my senses, I head to Ladbrokes where I am shocked into shame to discover that Tranmere v Eastleigh has its own coupon. I pick up a generic one, which has Chester at 11/2 to win at Sutton. No takers.

As happened last season, I'm the first to show for Chester. The Plough is closed so I sit in the club bar, scene of an historic broken chair incident. On the box, Tranmere are already one up albeit drowned out by The Eagles and Fleetwood Mac.

In the ground, I have a brief chat with Jonathan Legard, BBC sports reporter and erstwhile Formula One commentator, probably the closest Chester have to a celebrity fan. We go down to a mildly entertaining 3-2 defeat, and I repair to the pub with a fellow exiled fan known as The Hack, because he's a hack. They're showing Luton v Barnet, albeit with no pint glass symbol and a pixelated ball. I can't swear that it's from an official source, and the barman may be streaming it from his Nokia. We watch the goalless first half and fuck it off.

I eventually crawl home for the snooker, presented by Jill Douglas, the ITV Hazel Irvine. Murphy gets past Williams and gives a very technical post-match interview. Even Stephen Hendry looks bored. At least he's got an evening in Llandudno with Neal Foulds to look forward to.

Tired and emotional, I fall asleep trying to watch a replay of the women's boat race, which has mystifyingly been moved to Saturday. This country.

SUNDAY MARCH 25TH

Sandpapergate breaks overnight via Test Match Special. The dirty filthy cheating Australians have been tampering with the ball and we're going to be hearing a lot about it.

Still in Australia, the first Grand Prix of the Formula One season has taken place and I haul myself onto the day bed for a repeat. It's a sport that I've sporadically attempted to enjoy since the 1980s, with minimal success. Maybe this will be the season that it clicks. In Melbourne, Vettel beats Hamilton due to a virtual safety car loophole and the whole thing is a mess of rules and regulations. Again, it's sport for people who don't like sport.

Perth beat Melbourne Victory 1-0 and South Africa v Australia continues under a cloud. The clocks have gone forward, but it's forever 1pm at Venue Cymru where John McDonald slightly lets himself down with his pronunciation of "Clandudno". Ronnie comes out to Rock 'n' Roll Star by Oasis and commentator Clive Everton declares him "the greatest player we've ever seen". Go on Ronnie. He's favourite, although Murphy did do him in November. The match gets underway, but there's an instant interruption with both players looking up at a mystery object. What a sport. With normal service resumed, Ronnie takes the first session 6-3. Go on Ronnie!

At the bottom of League Two, Chesterfield beat Notts County 3-1 to give them a lifeline and deal a further blow to Barnet. Australia collapse in South Africa and the cheat Smith is booed off on 7. Australia all out for 107 on what is described as "a dark day for Australian cricket".

I have a backfield kickabout with The Boy, who gets the better of me, forcing me to introduce the dark arts of defending. We head back in for the end of Portsmouth 3-0 Oxford. John Portsmouth Football Club Westwood is there, ringing his fucking bell. He once shot me with a water pistol in a pub during Euro 2000, and I wish him nothing but misery.

Ronnie wraps it up by 8:30pm, and Clive Everton describes him as "snooker's answer to Tiger Woods and Roger Federer". A GOAT. Jill Douglas has her pins out for the final, and the kowtowing Murphy describes it as an "an honour to share the stage". with Ronnie. As for the man himself, he confesses to "heebeegeebees" and commends the Players Championship on its top 16 policy of "no numpties". And in an obligatory swipe at the authorities, he compares other tournaments to being in a zoo. Go on Ronnie.

MONDAY MARCH 26TH

After a bit of fitful TMS, I watch England's last stand on the iPad over breakfast with The Boy. Her Indoors is on the 5:40am Eurostar to fuck knows where. I'm in the shower for the final wicket, relayed by a shout of "Gone!" from The Boy.

Back from school, it's only The China Cup again, albeit with more limited viewing options. I tune into S4C for Cymru v Wrwgwai where I disturbingly find John Hartson chatting in fluent Welsh. Bale and Suarez embrace in the tunnel, and the big-toothed Uruguayan hits the post in the first two minutes. Half an hour later he hits the other post, but we reach the break goalless. Cavani notches early in the second half and that's your lot, Bale anonymous amid a slew of substitutions.

At Monday night soccer school, it's trophy night. Due to health and safety political correctness gone mad, pretty much everyone wins something, singularly failing to prepare them for a life of endless disappointment. Mini-Ronaldo has accrued the most skill points, and is rightly rewarded. There's also a special merit award, and as Big Rory reads out the attributes of the recipient, it becomes apparent that all of these could apply to The Boy. As he reaches the climax of his keynote address, I am already on my feet, tears welling as indeed my son and heir has achieved immortality, proud winner of a tawdry plastic trophy.

Suffering from snooker withdrawal, I watch a recording of Williams v Murphy. Elsewhere, the Red Button is offering the U-21 match between Ireland and Iceland. 0-0. There must be more to life than this. There is, in the shape of Danny Dyer's International Football Factories, which heads to Brazil where hooligans simply shoot each other. Lovely stuff.

I round off this momentous day with England cricket highlights, and we've come full circle.

TUESDAY MARCH 27TH

There's something of a departure on talkSPORT as Alan Brazil considers the existence of alien life. He's open to all possibilities, the Loch Ness monster, the lot. Ray Wilkins is more circumspect, adamant that we are alone in the universe, and that money squandered on space travel would be better spent on "kiddies". Some thoughts there.

Closer to home, with Her Indoors still touring Europe, we're having a boys' night in, which consists of getting as much football into our eyes as is humanly possible. England U-21s v Ukraine? We'll take it. They secure a late 2-1 win at Bramall Lane as the seniors emerge at Wembley. Assembling at the back door, we both shout, "Good luck England!" in the general direction of the Wembley Arch. They don't hear us.

Well-versed in the European game, The Boy recognises the AC Milan keeper, which is more than I do. I'm not even sure I really like football, I just go along with it. On the iPad we have Germany v Brazil, their first meeting since the historic 7-1 thrashing at the Brazil World Cup. Only 80 days to Russia now.

Prior to kickoff, Wembley hosts tributes to Jimmy Armfield, Cyrille Regis and Fiorentina's Davide Astori. England take a quick free kick, albeit from the wrong place, and it's slammed in by Jamie Vardy, or as he's known our house, The Rat. At half time we move the entire operation upstairs, closing the curtains on the luminescent Wembley Arch. Brazil exact a modicum of revenge on Germany with a 1-0 win, whereas Spain tear Argentina a new arsehole 6-1. Significant pointers to the forthcoming World Cup, or meaningless friendlies? You decide. At Wembley, a late VAR penalty denies England a long overdue win against the Azzuri. Fuck VAR.

WEDNESDAY MARCH 28TH

Some Australian cricketers have been banned for cheating, the silly cunts. No sport for me tonight, I'm off to the Vive Le Rock magazine awards with Sky Sports luminary and celebrity Ipswich fan, Bealesy. Behind us in the guest list queue is none other than punk fan and former England international Stuart Pearce.

"Have you got training tomorrow?" asks Bealesy.

"I have as it goes", reveals Pearce.

Almost 22 years after I saw Pearce utter the immortal line "Ladies and gentlemen, The Sex Pistols" on stage at Finsbury Park, he introduces The Damned. Later he appears in a high-kicking routine with Captain Sensible and I don't know what's real anymore.

In a further sporting snippet, Richard Jobson of The Skids reveals that Robert Smith of The Cure was an extremely hard-tackling defender. Who knew?

THURSDAY MARCH 29TH

Tears of a clown. Australia's Steve Smith is blubbing because someone rubbed sandpaper on a cricket ball. Now the coach, Lehmann, is crying. Now he's resigning. An endless cavalcade of sobbing cricketers appears on my screen throughout the day. Really? How many dead children in this scenario? Take the ban, pay the fine, and fuck off out. Meanwhile, PAOK Salonika's president has been banned for three years for coming onto the pitch with a gun. But what if he had a knife?

"Welcome back to the ballpark, America." Spring has sprung and the Major League Baseball season is underway. I watch the opening game, the first of a testing quadruple header, something of a commitment given that the average game generally exceeds three hours. Astonishingly, the season begins with a home run off the first pitch. Scenes, although I am legally obliged to point out that baseball is boring and 'like rounders'. Both of those statements are hard to dispute, but that is not to dismiss it out of hand.

Premier League Darts heads to Belfast and we are finally offered a solution to the Exeter debacle. The missing fixtures will now be played as part of a double-header in Rotterdam. I consider going. Of course I won't.

Blackburn beat Bradford 2-0 to regain top spot in League One, and I flick over to the final minutes of Wakefield v Castleford, both teams caked in mud and indistinguishable from each other, or humans.

The darts dovetails elegantly into the second test against New Zealand. The last test of the winter. Usual crap, Cook out for 2.

Midnight on BT Sport, we're live from Dodger Stadium for the visit of the San Francisco Giants. The home of the LA Dodgers is one of two baseball grounds I have visited, and scene of no small embarrassment. Arriving via stretch limo courtesy of Electronic Arts, stuck in traffic on the approach to the stadium, I was desperate for a piss. Taking my chances, I leapt out and headed for the bushes, my humiliation compounded when I attempted to get back into the wrong limo.

And finally, the Oakland Athletics get off to a winning start, 6-5 in extra innings. Let's go A's! Only 161 games to go, plus hopefully the post-season.

More bat on ball, I head to bed for TMS.

FRIDAY MARCH 30TH

Cricket never sleeps, and I simply pick up the TMS commentary where I left off. The South Africa v Australia 4th test continues without Smith and the Sandpaper Three. Not a Good Friday for those boys.

The football fixtures are all over the place, with Oxford v Scunthorpe going up against the Chinese Super League. Remember that? In a less exotic Super League, it's also a big day in the north, with Hull KR v Hull FC followed by St Helens v Wigan. And in a worrying development, Ray Wilkins has been hospitalised.

This month's biggest boxing match in the history of the sport is between Anthony Joshua and Joseph Parker. Astonishingly, the live weigh-in in Cardiff is absolutely rammed, people presumably paying to watch large men step on some scales. You can see that in my bathroom every morning for free, and it's not pretty. Joshua turns up in obligatory oversized headphones, with Parker on message in a Parka.

Infinitely more important is Chester's home match with Torquay. Tuning into BBC Devon, we match The Gulls for a full two and half minutes before conceding, eventually going down to a desultory 2-0 defeat with relegation a near certainty.

Woking are in danger of joining us, and BT Sport show their home game against high-flying Macclesfield, which ends in high farce. Deadlocked at 2-2 with seconds to go, a Macc player thinks he's scored and wheels away to celebrate. However, the ball sticks in the mud and doesn't cross the line. Unfortunately, the Woking keeper is oblivious to this, thus enabling a further Macc player to bundle it in for the winner amid scenes of confusion. What a league.

In the Egg League, Hull beat Hull and St Helens beat Wigan for the first Good Friday in nine years. South Africa put on a decent knock, and we're straight into Middlesbrough v Wolves then Derby v Sunderland, on what really is a good Friday if you like nothing more than to sit on your fat arse and watch hours of endless, pointless sport.

Channel 5 Goals has to share the screen with cricket as Bairstow posts a century, a fairly commonplace landmark given ludicrous significance: score 100 and you're a hero, score 99 and you're a worthless moron. New Zealand then take a shit with their trousers on, falling to 17 for 4 at one point.

Australian cheat David Warner has a press conference scheduled for 1am, our time. Please don't cry. Wheeled out like a child catcher, he unconvincingly reads a prepared statement. Please don't cry. He claims that his involvement in what is in the history of the species a relatively minor event is something that he will "regret for as long as I live". Please don't cry. He starts huffing and puffing, and here come the tears as he goes into a comedy high-pitched voice.

I watch New York Yankees at Toronto Blue Jays, a sport in which institutional cheating is routine, with some players spending decades on the 'roids. I retire for a bit of early TMS, for tomorrow I have business at Vicarage Road.

SATURDAY MARCH 31ST

TMS picks up where I left off, and the New Zealand middle order batsmen are burrowed in like a pair of Alabama ticks. I watch Melbourne Victory 3-1 West Sydney Wanderers. In a farcical VAR decision, there's a six-minute delay between a penalty being awarded and taken, during which the ref produces a flurry of red cards.

I listen to Palace v Liverpool on the overground to Watford High Street, then meet up with The Watford Gap and family in a nearby eatery. The service is so incompetent that they compensate us by waiving the drinks bill, making the mistake of telling us this in advance.

Watford v Bournemouth is the battle of 11th v 10th and I attempt to enliven it with a small wager on both teams to score plus a Bournemouth win. The Cherries have travelled in decent numbers and are singing about the Scummers going down, a reference to their south coast non-rivals Southampton. Until Bournemouth's improbable surge to the Premier League, most people in Bournemouth supported Southampton, but keep it up lads.

Compared to the shit I watch, the football is notably faster and imbued with pointless flicks and tricks before the ball is inevitably launched into the mixer. Watford score, Bournemouth equalise and we pour half-time lager into our heads. Watford then score again, but The Watford Gap misses it as he is taking an ill-timed shit. To compound his misery, Jermain Defoe nicks an injury-time equaliser for The Cherries.

We pile into a pub for Everton v Man City and see Sané score a ridiculous goal, incongruously accompanied by overloud Dolly Parton. Everton miss a header, then Jesus scores for City at Easter. I would stay, but the shit music makes it untenable. The One Crown, Watford High Street, you have lost a customer.

I hear City's next goal on the train, then wake up for the second game of Match Of The Day. A touch of cricket paves the way for Chicago 2-2 Portland, with the home team fielding Bastian Schweinsteiger, a man with whom I once had a brief canapé-based chat at a wedding in St Tropez.

Sadly I miss LA Galaxy beating LA 4-3 courtesy of Zlatan heroics, but listen to a talkSPORT catch-up of Anthony Joshua stoving some bloke's head in. Meanwhile in New Zealand, Cook is out during a severe bout of diarrhoea. Oh shit.

SUNDAY APRIL 1ST

Harry Kane has signed for Arsenal. Of course he hasn't. The transfer window isn't even open. Nevertheless, my hilarious April Fools' joke gets some traction from Her Indoors and The Boy. The fun never stops.

A bit of cricket catch-up segues into Arsenal v Stoke, and I endure the stultifyingly dull first half on Sky. It's so dreary that I make an informed decision not to watch the second half. But then we hear a penalty awarded on the radio. Gambling on the time delay, I sprint to the TV, switch on the PS3, select Sky Go and see it converted. Phew. We hear Arsenal's next two goals in the car en route to clearing out Her Indoors' former family home, The House of Doom. I don't really put a shift in, instead playing football with The Boy while listening to Chelsea v Spurs blaring out from the parked car. The Boy does a lap of the garden when Eriksen scores, some goal by all accounts.

We repair to Her Indoors' brother's house where the teenage son has been enjoying a lot of women's tennis. In men's tennis, we watch someone called Isner win something called the Miami Open.

The balance of power is shifting in the capital, and Match Of The Day 2 makes a big deal of Tottenham's 3-1 win being their first at Stamford Bridge since 1990, showing a clip of Gary Lineker scoring in that game. The presenter, Manish Bhasin, asks whatever happened to him? He became the presenter of Match Of The Day, advertised some crisps and became a regular subject of abuse for six-fingered Twitter users.

Away from my own bed, TMS is more fitful than usual as England set New Zealand a record run chase.

MONDAY APRIL 2ND

In a deeper bath than usual, snooker's China Open competes with South Africa v Australia, each essentially involving men hitting balls with wood. No time to tarry, Macclesfield awaits. Heavy rain. A solo drive. Snow on Easter Monday, Jesus Christ in reverse. Games are being called off all around me, but still I press on, the Shackleton of non-league football. Alan Pardew has been sacked, and still the world turns.

I successfully traverse the tundra and get to Macc early, using this time to wander around on my own listening to Joy Division. I head for a nearby pub that is so foul that I leave without buying a drink, albeit half a pound of Dundee Cake lighter. Outside I walk past the Chester fan known as K-Klass because he used to be in the cross-border electronic music combo, K-Klass, the traditional hatred between Chester and Wrexham put aside in the Summer Of Love. What I don't know is that he is still in K-Klass.

In front of a paltry, frozen, sodden away following, Chester actually play quite well and are denied a clear penalty because the fouled player attempts to stay on his feet. So what is a fucking penalty? Do both parties have to be complicit in it? We eventually succumb to a 1-0 defeat to the champions elect and I can't wait to get out of there.

Back in time for the cricket, Broad takes two wickets with his first two balls. Six hours later I awake for the final hour as New Zealand attempt to hold on for the draw and hence the series. Bad light stops play. Bring 'em home.

TUESDAY APRIL 3RD

Ronnie is four frames down to a "numpty" called Elliot Slessor. Unperturbed, he insouciantly knocks in a 147 to trouser £42,000. At 5-1 down in a first to six, I am dragged outside to play football with The Boy, squeezing into a pair of EA Sports shorts and Fulham socks, the latter a remnant of a training day with Kevin Keegan in the last century. It's all over for Ronnie, losing 6-2 in a conflicting day at the office with the World Championship looming.

The Champions League quarter-finals are worthy of our full attention. Real Madrid go to Juventus and brutally win 3-0, with The Boy pleased to witness a Ronaldo goal. Seville 1-2 Bayern is relegated to my phone, and Sky optimistically broadcast Fulham 2-0 Leeds on the iPad.

With no more cricket, I am forced to watch actual scripted television. The Walking Dead 2-1 Homeland.

WEDNESDAY APRIL 4TH

Selby is already 5-2 up against Woollaston by the time I immerse myself. With Ronnie gone he must fancy himself for whatever fucking tournament this is. Oh yeah, the China Open. The Jester from Leicester gets through 6-3, but what's this? Australia's Neil Robertson 5-4 down to the bespectacled Sam Craigie? Digging deep, the Antipodean former World Champion forces a tense decider and squeezes through.

Meanwhile, in Robertson's homeland, the Commonwealth Games is getting underway in torrential rain, which pleases me no end. The opening ceremony takes a philosophical, almost cosmic approach. Overseen by the unflappable Hazel Irvine, she sets the tone somewhere between awe and tedium, years of snooker analysis paying dividends.

"The earth as we know it begins to take shape", says Hazel of a cack-handed attempt to redress the despicable treatment of the indigenous people through the medium of interpretive dance. Suddenly it turns into a beach scene and Hazel wisely keeps her counsel.

I briefly spoke to her once in Tokyo during a minor altercation at the 2002 World Cup.

"We're not at the snooker now", I said.

"No, we're not", she confirmed.

And still the ceremony continues. Steve Cram joins in for an extended and hugely incongruous towelling off section, with tits hanging out all over the place. Prince Charles and Camilla look on. There are eleven days of this to come – the games, not the ceremony – and I don't intend to watch any of them. If the Olympics is the Champions League, then this is the Checkatrade Trophy.

Forced out of the house to run some errands, upon returning I flick on talkSPORT before getting out of the car. They appear to be talking about Ray Wilkins in the past tense. What a shame. RIP Butch.

There's a moving tribute prior to AC Milan v Inter, where of course Wilkins played.

The football continues forever, and Robbie Savage is on 5live ahead of arguably the biggest game of the season, Liverpool v Man City in a Champions League quarter-final first leg. Scenes.

"The only way it's going to be a 0-0 is if it's postponed!", screams a hysterical Savage. Postponed is not 0-0 though, is it? Try getting it past Ladbrokes.

Hours ahead of kickoff, the atmosphere is febrile. In a moronic, shameful incident, the Man City team bus is attacked on its approach to Anfield. Nice one lads.

The match itself is an absolute ding-dong-do, Liverpool blitzing City with three goals in barely half an hour, a 3-0 win leaving them with one foot in the semi. They will almost certainly be joined by Barcelona, who similarly dismantle Roma 4-1. What a night. I watch the highlights upstairs on ITV+1, with some heartfelt tributes to Wilkins.

Decompressing with a nightcap of Mark Allen 6-4 Yan Bingtao, I then have the briefest look at the Commonwealth Games where the parallel bars is underway. Not for me, Jeff.

THURSDAY APRIL 5TH

I have a high noon underwater meeting with Mark Selby as he eases past Lyu Haotian 6-1. This takes us straight into the marquee game, Williams v Allen, the fiery Celts locking horns in old Beijing. The Welshman puts down a marker with a confident 130 clearance in the first before blitzing the next, Allen yet to pot a ball. He forces a re-spotted black in the third, but Williams eventually slots it in for 3-0.

In the baffling word of golf – Gentleman Only, Ladies Forbidden – The Masters has started, and much is being made of Ian Poulter winning the Houston Open in order to qualify. Back at the snooker, Mark Allen claws one back to hit the mid-session interval at 3-1, but I have to leave it at 3-2 to play football with The Boy. On the plus side, I score a double hat-trick, but also inadvertently launch the ball into some kid's face. In other football news, Arsenal beat CSKA Moscow 4-1, all the goals coming in the first half.

Premier League Darts has come to Liverpool, where it's 'Judgement Night', starting with Peter 'Snakebite' Wright v Daryl 'SuperChin' Gurney, who became a father this morning. I briefly leave them to it to catch up with Williams v Allen, which has gone to a deciding frame: Allen misses a crucial red to let Williams clean up.

Back to the darts and some of the crowd are holding up placards bearing the name of Eric Bristow. Oh Christ, no. RIP Eric, who has actually died at the event. The match is a footnote (6-6) as the crowd choruses "One Eric Bristow". Snakebite is in tears. I'm in tears. It's extraordinary television, and Keith Deller appears on stage, remarkably holding himself together and describing his friend and foe as "a massive loss to our sport".

I had the honour of playing Bristow once, backstage at The Circus Tavern with Sid on commentary. Both gone now. Despite shaking him to the rafters with an opening treble 20, I finally succumbed to the master. All hail The Crafty Cockney.

FRIDAY APRIL 6TH

I've been trying to avoid it, but it seems that the cage fighter or whatever he is, Conor McGregor, has attacked a bus. None of my business, and I settle in for the more genteel China Open, where Selby dispatches Williams 6-2, finishing with a 143 break. Nobody attacks a bus.

Footage emerges of the Par 3 event traditionally held before The Masters. Celebrating a hole-in-one, Tony Finau horrifically dislocates his ankle, before casually popping it back in.

I try to catch the first half of England Women v Wales, plus the opening minutes of Cardiff v Wolves in the Championship, but have to bundle into the car en famille. We drive to Watford Gap, where there is blanket coverage of The Masters, the children wincing at the ankle incident. Amid a bit of baseball, I manage to dip into the torpor of Cardiff v Wolves, where the home team miss two penalties in a 1-0 defeat. Neil Warnock not happy. Neil Warnock also an anagram of Colin Wanker.

SATURDAY APRIL 7TH

The Sussex-based Chester fan known as The Hack drives to Watford Gap and I drive us both to Chester for the final rites. We duck into an unfamiliar multiscreen pub for shit pies and a turgid goalless draw between Everton and Liverpool. There's a final desperate rally from the home team, resulting in a botched free kick. It's followed by a close-up of the Everton manager, Sam Allardyce, in which he clearly says, "What the fuck was that?". He speaks for us all.

Chester v Tranmere at The Deva Stadium is slightly more entertaining. We dominate the first half although Tranmere hit the woodwork twice, and then score from an injury-time corner. They seal victory with a second, Solihull are winning, and our time in The National League is coming to an end. Both relevant results are consecutively confirmed on the Blues Bar TV, and that is that. There's no great outpouring of emotion, just resigned gloom at a conclusion that has seemed inevitable almost since the season began.

Back in the car in mute despair, we listen to another North West derby between the two Manchester teams. In what sounds like an incredibly one-sided game, City race to a 2-0 lead at the break. Robbie Savage is going off his nut, branding United "embarrassing" and "a disgrace". But they nick one in the second half, somehow fashion an equaliser and then only go and win it 3-2. It's breathless stuff, and Savage is on the verge of exploding, his hysterical approach for once seeming apposite.

Back at Watford Gap, we watch The Masters in the pub, where some people have been to watch a nearby rugby union match that ended Northampton 13-63 Saracens. Extraordinary behaviour.

Match Of The Day doesn't quite capture the madness of listening to the Manchester derby, but it does show City fans actually crying because they couldn't clinch the Premier League at home to their rivals. We've just been relegated by ours. Get to fuck.

SUNDAY APRIL 8TH

The Watford Gap is bellowing at rugby league, which makes for a relaxing Sunday morning. His team, Wigan Warriors, were 21-0 down at Catalans Dragons before turning it round to win 32-23. That's good apparently. Yeah, bye then.

Heading home, those of us in the car who remain awake listen to Arsenal 3-2 Southampton, and we get back for the last knockings of Chelsea 1-1 West Ham. I fall asleep for the start of the final round of The Masters, waking up to see Rory take a shit with his trousers on, handing a joyless victory to a great big American frat boy.

MONDAY APRIL 9TH

Back on the road again, destination Bournemouth. Stopping at Fleet Services, The Boy gets his first Panini Sticker book, free with FourFourTwo magazine, and is very pleased to snag a brace of Spurs players in his debut pack.

It's at this point that I should get all misty-eyed and reminisce about completing sticker books over the years: got, got, need. But I had little or no knowledge of football as a child, and by the time I was into it I had better things to spend my money on than pictures of men in polyester shirts. On the rare occasions that I dabble, I get too nervous to put the stickers in, perennially terrified that I'm going to involuntarily buck and thus condemn a journeyman midfielder to a jaunty angle for all eternity.

Furthermore, for all the faux-nostalgia and pseudo-ironic man-child obsession, it is basically low-level admin. The same people who pay a fortune to fill their albums would probably refuse to do it for minimum wage.

TUESDAY APRIL 10TH

Champions League quarter-finals, second legs. No fucking about, these need to be watched, and watched live. Still away from my control centre, in a sport-free environment, I am reliant on iPad and mobile phone, basically draped in screens wherever I go. I sometimes think I'm addicted to the technology as much as the sport. And while mul-tiscreening may be considered a nowadays pursuit, I consider myself something of a pioneer of the discipline. As early as 1993, I distinctly remember dragging the alleged portable out of the bedroom and placing it next to the main TV in order to simultaneously watch two games. Why wouldn't you? Have a good time all the time...

It's a more elegant solution tonight, with slabs of technology nestled into the soft furnishings. For once, the atmosphere at The Etihad is febrile. 3-0 down from the first leg, City need an early goal to have any chance. Jesus Christ, Jesus scores on two minutes and we have a game on our hands, or more accurately propped up on a cushion on the sofa. It's a compelling affair, but a brace of second-half Liverpool goals skewers any hope of a comeback, and Klopp's Kop Kings march on to the semi.

The other quarter-final is arguably even more dramatic. 4-1 up from the first leg, presumably Barcelona simply need to turn up to the Olympic Stadium to progress. An early Roma goal wobbles the nerves, and when they slot a penalty just before the hour mark, it's feral. It's arguably next goal wins, and the next goal is scored in the 82nd minute by Roma, who hang on to progress on away goals.

It's been an extraordinary night of Champions League football, all overshadowed by live commentary of Chester v Bromley of course. Playing with the freedom of relegation, we squeak a 3-2 win in the 90th minute. Something of a goal, by all accounts.

WEDNESDAY APRIL 11TH

We go again. More Champions League. Same format. Bayern get past Sevilla with a goalless draw. Forget it. The real action is to be had at the home of the holders, Real Madrid, who come into the game 3-0 up against Juventus. Foregone conclusion, Juve without a chance. Again an early goal! Juve on two minutes. And another! They score again on the hour, and improbably the tie is level. Injury time arrives, and it really is next goal wins. Penalty! To Madrid! Absolute bedlam. Juve keeper Buffon is sent off. Chaos reigns, as Ronaldo stands and waits. He finally gets to take his penalty in the 97th minute, drilling it high into the corner where no keeper on earth could save it. Absolute scenes, although the best goal of the night is scored by Wolves, a ludicrous long-range effort in a 2-0 win over Derby.

The Commonwealth Games can't really compete, but I have a swift look at the Lawn Bowls. Not for me, Jeff. And finally, Chester manager Marcus Bignot is sacked in a car park.

THURSDAY APRIL 12TH

To fill the void, I watch some Commonwealth Games hockey, specifically the semi-final between New Zealand and England Women. Come on England, get into these! Goalless after four quarters, it goes to a shootout and New Zealand chip an audacious winner. "It was perfect", says The Boy.

Thursday night is Europa League night, and I settle for ITV highlights of CSKA Moscow 2-2 Arsenal, which sees the Wenger Boys comfortably progress. Sadly the occasion is marred when Glenn Hoddle drops two "lacksadaisicals" in quick succession. Meanwhile, Roy Keane phones in some perfunctory drivel about "confidence". Over at the Commonwealth Games, somebody calling himself JJ Chalmers is presenting barefoot. The Games have gone.

FRIDAY APRIL 13TH

It's the last day of what has been a logistically testing stay in Bournemouth. I discover The Boy watching the 10,000 metres and a bit of shot put. We also see a Canadian pole-vaulter who appears to have paid a pound for a pair of shorts and has 50 pence worth up her arse.

In the real world, it's the European semi-finals draw. Arsenal get Atlético Madrid and Liverpool will face Roma. We finally get back home for the second half of Aston Villa 1-0 Leeds, Steve Bruce surely back on the piss. Meanwhile, actually in Leeds, the Rhinos are 8-0 up against Wigan Warriors with ten minutes left and conspire to lose 9-8.

Checking the post, they've arrived: two tickets for the opening day of the World Snooker Championship.

SATURDAY APRIL 14TH

Boreham Wood away, en famille. The family that watches non-league football together, stays together. That said, Her Indoors takes one look at the shit pub I find and fucks off to the shops. We pour fizzy muck into our necks and watch Southampton take a 2-0 lead against Chelsea.

"West Brom are gone", says The Boy, a sentiment echoed word-for-word by some bloke at the bar. However, three Chelsea goals in a nine-minute blitz turns the game on its head and it's on for young and old. What a sport.

I receive a message from my departed friend, The Driver, who has abandoned The Mighty Chester to live in France and support Bordeaux. He tells me that he is only six games away from completing La Carte – every match, home and away. I did The Card last season with Chester and it almost killed me. But due to the staggering distances involved, the French version is an even more unhinged venture.

He'd much rather be with us in Borehamwood though.

"Because Chester are relegated, there's no pressure on them", says The Boy.

He makes a valid point, but it doesn't stop us from being turned over 4-2. After the game, we pile into a nearby pub to watch the Grand National. It's won by Tiger Roll, a horse that The Boy claims I have previously bet on, something I have no recollection of.

Via another pub, we get home for Spurs 1-3 Man City, which takes me under. Regaining consciousness for the Commonwealth Games marathon, there are disturbing scenes when a runner called Calum Hawkins becomes delirious and starts falling over. It's macabre. Clearly not a sport, the marathon is simply an endurance test for people with no discernible skills.

Match Of The Day restores sanity. Back in Australia, I scrape the barrel with Women's Rugby Sevens, where England are thrashed 26-5. This JJ character still hasn't found his shoes. England men then lose to New Zealand. What have we done to upset New Zealand?

Thankfully, the stricken marathon runner is now talking, and it transpires that his team-mate ran past him to claim bronze. Still seeking footwear, JJ Chalmers runs into the sea, while Hazel Irvine is presumably prepping for the snooker: Sheffield awaits.

It's been a long day, but as a final act of glory hunting I watch England v Australia in the netball. Struggling for consciousness, I listen to the second half in bed, but pass out before the climax as England dramatically nick it 52- 51, followed by a Razzle pile-up as I sleep through an entire Chinese Grand Prix.

SUNDAY APRIL 15TH

Easy like Sunday morning, I flick between Channel 5 and Channel 5+1 to enjoy a touch of EFL Goals, and then immerse myself in hot water to watch newly-promoted Wolves take on Birmingham City. Annoyingly, it overlaps with Newcastle v Arsenal, where Gazza is in the crowd sporting a creative hairstyle. I miss the opening goal of a 2-1 home win as I am checking the end of the Chinese Grand Prix. Must prioritise.

The shifting of the seasons sees the Indian Premier League get under way, along with county cricket. No interest. The Boy has a new Champions League ball and I am railroaded into a kickabout, one eye on the iPad as Celtic turn over Rangers 4-0. We head indoors for Man United 0-1 West Brom, and Manchester City are crowned Premier League champions.

The Commonwealth Games closing ceremony is an absolute atrocity, reaching a nadir when #BRUM is spelt out by human bodies. Presumably the next games is in Birmingham. I simply won't be there.

There's a swathe of European football to get through, including PSG thrashing Monaco 7-1 to clinch the French title. The football is slipping away, although there's still a bit of MLS on Sky. Then we're into Match Of The Day 2, where Pep Guardiola goes golfing with Tommy Fleetwood, who may or may not try to sell him some whizz.

MONDAY APRIL 16TH

At Monday Night Soccer School, there's no sign of Merson, who seems to have taken the money and run. On the pitch, The Boy attempts an audacious overhead kick to gales of laughter all round. Back home, he insists on watching Golden Gordon again, perhaps to pick up some tips.

This takes us to West Ham v Stoke, a turgid affair enlivened by late goals from two big subs, first Peter Crouch for Stoke, and then Andy Carroll. Meanwhile in Germany, Mainz v Freiburg sees the players recalled from their half-time break in order for a VAR penalty to be taken. I foresee no problems with this technology in the forthcoming World Cup.

TUESDAY APRIL 17TH

The World Snooker Championship is almost upon us, but there are still qualifiers taking place, and they're live on YouTube. I have somehow worked this out and am watching them in the bath. I am winning at life.

Less interesting is the evening's Premier League match, Brighton 1-1 Spurs. It's so boring that I listen to second-half commentary of Guiseley 0-1 Barrow on Radio Cumbria, taking negligible pleasure in Gizlee being relegated and staying below Chester. The result also sucks Woking in and gives Barrow a chance of staying up, meaning I won't have to go there next season. I'm not welcome in Barrow.

Barcelona's 2-2 draw at Celta Vigo means they are still on course to be the first team ever to go unbeaten in La Liga. Closer to home, Accrington Stanley are promoted, a Rochdale fan has confronted the referee, and Joey Barton has been made Fleetwood manager, where he will no doubt see out his contract without incident.

WEDNESDAY APRIL 18TH

Snooker's Judgment Day continues in the bath. Spring has sprung, but I'm underwater watching the latter stages of Alfie Burden v Thepchaiya Un-Nooh, the former chasing his first Crucible appearance in 20 years. YouTube flips between tables as results come in, with Neal Foulds comparing it to a general election. Rob Walker even conducts post-match interviews for an online audience of barely a thousand, asking Robert Milkins about his Wurzels walk-on. Despite an outburst from Burden, Neal Foulds assures us he's a nice guy. But he will not be at The Crucible this year. Oh no, Un-Nooh through. It's a curse, it's a burden. Or not, in this case.

On the school run I am invited to a Sunday lunch and immediately try to think what sport this will clash with. Back for more snooker, I watch Premier League Darts in the garden with a gin & tonic as the sun goes down. But it's only Wednesday? As I explain to the returning Her Indoors, it's the first night of the Rotterdam double-header to make up for the snowbound Exeter postponement. In front of a packed house, there's a wall of noise for the ever-popular Barney. Here comes MvG, losing in front of his home fans. And now Gary Anderson, a cunt hair away from a nine-darter. Scenes. We go again tomorrow night.

Bournemouth 0-2 Man United is a footnote, along with a trio of Italian games and a touch of Real Madrid. The big story of course is Oakland A's beating Chicago White Sox 12-11 in six hours and 14 innings. That was a test.

THURSDAY APRIL 19TH

Despite the baseball-afflicted late night, I'm up at the crack of ten for the World Snooker Championship draw, live on Facebook: "Due to technical issues, the draw for the Betfred World Championship is delayed until 12 noon."

Fuck that. Tick follows tock. It's a shambles, and I eventually have to conduct my own impromptu draw by scrolling down my phone and reading them out loud. Ronnie v Stephen Maguire is the pick, described by Rob Walker as "seismic". And I've got two tickets for it.

Due to circumstances beyond my control, Premier League Darts and Burnley v Chelsea are cut short. Waiting for late-night highlights, I finally get round to watching the iPlayer snooker drama, The Rack Pack. As with all real-life dramatisations, you have to take it with a pinch of salt, but it's entertaining fare. At the end, Steve Davis is quoted as describing Alex Higgins as "the one true genius that snooker has produced". I shall ask him to clarify that on Saturday.

With more time to kill, I tentatively have a look at something called The Real Football Fan Show on Channel 4+1, which promises "real banter". As opposed to what? Fake banter? Imaginary banter?

My expectations aren't high, but nothing could prepare me for this, the depths of so-called Fan TV given oxygen by a mainstream broadcaster. During a heated debate, one fan appears to claim that "Arsenal had no impotence".

2am finally ticks round, and I watch highlights of Leicester 0-0 Southampton, followed by Burnley 1-2 Chelsea, a scoreline that I had already inadvertently stumbled upon. In the darts, it's a Dutch derby between vans Barneveld and Gerwen, with the crowd seeming to favour Barney despite MvG's dominance of the sport. Barney comes out on top to ensure that MvG will leave Rotterdam pointless. The repeat of Daryl 'SuperChin' Gurney v Simon 'The Wizard' Whitlock takes me to 3:30am and I am struck by a very real sense that I am wasting my life.

FRIDAY APRIL 20TH

Gone! Arsène Wenger is to leave Arsenal at the end of the season. Talk-SPORT is in absolute meltdown. This is their Diana moment, an uncontrollable outpouring of hysteria. Somebody get Tony Hadley on the phone. The former Spandau Ballet crooner describes Wenger as "an amazing man". He's not dead. Sky Sports News dedicates noon until 11pm to Wenger – End Of An Era. Is he dead? I don't think so, although he will be missed. Wenger has been managing Arsenal for the entire time that I have lived in London, but has finally been hounded out by the baying hordes of Fan TV. Presumably they'll win everything now.

Still reeling, I watch Melbourne City beat Brisbane 2-0 in some kind of elimination game, the trademark seagulls flying around the pitch presumably oblivious to the ramifications. I take the second half of Chelsea Youth 2-2 Porto Youth in the garden, Chelsea progressing to the final on penalties.

School run interrupts sport, but we reconvene in the garden for Millwall 0-3 Fulham. In a rare show of affection, The Boy wants a cuddle so I miss Sessegnon's opener.

SATURDAY APRIL 21ST

To Sheffield, and destiny. I have often said that the World Snooker Championship is the best 17 days of the year. The weather is on the turn, the football is coming to a head, and there are numerous hours of serene green to stare at, a marathon for players and viewers alike. I warm up with a touch of Mark Selby v Joe Perry on the train. First class of course, I'm not an animal (and it was about a quid to upgrade). However, the wi-fi is shit, rendering the snooker unwatchable.

The route from Sheffield station to The Crucible is lined with snooker paraphernalia, and you can basically walk into the TV set. I see Hazel Irvine, seemingly oblivious to our brief exchange in Tokyo almost 16 years ago. Also present is John Parrott, who I once spoke to on the tube – as he disembarked he generously gave me his copy of the Daily Mail. And of course Steve Davis, who recognises me and comes over. I half expect him to drop to his knees. Improbably, there was a brief period in the last decade when the six-time world snooker champion would in fact kneel every time he met me, out of respect for a regular feature I used to write in a now-defunct poker magazine. There are witnesses to the phenomenon, as well as photographic evidence. Strange days indeed. He's more business-like today, and we arrange to meet after the Ronnie match for an interview, as previously discussed by text.

Sheffield is resplendent in the sunshine, only sullied by an unsightly and incongruous BMX display outside The Crucible. I meet up with a friend that I haven't seen for about ten years, local author Steve McKevitt. He lives in the city and has been lured out by the prospect of a free ticket for the snooker. We go for a quick pint then take our seats, at which point he tells me he's colour blind and promptly falls asleep.

Ronnie is misfiring and I feel short-changed. I came here to watch The Rocket score centuries, not Maguire, but that's what's happening. McKevitt snaps out of his power nap and rallies strongly with a whispered anecdote about the French-Canadian Alain Robidoux once coming back to win a frame from four snookers behind. I counter with the tale about the same player once complaining that Ronnie was being disrespectful to him by beating him ambidextrously. We should probably have our own show.

Mercifully, the mid-session interval comes, and the man that we thought was Irvine Welsh turns out to be Damien Hirst, who follows

Ronnie everywhere. We also see the famous Cov Kit, a man who has a season ticket for the front row every year, turning up for each match in a variety of Coventry City replica shirts. But not this year. In what seems like a personal vendetta, snooker supremo Barry Hearn has banned football shirts, and is planning to abolish the season ticket system, meaning that after this year Cov Kit will have to take his chances with the rest of us.

Fuck knows how he sits there for all 17 days. If ever a sport was made for TV, snooker is it. While it's a thrill to be up close and personal with the players, and an honour to be at the home of snooker, you can't sing, you can't talk, you can't eat, and you can't drink. You can sporadically bellow "Go on Ronnie!" though, something that I take advantage of. And you can sneakily check football scores on your phone. Chester are 2-0 down before I know it, while my colour-blind associate celebrates a successful day for Wigan Athletic.

Ronnie eventually manages to reel off a century, and gets out of the session 6-3 down. Hungry like the wolf, we to head to Greggs. While the snooker is a massive TV event, it arguably has very little impact on the city. Two minutes from the venue and we're basically on the set of Threads.

Pastry item demolished, we meet Steve Davis in the foyer of his hotel, three Steves sat at a table. Intros over, I proceed to interview him, some 22 years after the first time. As an opening gambit, I ask him if there's too much snooker these days. He gives it a lot of thought.

"You could argue football's like that", he says, citing the incisive Mitchell & Webb sketch.

"For the hardcore fans it's brilliant. For the casual fan they're probably not watching it all anyway. You're doing an unusual thing by bombarding yourself."

I ask him if he would have fancied doing the entire card in his pomp.

"Yeah, I think so", he says with some relish. "The worst thing is twiddling your thumbs for too long and then having a massive time off. We got used to that, but you look at the players now, they've got a full season. It's more like a job, it's like a proper profession now. It's also given some of the older players longevity because they're actually benefiting from having regular competition. I don't watch all snooker on telly. I wasn't really a watcher anyway."

Traditionally associated with the 1980s, snooker is actually now a much bigger sport, and an estimated 500 million people will be watching the action unfold at The Crucible.

"Oh it's fucking massive now compared to the 80s", says Davis, dropping his first, but not last, F-bomb. "It's ridiculous. It's quite interesting how people in the UK are not as aware of what's going on in the snooker world even though there's a bombardment on the television. People go, 'Oh I don't watch it anymore, it's not as fun as it used to be' whereas worldwide, across Eurosport, across all of the European countries, it's massive, the Far East, more countries around the world watch it."

Snooker's audience is widely considered to have peaked when Dennis Taylor pipped Davis in the famous Black Ball Final of 1985, with approximately a third of the country tuning in until after midnight. I was among them, as unwittingly was my old dear, who at one point remarked: "No wonder it's taking so long, they keep putting the balls back on the table."

Like many, I was supporting the underdog Taylor, but I don't tell Steve Davis that.

As he says, "the 18 and a half million that tuned in for the '85 final was surpassed fourfold when Ding Junhui played in the final of the World Championship. Through the night in China there was 60 million people watching, and that was during the night. If there'd been the same time difference, god knows what the figures would be."

Having lifted the World Championship six times, Davis admits that it's a slog.

"Physically it does take its toll even though it wouldn't appear to be a physical sport. In the 80s when I was young I lost half a stone during the tournament, and I didn't really have a lot to lose. Nervous tension, perhaps not eating as much as you would normally. You're knackered by the end of it, you are drained a bit, so whilst it's not a game where you're sweating, it is incredibly draining. You're on your feet in the latter stages for two lots of four-hour sessions, and practising beforehand, and then getting out of your chair, sitting back down again. I know that sounds ridiculous, but the whole day, the mental concentration required and the adrenaline, you're exhausted at the end of it."

I repeat my long-held view that it's the best 17 days of the year.

"That's a great accolade", says Davis. "I'm too close to it. I suppose it depends where your allegiance lies. There are people that would say their year revolves around the Masters golf or the British Open. But this has stood the test of time. Laughably, still journalists in newspapers call it a pub game. It's laughable how they've got a job. Do they not understand what's required from competing at the highest level? It shows an amazingly inadequate understanding of what they're supposed to be good at being a journalist at. And they'll write reams about motor racing, which is really an unfair playing field. Horse racing gets loads of exposure at certain times, which is once again the horse, not the person. There's a load of sports out there that aren't level playing fields. Snooker is a totally level playing field, and journalists still snub their noses at it even after this amount of time. It beggars belief really."

Not me. It's a powder keg, and Davis concurs with my analogy of turn-based tightrope walking.

"It can be a very cruel game as well in as much as you don't get equal table time. Once the other guy's at the table you just have to sit there until he misses. In football at least you can try and tackle the guy."

That's almost verbatim what my six-year old son said, and they're both right.

Davis takes particular exception with those who question whether snooker is a sport, or indeed what that actually means.

"Archery's been in the Olympics for fucking ages", he blasts. "Snooker is as deserving as any other game to be in the Olympics. Anything that takes dexterity and skill. But the Olympics has never been a fair playing ground in as much as they choose what has a certain amount of popularity. Apparently if you go back in time, the Olympics used to have poetry in it. I saw this on QI."

On the subject of TV, I tell Davis that I found The Rack Pack broadly entertaining and am surprised to learn that he loved it, vouching for the veracity of everything bar one scene.

"It was a snapshot of folklore history with embellishment", he claims. "Obviously they made it funnier, but it was to some degree how it happened. A lot of it was written from biographies and reports in the newspaper. I thought it was a pretty good reflection of the time."

It's a much-revered time that seems hugely at odds with the ruthless professionalism of sport today.

"You don't see a footballer with a fag in his mouth just before he goes out to play", agrees Davis.

"But not every player in the 80s had a beer in their hand. Bill [Werbeniuk] was drinking, Jimmy [White] would have a few beers at the table, Alex [Higgins] would have a couple of beers every now and again, but most of the players didn't. But I think the attitude's more professional, same as the attitude in golf is more professional. There's probably more players going down the gym and working out now than there ever was in the 80s."

Indeed. In fact, I still consider this the Embassy World Championship, tobacco sponsorship long since jettisoned from sport in favour of wholesale gambling promotion. You pays your money, you takes your vice.

I remind Davis of his old quote about Alex Higgins being the only true genius snooker has produced. Unsurprisingly, he is happy to amend it.

"I would say Ronnie's the biggest genius we've ever had. I'd say Alex is the second biggest."

I also remind him that he described Ronnie as "shamanic" earlier in the year.

"I got that word in because I'd had a bet with somebody", he reveals. "My mate said, 'I dare you to say that.' Well it wouldn't be out of place to say it, so the first chance I got I said it."

Almost misty-eyed, Davis talks of Ronnie having "that other worldliness" of a shaman.

"I'd love to see through his eyes to see if he sees different pictures to the ones I saw, and the same for Alex Higgins. Those two, I think they may see different pictures, as if there's a different type of sporting spectrum, you're seeing something that others don't."

Yet Ronnie was shit today.

"Anybody can get caught cold, and if you haven't relaxed it shows you the minute difference between being good and being just average. Everyone's human, everybody's allowed bad days, but what he can do is he can turn things around very quickly."

Ever generous with his time, we spend another ten minutes discussing music, with Davis now a renowned underground DJ, and indeed playing a gig in Sheffield. It's been a solid half-hour chat, but we are eventually interrupted by some random who claims to have played him in Swindon once. Never one to disappoint his fans, selfies ensue, and we bid him farewell as he heads directly to a live television broadcast. What a legend.

A couple of scoops and I'm back on the train, watching Davis on the iPlayer. Due to being out of the house, I have successfully managed to avoid the result of the FA Cup semi-final between Man United and Spurs. Disembarking at St Pancras, I keep my head down, but unavoidably spot a big fat Manc with a flag stuck in his arse pocket, feet at ten to two, swaggering around like he owns the place. That is not the gait of a losing semi-finalist.

"I'm home dear. Ronnie played like a cunt."

Football highlights on, my instincts are confirmed when Spurs take the lead but succumb to their ninth successive FA Cup semi-final defeat. The day comes full circle with snooker highlights: Selby gone! No hat-trick for the Jester from Leicester.

SUNDAY APRIL 22ND

I wake up at exactly 10am to see Ronnie rattle off the first three frames to go level. In non-sport news, it's the hottest ever London marathon. Weren't we sledging a few weeks ago?

Sadly, I have to miss Arsenal 4-1 West Ham for lunch at the home of Saints Dad, where I am ridiculed for turning up late because I have been watching snooker in bed. It was worth every second. As predicted by my close personal friend, Steve Davis, Ronnie put on the afterburners to cruise past Maguire. Shame he couldn't do it when we were there.

Chelsea Dad is also present, albeit with a ticket for the FA Cup semi-final against Southampton. He regales us with tales of travelling away with Chelsea as a schoolkid, plonked onto Gary's Coaches with his Roland Rat lunchbox for midweek encounters at Leeds or Sheffield Wednesday. It's more straightforward today as he sups up and gets an Uber to Wembley.

Not only is Saints Dad not going to the match, there's some suggestion that he's not even going to watch it because they have guests, an astonishing set of priorities. For starters, don't invite people round on FA Cup semi-final day, or if you do then make sure you're showing the game on a massive television. But he doesn't even have BT Sport. It's like a third-world country. Reduced to watching it on my phone, in the end I log onto his laptop with my account and we watch it under a parasol, a perfunctory 2-0 defeat for Southampton. Chelsea Dad returns from Wembley in buoyant mood, and I eventually crawl home to catch up with the snooker.

MONDAY APRIL 23RD

I have cleared the decks for a full week of snooker and football. That's living alright. Up early, I kill time by watching looping FA Cup highlights on the Red Button. I dabble with the snooker, but it's a long haul.

Interrupted by the school run, I get back for the second half of Chelsea v Barcelona in the UEFA Youth Final. I have to leave before the end for Soccer School, where I am reprimanded by The Boy for not watching him. I tell him I saw him let a goal in.

Back for the snooker, Sean Murphy is gone, beaten 10-9 in a Jamie Jones war. In the Premier League, Everton beat Newcastle 1-0, with a banner on displaying shouting: "OUR SURVEY SAYS GET OUT OF OUR CLUB". It's a reference to a fan survey held regarding current manager Sam Allardyce, with a nod to vintage quiz show Family Fortunes. Brilliant.

I triple-screen with snooker on the laptop and iPad, and dip into a bit of Italian and German football on my phone. At The Crucible, Hawkins v Carrington cannot be stopped, entering its eighth hour of live coverage, now overlapping with the highlights. I even watch two hours of Ding v Xiao even though I think I know the result. I have more or less been watching snooker from 10am to 2:05am. It is, as they say, a marathon of the mind.

TUESDAY APRIL 24TH

Ding takes care of business and is in the next round by 11am. Attention turns to former champion Stuart Bingham and his tit-for-tat bout with outsider Jack Lisowski. In one frame, Bingham sinks 11 reds and 11 blacks, sniffing a maximum 147 only 35 years after Cliff Thorburn notched one at The Crucible.

Following the desultory fare served up at Goodison Park 24 hours earlier, across Stanley Park it's Liverpool v Roma in the Champions League semi-final, which is preceded by despicable violence from the visiting fans. In one of the great European nights, Liverpool go 5-0 up before giving Roma a lifeline with a couple of late goals.

It makes up a brick in the wall of sport along with Derby 3-1 Cardiff and a pair of snooker matches. Former world champions are struggling in Sheffield, where Bingham is gone and Robertson is 6-3 down overnight to Robert Milkins, still accompanied by The Wurzels: "I am a Cider Drinker/I drinks it all of the day/I am a Cider Drinker/It soothes all me troubles away/Ooh arrh, ooh arrh ay, Ooh arrh, ooh arrh ay."

WEDNESDAY APRIL 25TH

50 days until the World Cup. You can almost taste it. Meanwhile, two previous world champions attempt to ease their passage at The Crucible. Mark Williams takes on Jamie Robertson and John Higgins is up against Thepchaiya Un-Nooh. Williams makes a 140 clearance, his first since 2005. Sadly I sleep through it, but I'm in the bath to see Higgins pot 13 reds and 13 blacks including an outrageous fluke that I shout into the pocket. Shades of Cliff Thorburn, who began his historic break with a fluke. Sadly, Higgins runs out of position and the dream is over.

Neil Robertson v Robert 'The Milkman' Milkins resumes, and The Wurzels walk-on has now evolved into a crowd clap-a-long. Trump takes on debutant Chris Wakelin, and I take on the school run, returning to see Wakelin post a 141 break, the highest ever on debut. Robertson is struggling against Milkins and crashes out 10-5 as The Milkman delivers.

In the evening session, Un-Nooh pots 14 reds and 14 blacks then just overruns the last, his fingers twitching in a vain attempt to slow down the cue ball as 50 grand and immortality slips away. Anthony McGill takes on Ryan Day, winner of the Gibraltar Open, which doesn't have quite the same prestige as the Worlds.

There is also the small matter of Bayern Munich v Real Madrid. In an attempt to get The Boy to bed, I allow him to listen to commentary in his room: In Bed With Ronaldo. It's not an entirely successful strategy as he bellows down the stairs when Marcelo leathers in an equaliser for Madrid. They go on to win 2-1. It seems a reasonable game, but after the fireworks at Anfield I can't really engage with it.

In Sheffield, for once a world champion makes it through as John Higgins seals victory against the plucky Thai. In the other game, Day hits 141 to equal the highest break, then ends the day with a 145, ten grand changing hands for the third time today.

On ITV's Champions League highlights, Roy Keane describes Roma's defending as "shameful". After a hard day, I take the snooker highlights in bed. Un-Nooh furious at fucking up a 147. Oh no, Uh-Nooh.

THURSDAY APRIL 26TH

There is no 10am snooker, an absolute disgrace. Instead I am forced to delve into Alan Brazil's Sports Breakfast, where speculation is rife over Gareth Bale's non-appearance v Bayern. Someone is also trying to buy Wembley Stadium in an £800m bid.

We're at the stage of the snooker where there's an overlap between the first and second round, something I'm never wholly comfortable with. At the mid-session interval it is revealed that Ryan Day's brother, Rhys Day, has played football for Manchester City and the Welsh U-21 side. Back from the school run, Jason Mohammed reveals that it is "not Ryan's day", and he's gone, presumably to polish his Gibraltar Open trophy.

I've bitten off more than I can chew here: two Europa League semis, two snooker matches, plus the Premier League Darts. I have to let the darts go after the first two fixtures, safe in the knowledge that I can watch it unsullied tomorrow. It's not as if it's going to be on the news.

Arsenal v Atlético Madrid sees the visitors reduced to ten men after ten minutes. Their manager Diego Simeone is also sent off. Good. Arsenal eventually take the lead, but while attempting to walk the ball in are caught by a sucker punch from Griezmann for a 1-1 draw. In the other semi, it's Marseille 2-0 Salzburg.

There's late-night drama at The Crucible where it's gone Trump 8-8 Wakelin, yet another seed fighting for his life. Trump, who has previously had Twitter spats during a match, has taken some time off from social media. But he misses a black for the match to let Wakelin in to force a final frame decider. This is tension, and Cov Kit is resplendent in a suspiciously new-looking light blue Ralph Lauren. It's an error-strewn finale, but Trump finally gets over the line. Modern snooker is all about potting, but I quite like an extended safety bout.

Europa highlights reveal that Marseille's first goal was hand-ball. The NFL draft is under way – not a clue.

FRIDAY APRIL 27TH

At 10am, Joe Perry knocks in a century against Mark Allen. I can't even get out of bed. There are three former world champions left - all from the so-called class of '92 – including Ronnie, who is in action against Ali Carter. The Captain takes the first following an extended safety bout, with Cov Kit looking on, defiant in short-sleeved sky blue. Ronnie casually replies with a century. Simultaneous mid-session intervals give me time to draw a bath and continue day seven of my snooker odyssey under water.

I become so engrossed that I forget about the Premier League Darts repeat, switching to the MEN Arena, Manchester. Barney 6-6 Cross is the big one, the old warhorse battling the younger man.

All snooker all day. Allen is first through to the quarter-finals, whereas a misfiring Ronnie is 9-7 down overnight. Cov Kit rocks up in a turd brown tracksuit, presumably a nod to the notorious 1978 away kit.

On the banks of the Thames it's advantage Fulham as they eventually overcome relegated Sunderland 2-1. At nearby Stamford Bridge, the FA Youth Cup Final first leg finishes Chelsea 3-1 Arsenal, with the young Gunners apparently coached by Charlie Merson.

What a Friday night, living the dream. The NFL draft goes into its second night, all six hours of it. Fuck that shit.

SATURDAY APRIL 28TH

It's the middle Saturday of the snooker, but sadly I have to let some of it go. In the A-League, it finishes Sydney 2-3 Melbourne Victory, with a very late Melbourne own goal forcing extra time, then the same player making amends with the winner. In Sheffield, Hawkins is through, and may or may not be off to Nando's.

It's the climax of the National League relegation battle, and BT Sport are flicking between Barrow v Chester and Woking v

Dover. The tension is exquisite. With both home teams losing 2-1, Woking are relegated. Liverpool 0-0 Stoke is a mere footnote.

Meanwhile at Sheffield it's all kicked off. In a niggly match between Ronnie and Carter there has been an unprecedented shoulder barge. Dennis Taylor has never seen the likes. But there's no sign of Cov Kit, presumably at Cheltenham 1-6 Coventry. What a life.

Society almost breaks down, but the game finishes 13-9 to Carter, and The Rocket has fizzled out. Conversely, a rejuvenated John Higgins goes 8-0 up against Lisowski.

And still the football comes, as Havant & Waterlooville pip Dartford to promotion to the National League. I once got hit in the face by a ball at Dartford so have very little sympathy. It's the business end of the season in all countries, and Juventus steal victory from the jaws of defeat to win 3-2 at Inter and keep the title in their hands.

SUNDAY APRIL 29TH

It's a brutal schedule with 10am dual snooker. It may be the perfect sport to watch simultaneously as there is a lot of standing about. The Boy and I still talk of the time that Ding took three and a half minutes to take a shot. He's marginally quicker today, going to town on McGill, whereas Trump and Walden share the first eight frames. Ricky Walden is from Chester, but he supports Liverpool and is therefore dead to me.

Celtic beat Rangers to claim a seventh consecutive title, then there's the Azerbaijan GP. Christina Aguilera is there, presumably promoting some tat. The commentator has a dig about her knowing who is using soft compounds, the implication being that she is little more than vacant window dressing for a turgid dying sport. Strange to think that the fundamentally different activities of snooker, football and Formula One all come under the umbrella of sport.

As everyone hopes, there is a first lap crash, which is then followed by a prolonged safety car bout. With Lewis Hamilton seeking his first win of new season, I reject Crotone v Sassuolo, very much the Watford v Bournemouth of Italy. There is chaos in Baku. Grosjean drives into the wall under safety car rules, and Bottas's wheel falls off while leading.

Less deadly, Lisowski makes it 10-1 v Higgins to avoid the first ever second round whitewash, greeted by applause all round. Both remaining former champions are in action, with the laconic Welsh-man Mark Williams taking on The Milkman on the other side of the divide. Higgins now on a maximum, but he loses position on the final black and tactically settles for a 146, thus guaranteeing 10k in his arse pocket.

Manchester City casually win 4-1 at West Ham, and Higgins finishes off Lisowski 13-1, with Cov Kit reassuringly back in place.

Ahead of Man United v Arsenal, Sir Alex Ferguson presents Arsène Wenger with a trinket, the two bitter foes now engulfed in mutual respect. With the game locked at 1-1, Jose Mourinho chucks the big man Fellaini up front. They lump the ball up to him, he gets his head on it and nicks a stoppage-time winner. Tactical genius.

It's a marquee night at the snooker, although with the black ball blocking a pocket there is 20 minutes of nothing before the referee calls a rerack. Should he have stepped in earlier? I could watch it all night, just for the embarrassment. Trump and Walden cannot be separated, locked at 8-8 after a long day.

I take a nightcap of Dodgers at Giants, then quickly switch coasts for Patrick Vieira's New York City v Dallas, played at Yankee Stadium, which is wholly unsuitable for football as well as aesthetically aberrant. The 3-1 home win includes David Villa's 400th career goal (a dubious VAR penalty) shortly followed by his 401st. Meanwhile in baseball, the Yankees are at Los Angeles Angels, but I don't have the heart for it.

MONDAY APRIL 30TH

The revised snooker schedule affords me a well-earned 1pm lie-in. For once, Ding is too quick for me, rattling off his requisite frame in ten minutes and 20 seconds to progress 13-4. It's a filthy rainy afternoon, perfect for the conclusion of Trump v Walden. Barry Hearn turns up, playing down the shoulder barge and banging on about saturation versus starvation.

I briefly spoke to Hearn in Las Vegas during the 2003 Mosconi Cup, effectively the Ryder Cup of pool. In the tournament Steve Davis, playing under the name Romford Slim, took on legendary US player Earl 'The Pearl' Strickland. A few of us interviewed Strickland prior to the match and he was absolutely full of himself before being roundly handed his arse by our man, 5-0, truly one of the greatest things I've ever seen. Perhaps with this in mind, a few years later, again in Vegas, this time at The World Series Of Poker, I needed a doubles partner for a game of pool in the Ladbrokes Lounge. Scanning the room, after some thought I selected the six-time Word Snooker Champion, Steve 'Romford Slim' Davis. Won 1-0.

Back at Sheffield, I have to leave the snooker with Trump 11-9 up to get The Boy and his Ipswich mate. Trump cruises through, spurred on by Walden trying difficult shots. At Soccer School, Chelsea Dad tells me he used to play with Peter Crouch. The Boy scores a decent goal and makes some solid saves. Charlie Merson is not there as he's coaching Arsenal in the second leg of the FA Youth Cup final against Chelsea. Arsenal lose 4-0 at home.

Chelsea Dad is still harbouring hopes of fourth place in the Premier League, stymied by Tottenham beating Watford 2-0 in a rapidly emptying Wembley Stadium, absolute torpor. Has Kane rushed back from injury chasing the Golden Boot at the cost of the World Cup? Don't know.

The snooker is all over by 8pm as Williams dispatches The Milkman. Cov Kit looking casual.

TUESDAY MAY 1ST

May Day. May day. M'aider. The quarter-finals get under way at The Crucible and Cov Kit looks particularly pleased with himself in a casual sky-blue T-shirt with chocolate coloured piping. An unscheduled lie-in has thrown my schedule into chaos and I am faced with a minefield of iPlayer catch-up, at one point triple-screening, although a glimpse of Eurosport sullies one of the scores. By the time the digital dust has settled, The Hawk is leading Ding 5-3 while Wilson and Allen are locked at four apiece.

The afternoon session sees Trump take on Higgins plus Williams v Carter. With the school run interrupting, I am very pleased at being able to pause both games. However, disaster strikes on the way home when I duck into an Italian delicatessen to buy The Boy a Portuguese custard tart. They've only got the snooker on the café TV, the whole world gripped by the unfolding action in Sheffield. I avert my gaze, but the familiar voice of Steve Davis informs me that Trump is 5-3 up. I also face technical difficulties when I get home and the whole thing is ruined. Proof if proof were needed that all sport should be watched live.

The evening fare sees Real Madrid v Bayern Munich on BT Sport, while Sky hit back with Scunthorpe v Plymouth. It's deliciously poised as a win for The Iron would secure a playoff berth, but victory for The Pilgrims would see them leapfrog their hosts.

Bayern take an early lead but are quickly pegged back in an absorbing contest that reaches half time at 1-1. Meanwhile at Glanford Park, Scunthorpe are a goal to the good. An appalling goalkeeper error by Bayern sees Madrid go ahead and brings The Boy downstairs in pyjamas to see it. But Bayern equalise as Scunthorpe get their second, overseen by club president Ian Botham, who briefly played for them.

In Sheffield, Hawkins has gone to town on Ding, taking an 11-5 overnight lead and proving a genuine contender, despite his Benny from Crossroads demeanour. Madrid squeak through to their fourth Champions League final in five years where they will meet Liverpool or Roma. Seconds later, Scunthorpe secure a League One playoff slot, Plymouth's late-season charge coming to nought. Kyren Wilson also leads 11-5 overnight against Mark Allen, and I consider a small wager on him to win the whole thing.

It's all over bar the highlights when I get sucked into the last knockings of San Diego Padres @ San Francisco Giants. 5-3 down going into the 9th inning, the Giants somehow manufacture a 5-6 walkoff win. Scenes.

WEDNESDAY MAY 2ND

By the time this day is over we will know the identity of the World Snooker Championship semi-finalists and the participants in the Champions League final. These are the days of our lives. The Hawk rattles off the first two and Ding is gone 13-5. It's a bloodless victory, but Barry is "over the moon". No Nando's required. We go straight to Trump v Higgins without the need for a second screen. As with all the quarter-finals, it's a left-hander versus a right-hander. What are the chances? Don't know.

A self-styled "international playboi" in his youth, Trump is gradually morphing into Nigel Blackwell from Half Man Half Biscuit, as indeed the singer himself has pointed out on-stage. Musically they remain at different ends of the scale however, and Trump's awful aspirational walk-on tune does little to endear him.

John Higgins rattles off four frames including an outrageous fluke while snookered to go 7-7. Higgins absolutely cannot be dismissed. Hewn from pure Scottish granite, he is a course and distance winner. You'd choose Trump to play for your entertainment, but Higgins for your life. The Scot forges ahead 8-7. Cov Kit seems to have moved seats. Trump stops the rot to end the session 8-8.

This is of course a repeat of the 2011 final, where the spiky-haired newcomer blitzed his way to the last two, only to come up against the immovable force that is John Higgins MBE, the Wizard of Wishaw. It's a match that I distinctly remember watching in a heatwave in the garden on a pre-digital portable TV, the screen notionally shielded by a cockamamie cardboard construction. But despite his spectacular arrival on the scene, Trump has not graced a world final since, despite trousering the best part of four million in prizes.

For the evening session, Cov Kit is sporting a white T-shirt that says GHOST TOWN TO HOST TOWN, presumably a reference to Coventry City being kicked out of their stadium and forced to play at Northampton Town. And of course Ghost Town being a song by

Coventry's finest, The Specials. It's a pretty laboured message all the same, and something of an eyesore.

Higgins is an absolute Terminator and even when he goes 11-9 down you still fancy him. He ruthlessly rattles off the next three, but Trump grabs the next to force a decider. What tension. It's the match of the tournament so far and I feel sorry for Trump as Higgins holds his nerve in the final frame to once more crush the Bristolian's hopes.

Meanwhile there's high drama at Aldershot in the National League playoff elimination game. Ebbsfleet equalise in the 119th minute and somehow win a preposterous penalty shootout. In the more exalted environs of the Stadio Olimpico, Roma conspire to beat Liverpool 4-2, coming within a goal of forcing extra time. But the Scousers progress 7-6 on aggregate and will face Real Madrid in the Kiev final.

Back at Sheffield, it's a case of After the Lord Mayor's Show as Williams dispatches Carter 13-8.

What a night of sport. Now for the highlights. Clive Tyldesley describes James Milner deflecting the ball into his own net off his face as "a freak goal". Milner says he'll be celebrating reaching the Champions League final with "a glass of Ribena or something".

THURSDAY MAY 3RD

I had assumed that the Tour de Yorkshire was a joke. Not so, and ITV4 are showing Beverley to Doncaster over the course of several hours. Not for me. Cycling is a mode of transport, elevated to a leisure activity for middle-aged men in lycra.

I am instead counting the hours until someone in Sheffield mentions the single table setup. This is it, John Higgins v Kyren Wilson, the Scotsman surely drained by his late-night arse-clencher, but the young pretender carrying the additional weight of my 11p bet. The BBC treats us to the obligatory stop-motion footage of the single table being prepared. We are also told that Wilson keeps himself fit and eats the right food. Blasphemy. Higgins won it 20 years ago: move over, old man.

Wilson – playing his hero at the home of the sport – starts the nervier, missing shots and leaving Higgins chances that he eagerly hoovers up, taking the first three frames before Kyren gets on the board in a turgid and lengthy opening half-session. Higgins holds the advantage 5-3, with reports of Wilson suffering a backstage nosebleed, something that was presumably commonplace in snooker's 80s heyday.

Boreham Wood beat Fylde 2-1 to progress to the National League semis. The Boy correctly points out where we stood for our last visit there. As usual, I gaze longingly at The Lunch Box, home of the best bacon sandwich in non-league: "Hello darlin', cup of splosh with that?"

Due to the sheer weight of sport, I again have to defer the Premier League Darts, which tonight is at the Birmingham Arena. I took The Watford Gap there one season, and I believe it may be the first time I ever saw a two-pint pot. It's also where I urinated next to Kirk Shepherd, and conducted my final awful interview with Phil Taylor. He brought his grandson with him and spent much of my allotted time discussing the children's television show Ben 10 with him. Despite express instructions to remain silent, The Watford Gap asked a bemused Taylor "Are you a GOAT?".

Hawkins takes a 5-3 lead over Williams, still days away from the final. Arsène Wenger has the chance to sign off with a Europa League final. Arsenal play an exquisite brand of frustrating football that results in neither goals nor real chances, mustering only one shot on target. With my close personal friend Rafa Nadal looking on, Atlético nick it with a goal from "Diego Costa the Elephant Man" as The Boy has been singing. Wenger will now bring down the curtain on his Arsenal career not in Lyon, but in Huddersfield.

In the other semi, Salzburg beat Marseille 2-1, scoring five minutes from the end of extra time with their only shot on target coming from an incorrectly-awarded corner. Which is as good a way to win as any.

FRIDAY MAY 4TH

May the 4th be with you. Ha ha ha, sounds almost exactly like May The Force Be With You. The snooker is draining. It's a beautiful day, but I'm sat inside watching callow men shunt balls around a green table in the north of England. One semi seems to merge into the other, with Hawkins v Williams notionally the more entertaining.

I inadvertently see the Premier League Darts scores in a discarded copy of The Sun. Fuck The Sun. For reasons unknown, Brighton v Man United is on Sky, so I have it on the iPad while coming second best to The Boy at swingball, which is considerably more entertaining. Brighton beat Manchester United 1-0, a score and indeed a fixture that makes no sense at all. And still the snooker continues.

SATURDAY MAY 5TH

John Virgo is on The Danny Baker Show playing the Sausage Sandwich game and I am astonished to learn that he has no sauce at all. I had him down as a Brown Sauce man all day long.

'Where's the brown going?!'

Nowhere, as it transpires.

I have to leave the snooker to accompany The Boy to Saturday Morning Football. I barely see him as against my wishes I am given the managerial reins of Team B, a raggle-taggle outfit of insolent, uninterested little shits with no tangible skill or discipline. Astonishingly, we squeak a 1-0 win, and then grind out a 0-0 to get through the group stage - shades of West Germany v Austria in the '82 World Cup. We meet our match in the final though, where we are turned over 3-0 in a shambolic defensive display. It's a stressful business, as indeed is refereeing, which I discover is largely guesswork.

I get back home to see a recording of Higgins clinching his place in the final. Wilson never really made up the opening three frames, and experience again trumps youth. As is traditional at this time of year, there is a swathe of crucial football to watch. Tranmere beat Ebbsfleet 4-2 after extra time and the horrible Plastic Scousers will be back at Wembley yet again. Not that I'm bitter that I can see the arch from my house, yet Chester have still never played there.

Stoke lose 2-1 at home to Palace and are therefore relegated. Fuck Stoke. I once got chased there. West Brom beat Spurs 1-0 in injury time and are astonishingly still alive. Barnet win, but Coventry and Morecambe grind out a 0-0 draw that condemns them. The commentator mentions West Germany v Austria, a fixture that hangs over the World Cup like a bad smell, ultimately leading to simultaneous final group fixtures long before splitscreen viewing was practical.

In order to avoid my family, I head upstairs for the 5:30pm kickoffs: Everton v Southampton, Rochdale v Charlton and Arsenal Women v Chelsea Ladies in the FA Cup final, all goalless at half time. What a sport. Rochdale must better Oldham's result at Northampton, an agonising 90 minutes of flip-flopping in and out of the relegation zone. With Oldham drawing 2-2, Rochdale go 1-0 up, which is how it finishes.

Chelsea Ladies win the FA Cup final, and Everton equalise beyond injury time to again offer West Brom a lifeline. Northampton v Oldham cannot be stopped. There's an agonising few minutes as Rochdale players stand around helpless, having done their job. It's over. Rochdale are safe, Oldham are gone. Cue a pitch invasion at Spotland, where a crowdfunded Spanish Rochdale fan is in attendance. Equally ludicrously, my acquaintance, The Driver, aka the Chester-betraying Bordeaux fan, lets me know he's in a minibus on his way to St Etienne. The tit.

As the second snooker semi resumes, news breaks of Sir Alex Ferguson having a brain haemorrhage. I watch Juventus 3-1 Bologna as the home team close in on the title. The snooker looks like going the distance and overlaps with Match Of The Day, which really has to be watched due to its short shelf life. And ideally watched on the big fuckoff TV in eye-watering HD. The snooker can tick over on the laptop, and I even catch up with the Premier League Darts on the iPad. A solid shift.

Simply gorging on sport, I also treat myself to a touch of Tony Bellew beating David Haye on talkSPORT. I think I prefer boxing on the radio, primarily because you don't have to pay for it, but also because it somehow seems to capture the drama more eloquently than footage of two fat men cuddling each other.

The non-contact sport resumes in the white-hot crucible of The Crucible, where Williams has finally overhauled The Hawk and now leads for the first time, 16-15 in a race to 17. I desperately want a decider, but in a 40-minute frame Williams clinches it 17-15. I manage to miss the key shot due to the delay in flipping from the laptop back to the TV. Bollocks. Out on their feet like a pair of heavyweight boxers, it's close to midnight, but we have our final: John Higgins v Mark Williams. The class of '92.

SUNDAY MAY 6TH

Phew, what a scorcher. I'm in the garden, but there are all kinds of ups and downs to be decided in the world of football. I watch Cardiff 0-0 Reading, which sees The Bluebirds promoted to the Premier League. It's a result mirrored at The Etihad where Man City, presumably with one foot on the beach, grind out a goalless draw with a grateful Huddersfield. The real action is to be found in the National League playoffs where Boreham Wood are taking on Sutton United in what nobody is calling the Thameslink Derby.

This all takes place against a backdrop of the World Snooker final. Despite being seen wolfing down a kebab at 2:30am, Williams goes 4-0 up and helps himself to Cov Kit's sweets, our man on the front row resplendent in a sky-blue and white striped shirt.

The game at Sutton is delayed due to a pair of drones. What if they had a knife? It finally finishes 3-2 to the visitors, and Boreham Wood will go to Wembley with an average home attendance of 300. Fuck Boreham Wood. In Italy, Napoli draw 2-2 with Torino, all but handing the title to Juventus.

Nobody escapes The Terminator, and the opening session in Sheffield ends 5-3 to Williams. There are still Champions League places up for grabs, and Chelsea beat Liverpool 1-0. In Barcelona, El Clásico gets under way in front of an estimated 500m viewers in 182 countries. Adios, Iniesta.

Michael Carrick is at the snooker for the evening session, where Williams is yawning. There's a change of shirt for Cov Kit, and indeed a mid-session feature about him. His name is Brian Wright, and he has been coming since 1989. He actually proposed at The Crucible in 2012, but is yet to actually marry his betrothed. Presumably he can't find the time.

El Clásico finishes Barcelona 2-2 Real Madrid, ensuring that Barça are still unbeaten. Williams finishes 10-7 up overnight, and he draws closer to fulfilling his promise to do a naked press conference if he wins it. One more day until I get my life back. Match Of The Day 2 features Arsenal 5-0 Burnley, Wenger's last home game. Au revoir, Arsène.

MONDAY MAY 7TH

Bank Holiday Monday. Good for them. It's absolutely sweltering and there's no sport 'til Sheffield. As such, I am faced with filling the meaningless hours until 2pm. I even read a book – it'll never catch on. Finally it's time, and I take the final in a hammock on the iPad, my fat face in a straw hat staring back at me from beyond the baize. There's a theory that you end up with the life you want.

Cov Kit is living his best life, sporting an atrocity of a top that blurs the line between what is and what isn't a football shirt. Settling into the hammock with a side dish of England Kids 2-1 Italy Kids, there's a disturbing creak and suddenly my arse is touching the ground with the supporting tree on the verge of collapse. What a way to go.

Somehow I survive to see Williams go 14-7 ahead, and then 15-10 going into the final session. John Virgo has taken to repeating "right in the heart of the pocket!" like someone is pulling his string.

There's a brief respite for Monday Night Soccer School, then I'm back for the final session. Cov Kit is in an eyesore of a jacket, whereas the pundits are in suit and tie as tradition dictates. I like that, and almost consider following suit, despite the heat.

15-13 now, and Steve Davis mentions The Terminator. Great minds think alike. The bloke next door is mindlessly watering his garden, oblivious to the high drama at The Crucible. A seven-frame lead has been slashed to two. 15-14 at the mid-session interval. Williams can't find his extension. 15-15 now, should have had a bet. Higgins' kids look like The Proclaimers. Williams' kids weren't born the last time he won it, but they're here tonight.

Steve Davis has never seen the likes. I am firmly in the Williams camp, and at one point find myself screaming "miss you fucking tomato" at the ruddy Scot.

Williams regains his mojo and goes 17-15, one frame away from glory. Out of respect I go indoors to watch what might be the final frame on the big TV. Williams has a pink for the title. Missed it! 17-16 now. Hazel describes it as "absolutely astonishing". Davis: "the greatest final I've ever seen here". Shades of '85. I can't breathe, and resort to watching through one eye. Higgins needs three snookers. Whither Alain Robidoux...

It's over, Williams has done it! He is mobbed by his family, and it's almost tearful. Shades of Alex Higgins in '82. Williams watched last year's final in a caravan, drunk and pissed up on booze. Now he's holding a victory press conference bollock-naked apart from a towel, an addition made at the behest of Barry Hearn. Celebrating long into the night, he is still tweeting at 7am.

TUESDAY MAY 8TH

What a fucking nightmare. For reasons beyond my ken, I have agreed to drive a pair of cackling hags to Norwich. They are comedy duo The Scummy Mummies, and I am the friend of at least one of them. I must be, as this road trip has eaten into my options of watching the crucial relegation match between Swansea and Southampton, both in trouble, and with anything but a draw fatal for West Brom.

It's too much to bear and I take to the mean streets of Norwich, ducking into the Prince of Wales, which is showing the game. Nursing a pint of pissy lager, I watch the goalless first half, which is incongruously accompanied by Jimi Hendrix – it's what he would have wanted. With tensions running high, it's an absolute shit sandwich, or as the commentator says with some understatement "not for connoisseurs of the beautiful game".

In disgust, I head back to the theatre and find an unauthorised seat high above the action. Sat in my eyrie above 500 oblivious pissed-up women, I listen to the second half during the show. Gabbiadini comes off the bench to score a winner for Southampton, and West Brom are finally relegated. Saints are safe barring a freak goal swing, and Swansea are now in a world of shit.

WEDNESDAY MAY 9TH

Back in the fold, I head upstairs for Chelsea v Huddersfield with a side of the Coppa Italia final between Juventus and Milan, the latter still managed by Ray Winstone. Juve win 4-0, but the real action is to be found at Stamford Bridge where lifelong Huddersfield fan Sir Patrick Stewart has beamed himself down. Approaching the end of the first half goalless, Chelsea are awarded a corner, but the ref blows time before they can take it – shades of Clive Thomas in '78. Tough shit, they should have been quicker. The players don't see it this way, and crowd the ref, Lee Mason. Premier League referees have now evolved into bona-fide football personalities, but I would struggle to name more than a handful in a line-up. I simply don't care. All I know is that George Courtney came from Spennymoor.

Fighting for their lives, Huddersfield take an early second-half lead. Chelsea soon equalise, but The Terriers hold on for the draw that secures their Premier League status. It also hampers Chelsea's top four push, which makes it all the sweeter.

A quick tour of Europe sees Real Madrid and Barcelona both in action, with the latter still unbeaten this season. At some stage during the proceedings, The Boy appears to tell me that the Wembley Arch is flashing. Sure enough, Harry Kane has scored the only goal of the game against Newcastle, strengthening Tottenham's Champions League push and boding well for England. The World Cup is within touching distance.

THURSDAY MAY 10TH

I'm on the road again with The Scummy Mummies, destination Winchester. It's a diabolical liberty that means missing Premier League Darts plus Premier League football in the shape of West Ham v Manchester United. I listen to the opening minutes and then spot a man in a West Ham top running through the streets of Winchester. Is he trying to get back for the game? Does he know it's on? We may never know. I decide to watch the show instead of going to a pub on my own, sitting in the Theatre Royal oblivious to the action at the London Stadium or the arrows being slung in Aberdeen. Media lockdown commence.

FRIDAY MAY 11TH

I awake in a Winchester chalet with two women and immediately listen to catch-up of talkSPORT commentary of West Ham 0-0 Manchester United. Punditry is provided by Ray Houghton, who I have interviewed in his capacity as advisor for the Football Manager computer game series. He also once had a heated exchange with a friend of mine, with Houghton claiming that if you haven't played professional football then your opinion on the game is invalid. That is frankly bollocks. I'm not a professional chef, but I can tell you if I'm eating a shit sandwich.

Taking the scenic route to London, I get home in time for Derby 1-0 Fulham in the first leg of the Championship playoff semi-final. The Premier League that they are trying to get into is almost over for the season, and this Sunday sees the last round of games. Spurs are at home to Leicester, their final fixture at Wembley before moving into their new stadium. As such, I decide to treat The Boy to his first Spurs game, the club he professes to support, having been got at by a cousin.

What I want is two adult tickets and one child ticket together, but due to the utterly fucking hopeless online ticketing system this proves impossible. I'm so pleased I support a non-league team where you can simply roll up to the turnstile at five to three and hand over 15 notes. Computer continues to say no and the only available option is to buy two adult tickets for the best part of a hundred quid. An absolute disgrace. Fuck Spurs, and fuck Wembley.

SATURDAY MAY 12TH

Again I am forced out of my pit to attend Saturday Morning Football with The Boy, who is now a full squad member of the Shady Sharks. Again I am pressganged into refereeing, an awful experience that entails entitled little shits questioning my every decision. I wonder where they get that from? Respect my authority. This falls to pieces when I am forced to make a contentious ruling. One team celebrates a goal, yet the other team claims the ball went through a hole in the side of the net. Both outcomes are plausible, I didn't get a proper view of it and simply have to guess who's lying. In the end I rule out the goal, at which point a number of kids start crying and I abandon the game. Who'd be a ref? I have spent much of my adult life hurling abuse at officials, but may now think twice. Of course I won't.

With netgate casting a long shadow over the day, we are straight into a playoff frenzy. If you're not careful, they can get away from you, an endless cavalcade of random kickoffs: 12:30pm Scunthorpe 2-2 Rotherham; 3pm Lincoln 0-0 Exeter.

The real action is to be found at Wembley, where Tranmere Rovers and Boreham Wood play for a place in the Football League, with both outcomes sticking in my craw. It's a chaotic start as Tranmere have defender Liam Ridehalgh sent off after 48 seconds. Five minutes later they take the lead, with scorer Andy Cook having a bottle thrown at him. Wood then equalise deep into injury time, but Tranmere grab a dramatic winner. The dismissed Ridehalgh is interviewed live on BT Sport and admits to weeping and shaking during the game.

"The boys were fucking fantastic", he says. Ok, that's enough…

This takes me seamlessly into Middlesbrough 0-1 Aston Villa then Coventry 1-1 Notts County, basically a list of northern towns and binary numbers, but each scoreline carrying the hopes and dreams of thousands.

SUNDAY MAY 13TH

This is it then, The Boy's Wembley debut for Spurs v Leicester. Resplendent in his cousin's old shirt, we take the 18 bus and get talking to another dad and lad. Taking in the sights and sounds, there's all kinds of mither en route, with coppers getting on and off and various lunatics in evidence.

Wembley Way is baked in sunshine, and we enter the machine by scanning our grossly overpriced tickets that we paid for the privilege of printing ourselves. The day gets worse when I am served a dodgy pint, but improves immeasurably when I complain and am accidentally given two pints in return. Essentially designed to extract money from you, we loiter on the concourse and enjoy the panoramic view of London. We can see Wembley from our house, but we can't see our house from Wembley. Pints necked, we walk up the steps and The Boy is genuinely awestruck, almost overcome at that first intoxicating glimpse of the pitch.

"I'm shivering", he says, with visible goose bumps on his legs. The Boy has gone to Wembley, his knees have gone all trembly. In fairness, you don't get that at Braintree. After the ticket farrago, I am furious to discover that we are flanked by empty seats and constantly buffeted by an array of feral children. Sake.

As for the match, it's an end-of-season affair so we don't expect much. A goal for Leicester! The Rat on four minutes. Kane with the equaliser three minutes later! Dickheads wandering in with buckets of popcorn. Leicester swiftly score again and go into the break 2-1 up. Perhaps this will cure The Boy of his Spurs affliction.

When Leicester score again immediately after the restart I'm worried about his lower lip going, but Eriksen replies instantly for 2-3, and still people wander in like they're at the cinema. A Fuchs own-goal puts Spurs level and whatever happens we have seen one hell of a game.

Spurs finally take the lead on the hour mark and The Boy is in dreamland. It lasts for 13 minutes before The Rat hits a screamer for 4-4. Fuck me, shades of Swindon v Chester in '85, the only 4-4 draw I have witnessed live.

But it's not over yet. The Boy's favourite player, Harry Kane, scores again, notching what proves to be the winner. Spurs 5-4 Leicester. You couldn't make it up. Now wrap Kane up in cotton wool and ship him to Russia.

The Boy is walking on sunshine, and we have to spend hours in the garden, re-enacting the game. Dad of the fucking year. I pass out in bed during Match Of The Day. No surprise what the first match is.

MONDAY MAY 14TH

Playing catch-up with a 9am bath, I take in the highlights of the League One playoff semi, Shrewsbury 1-0 Charlton (2-0 on aggregate), having missed the first leg on Thursday. The drunken Shrews I saw at London Bridge in February singing "we're on our way to the Championship" may yet be proven right. They are at the very least on their way to Wembley.

A Grand Prix is hanging over me, Hamilton leading the last I heard. But the real story is in Spain, where Barcelona are two games from invincibility and hence immortality. Levante away shouldn't prove too troublesome, despite the lack of Messi.

Surprisingly, Barcelona are 2-1 down at half time, but I take my eye off the ball and get distracted by something else. Casually checking the modern-day Ceefax (yes, it still exists) I inadvertently learn that Barca have been beaten, such a seismic story that it infiltrates pages normally reserved for League Two injury news. Fuck it. I watch the highlights anyway, absolute madness, with Barca going 5-1 down before coming perilously close to equalising. Levante 5-4 Barcelona. You couldn't make it up.

Closer to home, Chelsea Dad has earmarked a kebab shop with half-price beer as a potential World Cup venue.

TUESDAY MAY 15TH

I'm all set for the 10am full replay of Fulham v Derby, but unbelievably see a clip of a goal on Victoria Derbyshire that looks suspiciously like a spoiler. I once saw Chester beat Fulham 7-0 in a league game, so have mixed feelings about them making it to the Premier League. They're going for it though and at one point the commentator describes Fulham as being "on fire, literally". He literally says that.

Fulham score early in the second half, confirming what I thought I saw earlier. Sessegnon with the goal, some player, not yet an adult. They score again to go ahead on aggregate, and with six minutes of injury time at Craven Cottage fans of both sides in are tears. Fulham win, sparking a pitch invasion to celebrate their first Wembley visit since the 1975 Cup Final.

I finally watch the Ireland test match, historic if painful viewing. It's an easy run chase for Pakistan, but the iPad battery dies with two runs needed, and I switch to the TV for the handshakes. I simultaneously get through mercifully brief Spanish GP highlights.

Aston Villa play Middlesbrough for the right to face Fulham at Wembley, the game preceded by applause for Jlloyd Samuel, who has tragically been killed in a car crash. It's an appalling game as Villa grind out a goalless draw for the aggregate win, sparking the obligatory pitch invasion and sea of phones. John Terry still in full kit....

WEDNESDAY MAY 16TH

I am guest of honour at The Non-League Paper Awards at Stamford Bridge. Well, guest anyway. I pen the occasional pithy column for them so the least they can do is give me a free feed once a year. Already running late from catching up with Match Of The Day, I get off at the wrong stop and then somehow get lost in a graveyard in broad daylight. Stumbling into the John Hollins Suite in a muck sweat, the ceremony is already under way and I skulk into my seat.

I have missed the intros and there appears to be a child at our table. It turns out to be Sutton United striker Tommy Wright, who this season scored against Chester at The Deva Stadium, presumably the greatest moment of his young life. Despite frequently playing in front of thousands of people, he admits to being far more nervous about picking up an award and muttering a few words to a room full of daytime drinkers. He also relates the tale of his name being spelt wrong on his shirt for a televised match, and reads out the newly announced England squad from his phone.

Essentially surrounded by players that I have spent the previous nine months hurling abuse at, I recognise the Boreham Wood keeper who responded to Chester fans baiting him by telling us to "enjoy the Conference North". It's actually called the National League North so the joke's on him.

In the pub afterwards I chat to a Macclesfield duo, boss John Askey and Player Of The Season, Danny Whitaker, frequent architects of my misery and perfectly pleasant people. I mine Askey for ex-Chester player gossip, and tell Whitaker that I'm always disappointed to see him on the team sheet.

The pub runs out of beer and we relocate to somewhere that is simultaneously showing the Europa League Final and the League One playoff semi. What a choice. Naturally, I watch both. Rotherham beat Marseille 3-0 to lift the cup, and Atlético Madrid turn over Scunthorpe 2-0 for a 4-2 aggregate win. Something like that anyway.

The best time to go home would have been three hours ago. The second-best time is now. I get the wrong tube and end up in a grossly overpriced black cab, goodie bag in the wind.

THURSDAY MAY 17TH

With no sport and a non-league hangover, I'm twitching like a mother. It's the big one tonight though, Premier League Darts finals night in front of 11,000 at the O2. MvG dispatches Cross despite a late rally and Michael Smith takes out his mentor, Gary Anderson.

Meanwhile in deepest Devon, Exeter beat Lincoln 3-1 in the playoffs for a place at Wembley. At half time I catch the last knockings of England U-17 0-0 Netherlands U-17, followed by penalty heartbreak for England again. Dutch legend Robin van Persie is at The O2 to see his fellow countryman give Smith an absolute towelling, 11-4 to van Gerwen for another Premier League title.

FRIDAY MAY 18TH

The World Cup of Pool seems to have been progressing without me. Sky are also showing a Chinese Super League match. Remember that? Intriguingly, the game between Tianjin TEDA and Shandong Luneng has a 12:29pm start, which is enough to pique my interest if not necessarily maintain it. Shandong nick an injury-time winner.

In the seemingly endless world of tennis, Nadal beats someone. Go on Rafa, lad.

And tonight's playoff match is between Notts County and Coventry. Blighted by offside injustice, Cov win 4-1 to book a return to

Wembley just 31 years after winning the FA Cup. Cov Kit no doubt in attendance.

SATURDAY MAY 19TH

It's an early start for the Shady Sharks as we head to Primrose Hill for a series of high-profile friendlies. With The Boy in defence, we are turned over 3-1 and then 4-0, leading to a clear-the-air meeting where we stress the importance of maintaining their shape and not running around like idiots. It seems to work as we win the final match 4-1, leading to much elation on the touchline.

We have at least managed to avoid the Royal Wedding, and listen to tedious live coverage in the car. David Beckham is there, presumably bored senseless, imagining free kicks.

We go straight to a kid's birthday party in the bandstand where The Jam recorded the video for When You're Young, directed by the man who would go on to make Mike Bassett: England Manager. It's a decent shindig, but I have to drag The Boy away as it's the FA Cup Final, and whatever you're doing you have to watch the FA Cup Final. It's the law.

I first watched it in 1979 at my Grandparents' place, where we had turned up presumably oblivious to the significance of the occasion. The unscheduled viewing also represents the first live football match I ever sat through in its entirety (but not the last) and as such it is burned into my psyche to the extent that I am still surprised when Arsenal aren't wearing yellow. In a thrilling encounter, the Gunners went 2-0 up at the break against Manchester United, who astonishingly equalised with two goals in the dying minutes, only for Alan Sunderland to immediately nick the winner for Arsenal, thus providing the genesis for a hoary old quiz question. Scenes.

The next few finals are sketchy, but from '83 onwards I could probably tell you what happened and where I watched it. I have seen two in an LA dive bar at 7am, and enjoyed the 2006 final with breakfast on the balcony of a cricket club in the Bahamas. I have even attended three finals, at old Wembley, The Millennium Stadium in Cardiff, and new Wembley. At Cardiff, I was pictured in the Daily Mirror sat behind former Chester legend Terry Owen and wife as their son Michael notched a brace. Perversely, it's the more recent finals that are harder to recall, what was once the showcase of the season now subject to the law of diminishing returns.

If it is remembered at all, the 2018 final will be remembered for watching it from my sofa on my big fuckoff TV with Saints Dad and respective sons. That said, the boys manage all of two minutes before repairing to the garden for a kickabout. It's a shrewd move as what follows is one of the most turgid finals in living memory. At some stage Phil Jones kicks Eden Hazard, who dispatches the penalty and Chelsea beat Manchester United 1-0. Stick it in the books. Arguably the highlight is when Saints Dad tells me that during the 1976 final he missed Southampton's winning goal as he had to go for a piss.

News reaches me from France, where The Driver has made it to Metz to complete La Carte avec Bordeaux. Zut alors.

SUNDAY MAY 20TH

The Driver makes it back to his ramshackle abode in the south of France for 9am, an utterly futile achievement ticked off. Closer to home, it's non-league finals day at Wembley, beginning with the FA Vase final between Stockton Town and Thatcham Town, notionally The Driver's former local team. Sean Cooper-Clark nets a first half penalty for Thatcham, his 62nd goal of the season, and the only one of the match.

I watch it in the garden with Wembley in the distance. There's a brief respite before the FA Trophy Final, enabling me to lather myself up like Ray Winstone in Sexy Beast. Too hot? Not for me, I love it.

Bromley take the lead and come within 20 seconds of glory before Brackley equalise and subsequently win on penalties. No one said it was gonna be easy, nobody said it had to be fair.

MONDAY MAY 21ST

I catch up with a bit of Match Of The Day with The Boy, then drop him at Soccer School and walk to the post office to pick up the new Half Man Half Biscuit CD, No One Cares About Your Creative Hub So Get Your Fuckin' Hedge Cut. It includes the football-themed track, Swerving The Checkatrade: "Let me look upon your curves/Instead of Ipswich Town Reserves."

Arsenal appoint Unai Emery. Without the mystique of Wenger, they are just another London club. Back home we finish off a week-old Match Of The Day, desperately clinging to the departed season. It's a gap that Roland-Garros qualifying simply cannot fill. Perhaps sensing my sorrow, The Boy gives me a spare Panini sticker. I catch a bit of Football's 47 Best Worst Songs on Dave, desperately peddling any old shit ahead of the World Cup.

TUESDAY MAY 22ND

Barren. Harry Kane has been confirmed as England captain for the World Cup. Manuel Pellegrini has gone to West Ham, presumably having failed his audition for The Walking Dead. There's some documentary on Channel 4 about Mo Salah. Nobody is singing that song anymore.

WEDNESDAY MAY 23RD

If there's one thing worse than watching football every day, it's not watching football every day. Ajaccio v Toulouse is being played behind closed doors, but I can't muster a great deal of enthusiasm for it. Without fans, football is nothing.

THURSDAY MAY 24TH

Practice is under way at Monaco, and cricket is back: England v Pakistan at Lord's. I find myself dancing round the kitchen to the iconic Test Match Special theme tune. I watch the toss in the bath: England win it and will bat. Stoneman gone for 4.

I take a second breakfast in the garden with TMS: "A hideous shot from Root taken very comfortably."

Cook incredibly makes it into double figures, probably still thinking about the time he shook my hand when he interrupted an interview I was conducting with Matt Prior.

There's still a semblance of football in the shape of the Women's Champions League Final between Wolfsburg and Lyon in Kiev. I take in the last half hour and it's goalless after full time. Wolfsburg score early in extra time, immediately have a player sent off and then concede four goals. What a sport.

FRIDAY MAY 25TH

I'm all set for a day of cricket when Her Indoors returns home and pressgangs me into accompanying her to The Chelsea Flower Show. Nobody expected that. She's got a pair of free tickets and amazingly can find no takers. Ground control to Monty Don...

I unsuccessfully try to get the cab driver to put on 5live Sports Extra for TMS, but have to settle for talkSPORT. He asks me my views on the forthcoming Champions League Final, and claims to support both Accrington Stanley and Manchester United.

The flower show is essentially one big piss-up with a few ornamental plants dotted about. Turns out it's nothing to do with Chelsea. I can't even find anywhere showing the cricket, and have to settle for the chirrup of wickets on my phone. By early afternoon, packs of predatory Sloanes roam the herbaceous borders.

Mercifully, we have to leave to pick up The Boy, and I manage the last half hour of the cricket in the garden with a gin & tonic. I am horrified to learn that my unscheduled floral outing has meant missing the afternoon session of the German Masters darts. I rectify this for the evening session, where barely a week after the conclusion of the Premier League, Snakebite beats Barney 8-7 and Mensur dispatches Cross by the same score. Sadly, I fall asleep for the semis then spend a fitful night trying to catch up with TMS.

SATURDAY MAY 26TH

Up early doors for Shady Sharks training in Queen's Park. It's interminable, and the team is now officially managed by one of the dads, who appears to be modelling himself on Alex Ferguson. I have absolutely no intention of contributing to the session and hide in plain sight, sitting perfectly still on a park bench and blending into the foliage. In keeping with the spy vibe, I listen to a miniature AM transmitter, flipping slavishly between talkSPORT and 5live for snippets of cricket. I eventually embrace the eight-hour Champions League build-up. Apparently, Kiev is somewhat tricky to get to, and various outlandish stories emerge of planes, train, and automobiles. A pair of Cockney Reds of my acquaintance have even gone, thus fulfilling their annual fixture.

But before it all kicks off in Kiev, there is the small matter of the biggest match in domestic football at Wembley. The Championship playoff final is variously described as the £100m game, the £120m game or indeed any figure in the environs that you want to pluck out of your arsehole. What is clear is that being in the Premier League is hugely financially beneficial compared to not being in it.

And it's live... on Sky at 5pm, the perfect amuse-bouche to the big one. Aston Villa and Fulham are contesting it, with more than 85,000 anxious fans sweating under the arch. With such high stakes, these games can often be low-scoring affairs, and this is no exception. Fulham take the lead in the first half, have a man sent off in the second, but hold on to secure their ticket to the Promised Land.

From Wembley we go straight to Kiev. Without going out of your door you can know all things on earth. Christ knows how they all got there, but got there they have, and this is a genuine occasion, Liverpool versus Real Madrid in the Champions League final. It's worthy of a European Cup Final.

Not a match to casually watch while pissing about on your phone, this is compelling fare. Where to begin? Ramos injuring Salah and sparking a thousand conspiracies. Karius rolling it out to Benzema for the opener. Mané's swift response. Bale with one of the most outrageous overhead kicks ever seen. Mané hitting the post. And then Karius throwing in another from Bale to seal it.

Not short of entertainment, still the feeling is one of frustration at not having seen a fair game, one with Salah on the pitch and without a couple of free goals. Still, at least I don't have to make my way back from Kiev.

SUNDAY MAY 27TH

Following the previous evening's drama, the cricket seems even more sedate than usual. England are all out in 27 minutes, and it's all over by lunch. As usual, the Monaco GP is blighted by a total lack of overtaking, the motor-racing equivalent of a goalless draw. Wembley is working overtime, today hosting the League One playoff final between Rotherham and Shrewsbury. Will those Shrews I saw at London Bridge singing "we're on our way to the Championship" finally realise their alcohol-fuelled prophecy? Having lost all four of their previous visits to the national stadium, it doesn't bode well when they go a goal behind. But they forge an equaliser and force extra time. Another goal for Rotherham seals their fate, and it is the Millers who are on their way to the Championship whereas The Shrews must start again in League One, a massive kick in the teeth. The agony and the ecstasy.

MONDAY MAY 28TH

Little more than two weeks until the World Cup, this is officially the last day of the football season. It is also the last time we will ever visit The House Of Doom, Her Indoors' family pile finally out of our lives. Following a final once-over, I slam the front door then realise I need a piss. Urinating in the garden, it affords me a final poignant glimpse into the sitting room, and all I can think is that's where I saw Barney beat MvG in the Worlds a few Christmases ago. What a game.

Due to being otherwise engaged, I have tactically avoided the result of the League Two playoff between Coventry and Exeter in order to watch the highlights and eke a tiny bit of pleasure out of this departing season. As we drive past Wembley, score still unknown, The Boy asks me if Cov Kit was there. I would be astonished if he wasn't, son. With hours still to kill until the Channel 5 highlights, I go for a piss and see the Wembley Arch lit up in sky blue. For fuck's sake.

TUESDAY MAY 29TH

School holidays. Sake. I drop The Boy at a daily Soccer School run by Charlie Merson's mob, essentially cheap childcare. Hours later it's abandoned due to torrential rain and I am forced to take two kids to the cinema when I could be watching sport on my own.

I eventually catch up with the playoff highlights, and there's Cov Kit, resplendent in blazer during a minute's applause for Cyrille Regis, Coventry and Chester legend. As relayed via the medium of blue light the previous evening, it is indeed a victory for Coventry, 3-1.

Ahead of the World Cup, the History Channel is showing non-stop football content. I watch something called The Three Musketeers: "The story of three of the most popular and most feted names in football, (Zinedine Zidane, David Beckham and Ronaldo) who, at the World Cup tournament in France '98, came of age in very contrasting ways."

It's a pretty tenuous link, but any footage of France '98 is guaranteed to raise the hackles as it is the first World Cup I attended, a pretty mind-blowing experience all round. Not to mention a few pints, a couple of cheeky wins and a hint of trouble.

There's also a fairly mindless debate as to the relative merits of Michel Platini and Zinedine Zidane. I fundamentally disagree with the entire concept, but begrudgingly watch it anyway.

WEDNESDAY MAY 30TH

Roland-Garros plays host to a four-and-a-half hour tennis match and by the end I'm still not sure who has won. Dimitrov? Some big lad called Cameron Norrie is also in action, but play is abandoned as it's too dark. Some kind of lighting system, perhaps? And where is Andy Murray?

THURSDAY MAY 31ST

Bereft of meaningful sport, I take The Boy to a local fairground. I manage a snippet of 5live where they are discussing Pochettino in relation to the Real Madrid job, seemingly departed by Zidane. I get back home in time for the last two hours of the World Cup of Darts. Finally.

FRIDAY JUNE 1ST

We're into June. The World Cup is in June. You can almost taste it. Until then, we sit and wait and watch inferior sports. I opt for a bit of cricket and tennis in the garden. I then forgo all sport to watch Echo & The Bunnymen at the Albert Hall with Bealesy. We also meet up with the associate known as The Evertonian, who has paid north of a hundred pounds to watch a Liverpool fan sing.

SATURDAY JUNE 2ND

I drive The Boy to Shady Sharks in Queen's Park, almost certainly over the legal limit (me not him). I am not physically or mentally prepared to help out and again hide from the coach, Shouty Steve. Back home, I half-watch Kyle Edmund crash out of the French Open as British interest evaporates on the middle weekend.

Again, music trumps sport as I reunite with Beales and head to Camden Rocks, a rock festival in Camden. By way of compromise, we go to The Enterprise pub and watch the last hour of the England friendly against Nigeria. England are already one up and I ask a random Geordie who scored. He appears to be saying "Kale". There is no Kale. Does he mean Kane? It turns out that Gary Cahill has given England the lead. Kane then does score to put us two up at the break, the experience largely marred by a coked-up Scouser at the bar.

Nigeria score two minutes into the second half and a man in an England shirt leaves for a bite to eat. What is the priority here? With a mere 12 days until the World Cup, England are competent, but not particularly inspiring. A woman calls a man a cunt and punches him two or three times in the face. Admirably he saves his pint and continues watching the game.

Back home late, I sleep-listen to a repeat of TMS.

SUNDAY JUNE 3RD

I'm ashamed to say it, but due to leaving the house, the World Cup of Darts has got away from me. I watch a repeat in the bath with live TMS. Repairing to the garden, both cricket and darts are now live, the correct way to follow sport.

In the darts, from Frankfurt, England have fielded an unfamiliar pairing of Cross and Chizzy. It's tense stuff, as when one player is at the oche, the camera cuts to a close-up of the other in the locker room, helplessly sweating it out. Partnered with emerging star Dimitri Van den Bergh, Belgium's Kim Huybrechts spends this time in headphones, perhaps listening to Celine Dion, as Wayne Mardle muses. Sadly, Chizzy plays like Celine Dion and Belgium beat England at the quarter-final stage. A chilling forebear of the actual World Cup, perhaps?

In minority sport news, footage emerges of a pair of Wigan Warriors – brothers apparently – monstrously arseholed and horrendously abusing a barmaid for refusing to serve them after the pub had shut. Not a good look, it has to be said. England comfortably win the cricket inside three days, the notion of a five-day test becoming increasingly hypothetical.

Back in Frankfurt, The Netherlands take on Scotland in the final, a dream team of MvG and RvB overcoming Snakebite and Anderson. Of course, neither team will be at the actual World Cup.

Both Spain and Switzerland will be, and draw 1-1 in a friendly. It's close now.

MONDAY JUNE 4TH

No cricket due to the early finish. In tennis, the French Open is still ongoing, although Serena Williams withdraws less than an hour before her highly anticipated fourth-round encounter with Maria Sharapova, citing a pectoral injury. Cricket and tennis, mere methadone in the sporting calendar. Ten days to go.

TUESDAY JUNE 5TH

Due to the paucity of sport, I watch highlights of England v Nigeria in the bath. My phone alarm pipes up at 11am to remind me of the commencement of the non-existent cricket.

ITV broadcasts a ludicrous trailer, attempting to compare the significance of Royal Ascot to the World Cup, both of which they will be showing. Pathetic. Most people could name a World Cup winner, not so many a Royal Ascot winner. It's simply somewhere to do your bollocks while pissed blokes in pointy shoes have a fight. Not a sport.

WEDNESDAY JUNE 6TH

D-day. Sharapova is gone in the seemingly endless French Open. For two weeks a year, ITV4 is reduced to mud, supplanting Minder, The

Sweeney and The Professionals with footage of a shit-brown clay court. At least the green of Wimbledon is visually soothing, like the snooker. Nadal's match rained off now.

THURSDAY JUNE 7TH

Nadal's match is back on. He cruises through, but I lose interest. My attention is grabbed by the BBC showing a full rerun of England v Tunisia, our opening group game of France '98. I am immediately transported back to that day. The early flight from Stansted to Marseille. The absolute chaos outside the Stade Vélodrome. The friendly Tunisia fans. Shearer's opener. His celebration by the McDonald's sign, sparking conspiracy theories as he was appearing in an advert for them at the time. Scholes clinching it with a second goal. The city on lockdown as we spent the evening on a yacht in an absolute two and eight.

It will be interesting to see if England's hooligan faction is as enthusiastic in Russia, where the repercussions may be more severe. England are actually playing tonight, in Leeds, a final friendly against Costa Rica before heading off to the tournament. Rashford rips in a belter, and The Boy asks if that is Navas, the Real Madrid keeper, in goal for Costa Rica. Indeed it is, The Boy's sporting knowledge already surpassing mine.

Welbeck scuffs in a header and with a party invitation hanging over me, I bolt early, listening to the last ten minutes en route, Stuart Pearce drawling in my ears, the occasional thrilling flash of the match glimpsed through a stranger's window. Pleasingly, the commentary ends almost exactly as I reach my destination. Cradling four cans of Polish lager, I am greeted by a plus size model and Ronnie Wood's daughter. Coincidentally, I was once at Wembley Conference Centre watching Ronnie O'Sullivan when Ronnie Wood and Jimmy White burst into our corporate box, having mistaken it for theirs. Go on Ronnie.

FRIDAY JUNE 8TH

Kop King Kenny Kops a Knighthood. Arise, Sir Kenneth of Dalglish. I actually saw Dalglish play once, and indeed score, curling in a screamer against Southampton at Anfield in a Milk Cup semi-final. Alongside a stellar playing career, his tireless work in support of the Hillsborough families is deserving of this honour. All the same, it would be amusing if he told the Queen to shove it up her English arse.

In the inferior sport of tennis, Nadal cruises through to yet another French Open final. Go on Rafa, lad.

SATURDAY JUNE 9TH

9am at Brent Cross is not on my menu, but here I am, present and correct for a seismic moment in sport. After months of intensive training, it's the first official game for the Shady Sharks. With our manager, Shouty Steve, prowling the touchline, much to the bemusement of other parents, we are roundly dismantled 6-1. It's a blow, but something to build on, and we reconvene in Queen's Park for extra training.

Afterwards in the café, an elderly Australian lady asks me when the World Cup starts, labouring under the misapprehension that it's in October? Five days now.

England Women are playing cricket. Having looked down and out, they have given themselves a chance. I drop The Boy at a Harry Potter party and sleep through Simona Halep of Romania winning the French Open at Roland-Garros. England Women lose the cricket. England Men lose some rugby union, 42-39 to South Africa.

In football, England U-21s are playing Mexico in the final of the Toulon Tournament. They only go and bloody well win it 2-1, lifting the trophy for the third successive time. Who knew? Come on England.

It seems that the MLS is still going, and I watch New York City squeak a 1-1 draw against Atlanta United at Yankee Stadium. Elsewhere, Spain grab a late 1-0 win over Tunisia actually in Russia, at the state-of-the-art Krasnodar Stadium.

And finally, Tyson Fury wins some shit fight, but it's all over before I see it.

SUNDAY JUNE 10TH

Jimmy Anderson out for six weeks. Sake. England are playing Scotland in a One Day International and I dip in and out of TMS and Sky, the perfect accompaniment to a sweltering day. Forcing myself out of my torpor, I pound the mean streets of NW10 looking for a copy of The Non-League Paper, which has published my debut poem, an ode to the lost joys of the National League.

Strolling back up the Harrow Road, I earmark World Cup venues, making tenuous and inevitably unfulfilled plans to watch different countries play in the company of their respective fans. On my odyssey, I listen to Nadal cruise to a preposterous and record-extending 11th French Open, getting back to watch the last knockings, which probably represents the most action I've seen of the entire tournament. I've got a busy schedule. Zinedine Zidane is there, as is Hugh Grant, the latter peddling A Very English Scandal.

Which is exactly what I witness in the garden as England are beaten by Scotland at cricket, prompting a pitch invasion. Shades of Wembley '77. Shocked and appalled, I go straight into the second half of the Canadian Grand Prix. Muck. Desperate for entertainment, I flip to Soccer Aid to see Cantona come on and Olly Murs miss a sitter. England draw 3-3 with a World XI, and face a penalty shootout with David Harewood out of 24 in goal. Fair play to him, he pulls off some heroics and England win on pens. Clive Tyldesley teases that Robbie Williams has a big announcement in the morning. Take that and party.

MONDAY JUNE 11TH

Stop the world. It is officially announced that Port Vale fan Robbie Williams will appear at the World Cup opening ceremony. Be still my beating heart, the fat dancer out of Take That is going to do a turn.

In the real world, Patrick Vieira has left New York City for Nice. It's nice in Nice. At the Monday Night Soccer School formerly hosted by Charlie Merson, Chelsea Dad is in a near frenzy of World Cup excitement, already planning for this time next week. Above the pitch, some tawdry bunting flutters, representing some but not all of the flags of the teams involved. The Boy is mercilessly scythed down by his Ipswich mate. Fuck Ipswich. At the Heysel Stadium, Belgium beat Costa Rica 4-1. Fuck Belgium.

TUESDAY JUNE 12TH

England are on their way to Russia. Physically on their way, in an aeroplane, in the sky. Breaking news: they've arrived. I watch live footage of them disembarking in St Petersburg. Please nobody trip over.

If there's one thing worse than watching football every night, it's not watching football every night. As a poor substitute I listen to England Women beating South Africa in an ODI while having a kickabout with The Boy. Despite minimal visible build-up and a fairly low-key approach all round, we are within 48 hours of the World Cup.

WEDNESDAY JUNE 13

Spain sack their manager two days before they are due to play Portugal. Not happy about him taking the Real Madrid job, apparently. You couldn't make it up. In the more distant future, USA, Mexico and Canada will host the 2026 World Cup, beating off Morocco. Not sure how that will work if Trump ever builds his wall.

It might be World Cup eve, but still the cricket comes. In the first of five One Day Internationals, England play Australia at The Oval, or as Her Indoors calls it, Yeovil. She once asked me how I was going to get to Yeovil by 11am. There are no such issues today. It starts at 1pm and I'm not going, settling in with the iPad in the garden, a constant battle against the sun. England make heavy weather of a run chase, but get home safely. We head out for a curry to celebrate (my debut book selling out).

THURSDAY JUNE 14TH

It's a momentous day for football. Firstly, it's the official release day for my book, The Card, about doing the card with Chester FC. But I still haven't seen a copy because they've all sold out as pre-orders. What a time to be alive.

Secondly, the Premier League fixtures are released. They go live at 9am, and Sky Sports dedicates three hours to what is essentially basic admin.

And finally, it's arrived. The World Cup begins today. Truly a time to be alive. If you're lucky, you might get 20 World Cups in your lifetime, and you should relish each and every one of them. I bump into Chelsea Dad at school. Head's gone.

And we are off. A festival of football and an absolute logistical minefield. Naturally I intend to watch it correctly, that is every minute of every match, ideally live. But the truancy laws forbid me from taking The Boy out of school for a month, and the 4pm kickoffs are not ideal.

As tradition dictates, the host nation is up first, with Russia v Saudi Arabia kicking off proceedings. And it's live... in Queen's Park café, meaning that I can dump The Boy in the playground and watch the action. They've gone to the bother of installing a television specifically for the World Cup yet insist on playing dog shit music over the top of it. I ask about turning the volume up on the TV, but am told it is not possible. Minutes later, I prove that it is actually possible by manually turning it up. If I'm paying £1.50 for a can of Diet Coke I would like to hear the television please. No HD though. Animals. Russia go 2-0 up before the break, and we cycle home in time for the second half as they complete an impressive 5-0 victory. Scenes.

I briefly nip into Covent Garden for an exhibition of photographs of The Cure, but eventually catch up with the opening ceremony. The good news is that it's ten minutes long. The bad news is that most of the ten minutes is Robbie Williams singing. He seems to be morphing into Morrissey, and the lead singer of Del Amitri tweets that "his whole countenance is redolent of an unsolved child murder in a car park in Mansfield", and that's pretty much all I can think of for days.

Clive Tyldesley lightens the mood by mentioning "Stalin's 'tache" and the fun really has begun. I watch the BBC highlights then a repeat of the full game.

Apparently, the US Open has begun.

FRIDAY JUNE 15TH

At 8:30am, I discover Robbie Savage's World Cup Breakfast. God, I wish I hadn't. Bring 'em home, and call the whole thing off.

The release of the Scottish fixtures garners a mere hour of coverage on Sky, and then we're into the 1pm kickoff. The school run clash notwithstanding, the timings of this World Cup are near perfect. Depending on the time zone, a World Cup can fuck you up. Japan and South Korea entailed getting up at sparrow's fart to watch England, whereas I spent much of Mexico '86 sat up in the dead of night on my own, a template eventually honed into a design for life.

The 1pm game sees Egypt take on Uruguay in a ground with a ludicrous extra stand that hangs out of the main stadium. Hilariously, the VAR officials are in full kit. There's a suggestion that Egypt's sluggish performance is as a result of fasting for Ramadan. And when they use all three subs, it becomes apparent that we are not going to see Mo Salah, presumably still injured from his Champions League grapple with Ramos. Even their manager, Héctor Cúper, is barely able to stand, and Egypt succumb to a forgettable 1-0 defeat. At this stage, the football barely matters. It's about the sights and sounds, the fact that it's actually happening.

The 4pm game sees a post-school dash to Queen's Park for Morocco v Iran. I watch while listening to AM radio commentary on headphones, but it's wildly out of sync, a rarely-mentioned casualty of the digital age. Checking that a nearby man on a laptop doesn't mind, I again sneak up the volume and stay to see Iran nick it with an own-goal winner.

Back home for Portugal v Spain at 7pm. Now we're talking. A heavy-weight encounter that lives up to its billing and then some. With goals flying in left right and centre, we are drunk on football.

"This is a brilliant game", says The Boy. Correct.

And when Ronaldo leathers in a late free kick to make it 3-3, even Her Indoors appreciates the technique. Alan fucking Shearer even cracks a grin. Day two and we have witnessed a classic. We are up and running and we have a month of this to come.

In what is an absolutely trivial footnote, England Women beat South Africa. And in an increasingly weird US Open, everybody seems to be over par. Poulter goes on a charge but shits the bed with a triple bogey. Golf...

SATURDAY JUNE 16TH

Up early doors for a Bournemouth runner. France play Australia at 11am in the first of four – FOUR – World Cup games – 11am, 2pm, 5pm and 8pm. Possibly one of the greatest days in the history of sport. We are driving to my old dear's in time for kickoff, and her birthday weekend. England are also playing Australia in an ODI, and in rugby, Ireland are playing Australia.

Perversely, I'm happy for Australia to lose at any secondary sport, but am supporting them in the football. We get there in time for cursory greetings, then camp out in front of the TV. France take a second-half lead through an historic VAR penalty. A mindless handball then gives Australia a penalty that they convert for parity, as nobody but commentators say. Sadly, France find a winner, squeezing the ball over the line by the shortest of cunt hairs.

We repair to a nearby hotel for Argentina v Iceland at 2pm, watching the second half in the games room with a bit of table football. I beat The Boy 10-0. Argentina are far more profligate, however, and are held to a 1-1 draw by Iceland. A disgrace. Messi even misses a penalty.

A quick dip sets us up for the first half of Denmark v Peru in the hotel room, then we nip back to my old dear's for the second half during dinner, plus cricket on the iPad. Peru 0-1 Denmark. Manners 0-1 Sport.

By the time the 8pm kickoff comes around, patience is wearing thin, and we decamp to the hotel for the second half of Croatia's 2-0 win over Nigeria.

In something of an historic day for Australia, they manage to lose at four international sports, if you include Kyrgios's defeat to Federer in Stuttgart. Wales also win some rugby in Argentina, including an extended bout of strangling. It's been an energy-sapping day of sport, and it's as much as I can do to make the World Cup highlights. It's a marathon, not a sprint.

SUNDAY JUNE 17TH

Happy Birthday Mum, who has graciously agreed to a celebratory brunch in order to accommodate the 1pm kickoff, Serbia 1-0 Costa Rica, a stinker. Then at 4pm Mexico beat Germany 1-0, accompanied by a lot of barking and more than a tinge of resentment. We have pushed our luck as far as it will go, and I tactically agree to withdraw from the 7pm game, strategically bundling into the car for the kickoff of Brazil v Switzerland.

As cliché dictates, a World Cup hasn't truly begun until Brazil have played. Sadly, we're on the M3 when Coutinho scores his wonder goal to put them ahead. At half time I switch off the commentary, gambling on getting home for the second half on ITV+1. As such I instigate a CD-only policy, safe in the knowledge that the score won't be ruined by My Bloody Valentine's long-awaited yet ultimately disappointing third album.

However, the media lockdown is put at risk when The Boy wakes up and claims to have seen the score through a pub window in

Acton. Following a nervy initial encounter with the remote control, ITV+1 comes up with the goods, delivering delayed standard definition coverage of the Swiss equaliser. Mission accomplished.

I decompress with the US Open, where Southport-based whizz dealer Tommy Fleetwood is beaten. A touch of World Cup highlights, and so to bed. England await.

MONDAY JUNE 18TH

Chelsea Dad is in a frenzy, phoning me before the first game is even under way. I watch the 1pm kickoff at home, Sweden 1-0 South Korea. For the 4pm we again hit Queen's Park, watching the first half with subtitles then cycling home in time to miss the first goal of Belgium 3-0 Panama.

This is it then. England v Tunisia, 20 years on. Minor logistics see me abandon The Boy at Soccer School, with instructions for Her Indoors to pick him up. From there I go directly to the nearest pub, The Royal Oak in Harlesden, where Chelsea Dad has reserved a table upstairs. It's a mixture of new and familiar faces, including supporters of West Ham United and Manchester United, each putting their differences aside for the greater good, otherwise known as behaving like normal adults.

In London, you are never more than 12 foot from a DJ, and there are at least three of them in our party. Joyously, we are situated front and centre in the glow of a great big flapping screen, the scale of which requires you to move your head around in order to follow the action. Gallons of lager, sweaty food, sundries. Shut the world outside, this is all that matters.

If you can't be at the match, the pub is next best, and England's opener is greeted with joy. Tunisia's contentious penalty equaliser: not so much. What follows is that familiar tension, frustration, and finally, improbably, absolute elation. With the game ebbing away, suddenly Harry Kane is wheeling away at the far post. He's only stuck in an injury-time winner, and it's all gone off. Chips, lager, random strangers; all coalesce in a blur of celebration. A man in Russia has headed a ball into a sack and it is everything. Now blow that fucking whistle.

England's win is only the beginning of the night. We bump into another DJ, a Newcastle fan. Finally kicked out of the pub, a hardcore repair to Chelsea Dad's soundproof rave shed to continue the celebrations. I finally return home to find the place bedecked in England flags like Tommy Robinson's cell. Paper plates, cups, the lot, adorned with tawdry patriotism. Apparently, The Boy fell asleep before the winner.

TUESDAY JUNE 19TH

In an unscheduled errand, I have to drop off The Boy's sports kit at his school. The outside world seems changed, with London basking in the glow of victory. Immediately returning home, I watch the first game through the fug of a hangover, an impressive 2-1 win for Japan over Colombia. I then have to pause the 4pm match – Poland 1-2 Senegal – to pick up The Boy. He claims to have sort-of seen the England winner, and even says Her Indoors claimed to know what was happening.

England are involved in yet another ODI, but as The Boy says: "Who cares about cricket? It's the World Cup."

Correct, although they do set a record one-day score of 481 as Andy Murray loses to the thoroughly unpleasant Kyrgios at Queen's, the traditional precursor to Wimbledon. Back at the main event, Russia are already on their second match, turning over Egypt 3-1.

WEDNESDAY JUNE 20TH

Alan Sugar, or fucking Lord Sugar or whatever he is, posts a deeply offensive racist tweet about the Senegal squad, suggesting that they sell sunglasses on the beach in Marbella. Similar twats will presumably also be appalled at the appearance of the first female World Cup commentator, Vicki Sparks. Yes she does.

Portugal 1-0 Morocco kicks off proceedings, but my World Cup marathon is thrown into turmoil by taking The Boy to a kid's birthday party in South East London. Picking up a dismal gift, we bundle onto the train, where Alan Sugar's moronic tweet has made the front page of The Evening Standard: this morning's tweets, tonight. As opposed to The Metro, which offers yesterday's tweets, today.

I make an aborted attempt to watch Uruguay v Saudi Arabia on my phone, but have to enforce a full media lockdown. At the party, the kid's grandfather – aka Jossy out of Jossy's Giants – is in full Crystal Palace kit, replete with Lionel Messi mask, a frankly disturbing sight. The birthday boy himself was apparently converted from Palace to Manchester City when the former missed a penalty against the latter. On such events are lives changed. As such, he has a cake in the shape of a Man City shirt. I briefly lived almost in the shadow of Maine Road, and had some sympathy with them, but like many find it hard to get behind a money-driven corporate behemoth.

It's a football-based party, and The Boy spends hours running rings round these South London slags before I finally prise him away. For reasons that will become apparent, I bundle him into the hosts' Skoda Yeti and drive it home to North West London. With a media lockdown still in place, I am pleased to find an Alan Partridge audiobook in the CD player.

I manage to avoid the scores and hit the iPlayer for Uruguay 1-0 Saudi Arabia, an absolutely turgid affair. Spain v Iran is on ITV, where Roy Keane expresses regret that when he worked under current Iran manager Carlos Queiroz, he didn't rip his head off. Lovely stuff. Women are not allowed to attend football in Iran and the support in Russia is cacophonous as Spain fail to break them down in the first half. At half time, news breaks that Gareth Southgate has dislocated his shoulder attempting a 10k personal best. The tit. Spain score. Iran score, but the rampant celebrations are quelled when the goal is ruled out by VAR two minutes later for offside. What a bollocks.

THURSDAY JUNE 21ST

Denmark 1-1 Australia makes me late, but I have to stay for the end. Anything could happen. As the final whistle blows, I leap into the Yeti and drive to Ascot racecourse where comedy duo The Scummy Mummies are enjoying a day out on the tab of failing retailer House Of Fraser. Foolishly, I have agreed to drive them from there to their gig in Harpenden.

With commentary of the fourth ODI for company, the Chiswick roundabout sets me back further and by the time I arrive there is mild concern, a flurry of phone calls and messages. Get in the back of the van. I don't ask them who won what, as I don't care, and they don't know. None of their bets have come in, and I'm not sure how much horse racing they've actually seen. Why bother when there's free champagne to quaff?

Further traffic hell is partially assuaged by live commentary of France v Peru, which sends at least one of them to sleep. It's the first match that I have seen no part of, and it doesn't feel right. If it's any consolation, it sounds like a stinker, with France winning 1-0. Garbage.

Having performed my executive tour manager duties, I head to the nearest pub for a pint, a sweaty burger and a prime seat in front of Argentina v Croatia. It's an absolute tear-up as Croatia twat in three goals without reply to leave Messi's mob hanging by a thread. Also watching in the pub is an excitable Bulgarian, downing shots and supporting Croatia on the basis that he hates Argentina. When the third goal goes in, he embarks on a spontaneous lap of the pub, not easy wearing sandals.

Following a difficult late night drive to South East London, I watch a repeat of France v Peru in its entirety with Scumbag number one, daughter of Jossy. Watching football with someone who has absolutely no interest is something of an eye-opener, enabling you to see it for what it is, essentially close-up footage of heavily tattooed men wrestling with each other. Although she is impressed by Giroud's cheekbones and the Carry On connotations of Umtiti's name.

"What percentage of your life have you spent watching football?", she asks.

Hard to say. Tired and emotional, I repair to the penthouse suite and watch the last five minutes in bed.

FRIDAY JUNE 22ND

Back in the civilisation of North West London, a minor timing aberration results me having to listen to the opening exchanges of Brazil v Costa Rica on headphones. I get home for ITV with 17 minutes played and am horrified to discover Brazil wearing blue, against Costa Rica in white. Brazil's iconic yellow shirt has been associated with the World Cup since its inception, and this unnecessary away kit is a disgrace. I then find myself cheering a VAR review that shows Neymar going down in instalments after his shirt is brushed. Two late goals seal it for Brazil.

A quick look at summer in the garden then we're into Nigeria v Iceland, the first half of which is little more than foreplay. Nigeria fail to muster a single shot. They make amends early in the second half with a thunderbolt from Musa. And another! Yet another VAR penalty gives Iceland a lifeline but it is spooned by Sigurdsson.

My Friday night? Serbia 1-2 Switzerland. Living my best life.

SATURDAY JUNE 23RD

Sake. We are scheduled to go to Her Indoors' brother's place in Northamptonshire. Naturally, I get us there for 1pm to see Belgium turn over Tunisia 5-2, making something of a mockery of England's laboured victory. This is followed by a little nosegay of England Women's cricket v South Africa and a touch of Djokovic at Queen's. 4pm sees Mexico beat South Korea 2-1 as England win the cricket.

I then decamp to the nearby residence of The Watford Gap for Germany v Sweden on the same TV that I saw Phil Taylor throw his final dart. I end up watching most of it on my own, barking "get fucking in you IKEA cunt" as Sweden take a first-half lead. Germany equalise early in the second half, but need to win to stay in the tournament, not helped when they have a man sent off. It's incredibly tense, but inexplicably The Watford Gap and son wander off as injury time approaches. In the 95th minute, Germany's Toni Kroos has a free kick and there really is only one place it's going. Astonishingly, dramatically, mind-bendingly, it rips into the net at a macabre angle and a nation is saved. Saturday fucking ruined.

Against all common sense, we decamp to the village pub for some kind of rugby league between England and New Zealand, inexplicably played at the Mile High Stadium in Denver. Altitude affected, it's a baffling watch, but at one point The Watford Gap starts pogoing in front of the television. A truly unique individual.

SUNDAY JUNE 24TH

The Watford Gap is watching State Of Origin. Not a clue. England's cricketers appear to be trying to get it over with in time for England v Panama at 1pm. I watch the build-up in the bespoke sports barn with The Boy, nervous as kittens. Eventually, we have a full complement of men, women and children, gathered in this humble barn for this holy occasion. Stones 1-0! Kane penalty! Lingard screamer! It's an absolute bundle, shrieks of joy all round, kids spilling everywhere. Stones again! Another Kane penalty! 5-0 at half time. I may need a tincture. Teams rarely play brilliantly in both halves, but Kane completes his hat-trick just after the hour mark. Panama finally muster a consolation, their first-ever World Cup goal, and celebrate it like they've won the tournament. We'll take a 6-1 win, thanks. Scenes.

I'm back in the barn for Japan v Senegal, also something of a ding-dong-do as they share four goals between them. Meanwhile, Djokovic blows it at Queen's, losing in the final to Čilić. I avoid the 7pm kickoff and get home to sleep-watch Poland 0-3 Colombia.

MONDAY JUNE 25TH

I'm annoyed at ruining the cricket for myself. Further despair awaits as the World Cup reaches the stage of simultaneous 3pm kickoffs. I manage the second half of Uruguay 3-0 Russia on the wi-fi in the playground at Queen's Park, but it's not ideal.

We then have to rush back from Monday Night Soccer School to dual screen the 7pm games, which descend into VAR chaos, Shearer incandescent. When the dust settles, Iran have snatched a late 1-1 draw against Portugal, and Spain have snatched a late draw 2-2 against Morocco. What a tournament.

As a change of pace, I repair to the garden to watch Oakland A's win 5-4 at Detroit Tigers. Let's go A's! Back upstairs for World Cup highlight on ITV+1. My life isn't my own.

TUESDAY JUNE 26TH

The 3pm games again provide a logistical challenge. I manage the first halves of France v Denmark and Australia v Peru at home, the only goal coming from Peru. "That was rubbish", says ITV's Mark Pougatch of the France game. Correct. Nevertheless, I take The Boy directly from school to the nearest pub to watch the last knockings of it, the first 0-0 of the tournament. On the other screen, Peru clinch it 2-0.

By contrast the 7pm action is breath-taking. Croatia beat Iceland 2-1 to qualify, while Argentina simultaneously overcome Nigeria by the same score to squeeze through the group stages. It's got it all, a sublime Messi goal, a dramatic late winner, and Diego Maradona giving it a double middle finger celebration. I want him to suffer for what he did to England 32 years ago, but mainly I crave drama and the game delivers in spades. There is also some conflict in wanting good teams to go out in order to theoretically help England, but wanting to watch the best players on the biggest stage. This lad Messi can play.

WEDNESDAY JUNE 27TH

It's a tense business as I pause both the TV and the iPad in order to pick up The Boy and his feral friend. It's a successful operation, but due to the time shifting I daren't look at my phone for fear of spoilers. As such I am actually forced to watch the football without distraction.

Sweden cruise through with a 3-0 victory against Mexico, but the real action is to be found on the other screen as South Korea take on Germany. It's an enormous mismatch, with Germany expecting to win and indeed needing to win to prevent a shameful exit. They dominate the game, but get to the break goalless. It's absolutely relentless, but still South Korea hold out, playing for nothing but pride. Injury time. It's in the net! The German net! But it's offside. Sake. Hold on, it's gone to VAR. On close inspection it appears that the final ball has come off the defender's leg so it can't be offside. As this fact dawns, I am on my feet roaring this information into the ether, kids scattering in fear. It's confirmed, 1-0 to South Korea. Germany need two in injury time to stay in the World Cup. Their keeper starts playing in midfield. He's lost the ball! Son of Spurs rolls it into the net for an historic 2-0 win. Germany, the defending champions, are gone. This tournament. This life.

Stuart Pearce calls it "the biggest VAR call ever".

Lothar Matthäus tweets, "This is a very sad afternoon...".

Fuck him. I once kicked a ball at him after he fell over during a FIFA press trip.

The 7pm matches are more straightforward. Switzerland confirm their qualification with a 2-2 against Costa Rica and Brazil beat Serbia 2-0. It concludes a strong month for Mitrović, from turning out in the playoffs for Fulham to taking on Brazil in the World Cup. It's a World Cup in which all 32 teams have now scored.

It's been a draining day, but I have managed to avoid the T20 score and treat myself to a nightcap on Channel 5, another cursory towelling for Australia. And finally, at 2:20am ITV4 shows England v Argentina: The Rivalry, forcing me to remember where I was for each game.

THURSDAY JUNE 28TH

Big Sam is on talkSPORT, and Wayne Rooney is on his way to DC United. If things had turned out differently, give or take a pint of white wine, they might both be preparing to take on Belgium tonight in Kaliningrad.

The first halves of the 3pm games are negotiated via a hybrid of home and The Whippet Inn, where I have a chat at the at the bar about England finishing second and getting squad players booked. Everyone's an expert.

We decamp to Queen's Park for the second halves via a combination of radio and café TV while The Boy does a Shady Sharks training session. Seemingly unperturbed by yesterday's result, a blonde German kid strolls past in full Die Mannschaft replica kit.

At the World Cup in which Germany are no longer involved, Japan v Poland descends into farce. With Japan set to go through on yellow cards, they gamble that Colombia v Senegal will remain 1-0 and spend the last 15 minutes simply knocking the ball round the defence - shades of West Germany v Austria. It's a strategy that bears fruit, and they indeed go through on yellow cards. The game's gone.

At the Shady Sharks training session, a lad called Dylan misses an open goal and Shouty Steve berates him: "How are you going to be able to look yourself in the mirror?".

The Boy wants me to stay at home for the big game, but Chelsea Dad is on the blower and I make the split-second decision to march the sweaty mile to the Royal Oak, 5live in my ears, a glimpse of a nervous Phil Jones through the window of a kebab shop. In the pub for the anthems, I bump into some other acquaintances who are forced to watch it in the pub garden. Much to their chagrin, we are upstairs again in front of the big flapping screen, two tables hosting an expanded group including Chelsea Dad's wife. It is their wedding anniversary, after all.

Following a tepid first half, I disloyally split off from the main group and watch it with the stragglers in the garden on a shit TV. I spontaneously applaud the Janujaz goal that arcs over fellow former Sunderland player Jordan Pickford. Belgium's Batshuayi kicks the ball into the post by way of celebration and it twats him in the face, arguably the highlight of the entire game.

Colombia await. What made Colombia famous made a prick out of you.

FRIDAY JUNE 29TH

A rest day. In the bath, I watch a repeat of Panama 1-2 Tunisia in its entirety.

SATURDAY JUNE 30TH

Shady Sharks win 4-1. Dylan is among the scorers.

And we're into the knockout stage of the 2018 World Cup, the so-called round of 16. France 4-3 Argentina. Don't cry 4-3 Argentina. Messi gone. This lad Mbappé looks like he can play. With a bit of pace, he'd be dangerous.

Clueless, Her Indoors had booked a babysitter for 7pm, now hastily revised for 8:45pm. I want extra time, but I don't want to watch it with a babysitter I've never met. Uruguay 2-1 Portugal. Ronaldo gone.

I get to the party at the same time as Saints Dad and Chelsea Dad. Astonishingly, the host is unaware of the scores. What is wrong with people?

SUNDAY JULY 1ST

Crippled with a monstrous hangover, I haul myself onto the sofa for Spain v Russia. It's like a training session, albeit imbued with extraordinary tension. Spain take an early lead with an own goal, but Russia equalise with a penalty. Extra time comes and goes, and The Boy returns from somewhere or other in time for the dramatic penalty shootout. Spain gone, the hosts through.

There's barely time to wince at the sun and we're into Croatia v Denmark. It's an explosive start as Denmark take a first-minute lead then Croatia level in the fourth minute. This is followed by two hours of absolute torpor then a remarkable ending. With prior knowledge, you could have watched a film then turned on at the end of extra time to see Kasper Schmeichel save Luka Modrić's late penalty. But sport is unscripted and it is impossible to say exactly what is going to happen (otherwise we'd all be down Ladbrokes). Schmeichel saves two more penalties in the shootout, but it's not enough as Croatia dramatically progress. This team of global superstars are already being talked of as dark horses.

It's been a long, painful day, and this takes me up to the highlights. I'm ashamed to say I don't manage the entire replay.

MONDAY JULY 2ND

The Boy requests to skive school with an alleged illness. For the sake of World Cup convenience, I am happy to allow it.

It's the first day of Wimbledon, a minor distraction at the best of times, and a mere footnote in a World Cup year. Nevertheless, I begin the sporting day at 11am in the bath with Venus Williams. She loses the first set, but seals victory as the second half of Brazil v Mexico kicks off. Three Mexicans have bleached their hair – shades of Romania in '98. The Boy has sufficiently recovered from his mystery illness to provide punditry, and shrewdly points out that "Mexico take too many touches". They won't be taking any more, as they are dispatched 2-0 by the cheat Neymar and Firmino.

The 7pm game is Belgium v Japan. It may seem a mismatch, but it reaches half time goalless. Alan Shearer reviews Neymar's preposterous rolling around from the previous game, describing him as "absolutely pathetic". He's not wrong and the memes were circulating almost before he got off the ground.

I am literally on the edge of my seat for the second half, partly because The Boy is asleep behind me, but also because it's an utterly compelling spectacle. Despite their underdog status, Japan come flying out of the blocks, scoring not once, but twice in the opening seven minutes. Scenes. Now this is a test. Martinez and Henry need all their tactical acumen to get back into this. So what do they do? Stick the big man up front and launch it. Pure alehouse.

Fellaini is the big man, coming on with Chadli. Four minutes later, they're back in it, Vertonghen of Spurs with a looping header. Five minutes after that, Fellaini gets his swede on it and we have a level game. What drama. Still Japan come, forcing an injury-time corner. Courtois plucks the ball out of the air and immediately rolls it out. Suddenly, terrifyingly, De Bruyne is on a charge. A cross comes in, Lukaku sublimely dummies and Chadli is there to apply the finish! You hate to see it, but it's a near perfect passage of play, keeper to winner in seconds. Japan are broken, but what an effort. What a World Cup. What a sport.

TUESDAY JULY 3RD

Today's the day we fuck them up. A bit of Konta in the bath does little to settle my nerves as England v Colombia draws agonisingly closer. But first, Sweden v Switzerland. Still goalless, I hit pause, establish a media lockdown, and usher The Boy home for the last half hour. Sweden progress with a deflected winner. With ludicrous timing, a T20 match starts.

Tick follows tock, and the game is almost upon us. It has been 20 years since England played Colombia in the World Cup, a match preceded by the Vindaloo incident. Stranded ticketless at a luxury hotel in Lens, Northern France, we spent the afternoon in the company of Chumbawamba, Keith Allen and briefly, Zoe Ball.

Still no tickets, hope receding, when suddenly a Colombian official stepped off a coach and simply fanned a swathe of billets in our faces. Hundreds of euros were exchanged in seconds, and I ran to inform Keith Allen of this joyous bounty. However, despite recording England's unofficial World Cup song, Vindaloo, he had no interest in attending the match, preferring to watch it in the hotel. Welsh or something. By way of compromise, he did walk with us to the stadium arm-in-arm bellowing the full version of Vindaloo, something of a moment. As a footnote, earlier in the tournament we had a kickabout with his son, Alfie Allen, who would go on to have his cock cut off in Game Of Thrones.

Naturally, the tickets were for the Colombia end, but their fans couldn't have been friendlier, or more attractive. Darren Anderton got the opener, Beckham's free kick sealed it, and we drove back to London in time to see England fans spilling onto the streets. Meanwhile, Keith Allen's helicopter home was diverted to Bristol because of fog.

It's a less elaborate build-up tonight as I take the hardest walk to The Royal Oak in Harlesden. It feels like I'm heading to the electric chair. It's the same table, the usual mob, Man United Mum & Dad now celebrating their 10th wedding anniversary. The tension is almost dripping from the ceiling. It's a hugely destructive drug, but thank fuck for alcohol.

In a painful encounter, England are subjected to absolute shit-housery from the Colombians, who employ every dirty trick in the library. It's finally punished in the second half and Kane emphatically, joyously dispatches the penalty. Do not fuck this up. Chances come and go, but we head into injury time still 1-0 up. Do not fuck this up. Do not fuck this up. Do not fucking shitting fucking hell. Colombia's equaliser seems to suck the air out of the pub, like a punctured football. Not again.

Extra time comes and goes in a blur of lager and it's penalties. Of course it's penalties. It's always penalties. We are but extras in an endless penalty shootout. England go behind and we act accordingly, heads dropped, stomachs clenched. Do we really feel it or are we simply going through the motions, enacting a timeless ritual? Fuck me, we're back in it, heroics from Pickford. Suddenly Eric Dier is making the hardest walk from the centre circle to the penalty spot, the hopes of a nation resting on his shoulders. Please score. Please score. Please score. Within seconds of the ball hitting the net, a man is riding me round the pub, fizzy piss and chicken wings all over the gaff. Never in doubt. Rave shed, anyone? What made Colombia famous made a prick out of me.

WEDNESDAY JULY 4TH

Another England hangover. I hope the players appreciate these efforts. I can't engage with Wimbledon, which does little to lighten my mood. At 1pm, the fixtures are released for National League North, a random list of northern towns that will define nine months of my year. We start at home to Spennymoor, whatever that is.

Flags are out on the school run, World Cup fever finally kicking in. I catch up with India cruising the T20. It doesn't hurt. I watch England v Colombia highlights with The Boy, who claims that he was sent to bed before the penalty shootout, an extraordinary act of cruelty. It's a much-needed rest day at the World Cup, so I watch a Barry Davies documentary: "Look at his face! Just look at his face!"

Sadly, I can't manage LA Galaxy v DC United at 3:30am, not even for Rooney.

THURSDAY JULY 5TH

I sit through a bit of Wimbledon, but really can't be arsed. The Shady Sharks are training in Queen's Park and I use up my entire data plan to watch the last knockings of Konta, gone. I get back to see the reigning women's champion, gone.

ITV4 comes to the rescue at 8pm, providing relief in the in the form of the World Series Of Darts from the Mandalay Bay, Las Vegas, former home of the Desert Classic aka DARTS. I recognise the Canadian Jeff Smith from his Lakeside performances. He even wins.

FRIDAY JULY 6TH

Her Indoors' birthday. The same day every year without fail. I've missed Wimbledon finals, Grands Prix and some other stuff I can't remember that seemed important at the time. The timing is particularly cruel this year. Off the back of two blank World Cup days, we're now into the quarter-finals. Astonishingly she doesn't want to watch either of them, instead preferring the rarefied delights of Sissinghurst Castle, in Kent. You couldn't make it up.

What the fuck do I do? The quarter-finals of the World Cup. What I do is drop Her Indoors and The Boy at the aforementioned National Trust property and hotfoot it to the nearest pub for 3pm. The Milk Room, nestled in the heart of the Kent countryside. Big screen, comfy sofa,

Wimbledon off, ITV on. That's as good as it gets, as the game is an absolute shit sandwich, with France boring their way through 2-0. I return to the car park of Sissinghurst Castle and listen to Venus Williams get knocked out of Wimbledon.

We check into a B&B in Crowborough in time for the start of Brazil v Belgium in the room. Her Indoors and The Boy form an advance party while I bring up the rear at half time – Belgium 2-0 up – speed walking with headphones on, destination The Blue Anchor. It's a successful operation on a beautiful summer's evening. It's always nice to get out of London, if only to remind you why you live there, as confirmed when a local openly refers to Romelu Lukaku as a "gorilla". What a country.

The game is being shown on a TV in the corner of the pub so I camp out in front of it while Her Indoors enjoys her birthday dinner on an outside table. It's certainly an improvement on the previous match and when Brazil pull one back I want extra time for the sporting drama if not the domestic drama. Belgium hang on and I finally join the birthday celebrations. Brazil gone. In the same way that a World Cup cannot be said to have truly started until Brazil have played, it can also be said to have lost something when they depart. At least we won't have to endure any more of Neymar's antics. Back at the B&B, I stealthily watch ITV highlights then sleep-listen to the 2nd ODI. Happy Birthday.

SATURDAY JULY 7TH

Today's the day we fuck them up. England v Sweden in the quarter-final of the World Cup. What a time to be alive. I contact the Sussex-dwelling Chester fan known as The Hack to see what his plans are. He and the wife are going to a friend's barbecue and we are welcome to join them. Touch. Following a hearty feed and a couple of nerve-calmers, we take our seats on the IKEA sofa. It's a comfortable 2-0 victory for England and we are in the semi-final of the World Cup. At the final whistle, the host puts on Abba's The Winner Takes It All and it all goes a bit Abigail's Party. I may never see them again, but we will always have this moment. And while I am naturally pleased with the win, it almost feels dishonest not to have suffered for it. Without pain, football is nothing. Ludicrously, Chester played a pre-season friendly against Liverpool at the same time as the England match. Lost 7-0.

We check into a hotel in time for Russia v Croatia and The Boy falls asleep. I briefly inspect the inside of my eyelids, bucking awake to find Her Indoors watching something on Dave. She then dines alone beneath our window as we continue watching the match. She brings up some food and takes The Boy somewhere, returning to make me miss the second Croatia goal. Then with ten minutes of extra time left, she arranges for a pair of staff to assemble The Boy's bed directly in front of the TV. This is nothing less than sabotage.

Russia dramatically equalise with five minutes left, and we are into penalties. Croatia squeeze through and I am struck with a sick feeling that this may negatively impact my life in the near future.

SUNDAY JULY 8TH

With the semi-finalists now decided, the World Cup goes back in its box for a few days. We take advantage of this break in play with a tetchy visit to the beach at Seaford, sunbathing under the gaze of Beachy Head. Commentary of the British Grand Prix is interrupted by a visit to Standen House, yet another National Trust property, all overpriced scones, cloying enthusiasm and rabid deference to a time long since passed. We get back in the car to hear the German national anthem as Vettel has beaten Hamilton by a couple of seconds. Back home, I watch a repeat of it. The Hack and wife were actually there on a jolly. Showbiz wankers.

Making up for lost sport, I then watch a repeat of the T20 in its entirety. Game and series, India. New York City v New York Red Bulls seems a step too far, and an 11th-minute use of "lacksadaisical" proves the final straw.

MONDAY JULY 9TH

Apparently it's Manic Monday at Wimbledon. I don't know what that is and I care even less. At noon, the BBC shows a replay of England's ill-fated Italia '90 semi-final, now nearer to 1966 than the present day. It's a frequently-told story, but what I didn't know is that there were only 4,000 England fans there and 40,000 Germans. I feel sick during the anthems, instantly transported back to that night. Germany's macabre deflected opener, Lineker's sublime equaliser and, of course, the dreaded penalties that would set the tone for the next 28 years. I also remember cinematically missing my bus by seconds and having to walk home after the match. What a tit.

I really can't be arsed with Wimbledon and fill the football vacuum with Danny Dyer's Football Factories. He spends some quality time with the Burnley Suicide Squad, and I fondly remember a brick landing near me when we turfed them out of the FA Cup in '88. In keeping with the international theme, Scotland and England also feature, including an interview with loaded photographer Grant Fleming, who drove me back from Lens after we stuck it up Colombia in '98.

TUESDAY JULY 10TH

England Women v New Zealand Women ODI in the garden. To be honest, I am struggling to care. I head indoors and splitscreen the ODI with Serena Willams. I watch the Gareth Southgate press conference on my phone, becoming almost tearful. It couldn't be, could it?

Meanwhile, Ronaldo has signed for Juventus. At 7pm, I settle in with The Boy to watch the first semi, France v Belgium, with one ear on Chester's preseason friendly at Ramsbottom. Won 1-0, as did France, bringing the tournament to an end for Belgium and Roberto Martinez, probably the only former Chester midfielder to manage in the semi-final of the World Cup.

ITV highlights segue into a Euro '96 documentary, reminding me of where I was for each England game. Old Wembley for the opener v Switzerland, sat with Billy Duffy out of The Cult for no apparent reason. In front of a big screen in Le Mans to see us beat Scotland with a Shearer bullet header and a touch of Gazza magic. A mate's house in Bournemouth to see us put four past the Netherlands. Redemption for Pearce, beating Spain on penalties in a pub in Bournemouth where a moron thought it would be amusing to urinate on my leg. Then the fatal error of switching pubs at half time against Germany, suffering the curse of ITV.

In football terms, this is Christmas Eve, reminiscing about days of yore ahead of the big one tomorrow. All things considered, it's a pretty fucking big one.

WEDNESDAY JULY 11TH

Today's the day we fuck them up. The morning school run is littered with people spontaneously bursting into 'it's coming home'. Flags are being waved from car windows. I spend all day pacing, listening to This Nation's Saving Grace by The Fall on vinyl. On the way back from the afternoon school run, I pick up 12 lagers as New Order blasts out from a passing car. Federer is out of Wimbledon, a minuscule footnote. Probably wants to see the match.

In a change from routine, Chelsea Dad is hosting at his house, on my street, which is easier than going to Russia. It's a family affair, with full complements from Saints Dad and Man United Dad, plus a solo West Ham Dad and a handful of stragglers. Everyone pretends to be normal, but everyone feels as sick as a dog. Rio Ferdinand seems to be assuring us that England are better than Croatia man-for-man, although I can't see many Barcelona or Real Madrid players in our side.

Still, it's a chance to get to a World Cup final in our lifetimes, 28 years after our last thwarted attempt. These kids don't know how good they've got it. That said, they stay for one minute and 35 seconds before trooping out to the astroturfed back garden to resume their kickabout.

I naturally expect the worst, but am surprised and delighted when Kieran fucking Trippier curls in a free kick after five minutes. Grown men on their feet roaring. It's coming home. It's actually coming home. Of course it's not, but we get to the break ahead and briefly repair to the rave shed.

It's evident that Croatia are the better side, and I spent the second half numb, awaiting the inevitable equaliser. It comes on 68 minutes and we crawl agonisingly into extra time, and the distinct possibility of penalties in a World Cup semi-final for the second time in most of our lives. We are saved that agony by a Croatia winner, and the dream is over. Adults numb, children spontaneously bursting into tears, a genuinely disturbing maelstrom of wailing and gnashing. It captures how we are feeling, and I am almost tempted to join in, instead surveying the wreckage in mute despair.

"Worst day of my life!", screams Chelsea Dad's youngest, eventually having to be sedated by being put behind the sofa to watch something called Poop Man on YouTube.

I finally crawl out of the rave shed at 3am, stagger across the road and sit in my own garden, listening to talkSPORT. I have always maintained that England will never win a major tournament in my lifetime, but it was fun to dream. We'd have been murdered by France anyway.

THURSDAY JULY 12TH

There's no time to wallow as it's the dreaded school sports day. I get there late, nursing a can of full fat Coke, described by a fellow parent as "the red ambulance". Other casualties of last night roll up with a thousand-yard stare. I've missed the hurdles, and The Boy takes an over-cautious approach to the egg and spoon race. Rubber eggs of course, political correctness health and safety gone mad. I tactically swerve the Dads Race, and The Boy picks up a bronze medal for something or other.

And so to bed, woken by the ping of wickets as England take on India in an ODI at Trent Bridge. Surely there should be some kind of sporting amnesty on a day like this, a respectful period of rest. But the sporting world continues to turn, and I have to sit through a Shady Sharks training session with only TMS for company, experiencing what appears to be a double hangover. The day after a World Cup exit feels like waking from a wonderful dream. Ostensibly everything looks the same, yet is tainted with disappointment, weighing heavy with freshly-writ history.

Back home, India win easily, something that barely registers on the scale of sporting pain. Preposterously, Rangers seem to be involved in a Europa League qualifier, live on BT Sport in front of a 49,000 sell-out at Ibrox. Unlikely, I know, but what if Scotland had made the World Cup? It's Steven Gerrard's managerial debut, and he appears suited and booted for his first day at big school. Rangers beat Shkupi 2-0. Not a clue.

FRIDAY JULY 13TH

Amid all the excitement, the Wimbledon semi-finals have snuck up on us, Isner and Anderson in a battle of the giants. In other news, Donald Trump is in town, hence the occasional sighting of unusual aircraft.

Isner is finally broken for the first time this tournament after 110 consecutive games. We head out for a family meal, and I watch the tennis on my phone, hiding it behind the menu until I am busted. It's another of those ridiculous situations where they simply keep playing in the final set until someone gets two games ahead. Surely time for a rule change.

It's still going when we get home, with furious punters waiting for Nadal v Djokovic. I somehow conspire to miss the end as one of them finally wins after six hours and 35 minutes. Mindless. It's not a huge improvement, but I watch Kilmarnock 0-0 St Mirren in the Betfred Cup. St Mirren then win on penalties for an extra point and I don't know what's real anymore.

Meanwhile at Wimbledon, the roof is closed and the lights are on, with Nadal in a muck sweat as he levels at 1-1 with time running out. Sadly, it's up against the Shanghai Masters in the World Series of Darts (non-UK legs). Djokovic leads 2-1 overnight, while in the darts, a heavily perspiring Gary Anderson's glasses have steamed up and he's gone.

SATURDAY JULY 14TH

It's an early start at Queen's Park for Shady Sharks. I overhear Shouty Steve saying he needs a ref, and give it a quick swerve. We then all bundle into the car, flicking between an ODI and Nadal v Djokovic on the way to a barbecue hosted by The Evertonian, a man who actually went to the World Cup semi-final, a very long, tiring, expensive trip.

England's defeat means we now have to play Belgium in the much-maligned third-place playoff. I throw some kids off the Xbox and watch the entire thing live. We lose 2-0 and it's now fashionable to undermine England's achievement by pointing out that they lost as many games as they won at the World Cup.

I attempt to keep a lid on the tennis, but a child reports that Nadal has won, and an adult reports that Serena has lost.

SUNDAY JULY 15TH

I catch up with the last knockings of Nadal v Djokovic, the latter of whom wins a classic worthy of the final. I then keep a cursory eye on the one-sided final as the Serb automaton overcomes either Isner or Anderson, assuming their game has ended.

The tennis overlaps with the small matter of the World Cup final. As established, England aren't in it and there is an inevitable element of what could have been. Imagine. It would almost be too much to cope with. Finals often fail to live up to their billing, but this one has it all. An own goal, a penalty, some inconclusive VAR, and even a shameful Fortnite goal celebration from Griezmann. If the game was run properly, the goal would be ruled out and the player automatically red-carded. When the dust settles, France have won 4-2, followed by a chaotic medal ceremony conducted in torrential rain.

I watch the highlights then a full replay. I feel that I am clinging on to something.

MONDAY JULY 16TH

There ain't no Monday like the Monday after a World Cup. Having put my life on hold for a month, it's a galling return to the grim reality of day-to-day existence. I draw myself a deep bath and catch up with the second ODI. India are demolished at Lord's as England level the series.

TUESDAY JULY 17TH

It's the third and deciding ODI against India. I watch it in a combination of bath, bed and garden, all the while pre-emptively being informed of wickets by the BBC Sport app. TMS is a lifeline on the school run, and we get back for the last knockings of Turkey v England U-19s in the opening group game of some tournament. Christ, give me a break.

TMS sees England home, with Root sealing victory and a century. In all the excitement, I miss Shkupi 0-0 Rangers. I relive the ODI on Channel 5+1 and then we're into Major League Baseball's All-Star Game.

WEDNESDAY JULY 18TH

"Tottenham shirt!" shouts The Boy at 7:50am. It is his birthday and there has been a betrayal. Without consultation, Her Indoors has bought him a Spurs top, thus fuelling his nascent support of a team that is not the one I follow. It's an absolute disgrace. Serendipitously, a bloke comes on talkSPORT moaning about £17 socks and a £183 Man United kit. The game's gone.

The Boy has requested a football-themed party so I have enlisted Chelsea Dad to referee a match on the backfield while I dispense cold bottles of lager from a carrier bag. I am the carry bag man. It's all going swimmingly until Chelsea Dad announces that he has to pick up his eldest from cricket and tosses me the whistle. It's chaos, with little shits questioning my every decision. In a brief moment of clarity, I give a penalty against Poop Man. I'm fairly sure he handled it, something confirmed when I catch him in a lie. Son of Saints Dad places the ball on the spot, and as one the opposition (and possibly some of his teammates) start chanting "Pressure! Pressure! Pressure!"

There are probably more pressurised situations. His team are 3-0 down, it's the last kick of the game, and it is after all a birthday party kickabout.

"Pressure! Pressure! Pressure!" He's missed it! The game's over! And the penalty taker is having an absolute meltdown. The only kid who didn't cry after England were knocked out of the World Cup reduced to a blubbering wreck by a scuffed penalty. I resist the urge to ask him how much pressure he was under.

THURSDAY JULY 19TH

The Open begins at Carnoustie, but it's far too early to be getting involved in that. Besides, I have a social occasion in town, The Scummy Mummies' fifth birthday party. It's an absolute horror show of Instagram states filming themselves dancing to tepid music, and a prescient reminder of why I stay in and watch sport. I salvage something from the evening by chatting to Jossy out of Jossy's Giants, about sport.

FRIDAY JULY 20TH

One of the highlights of the sporting calendar, it's golf's unofficial fifth major, the Mini Masters charity tournament at Duke's Meadow, Chiswick. I'm back for my second consecutive appearance following a five-year ban for alcohol-related offences on my debut. Of course I don't actually play any golf. I just sit around the various hospitality areas getting absolutely leathered for free while gawping at sporting icons and D-list celebrities. Something of a safe space for tabloid disgraces, Jamie Theakston is spotted getting stuck in. Jodie Kidd is also wielding her clubs, herself back from a ban for cheating, the only person ever to have suffered this indignity.

Someone else who won't be playing any golf today is David Seaman, having phoned in ill from his shitter at 4:30am. I camp out with a cocktail at the main bar and watch actor Phillip Glenister sink a putt with a celebratory dance. Scottish football person Alex McLeish looks on. Football manager Michael Appleton is on the phone, his dual sleeve tattoos on show in the sunshine. I watch Gianluca Vialli make the green with a champagne cocktail and a massage (me, not him).

Each of the nine holes has a bar, posing a challenge for even the most hardened drinker. On an outer hole I try the Butch Wilkins cocktail, out of respect. A random punter lets me have a swing with his pitching wedge and I make the cusp of the green. I could have been a contender, but I had a paper round.

Due to the gargantuan amount of free alcohol, the event always gets a bit feral when the evening sun goes down, as I have discovered to my cost. This year is no different and I become embroiled in a minor altercation with a square man who I later learn to be rugby player Max Evans.

"Don't touch me", I say.

"You can't kill me", says Square Man.

That escalated quickly. Anyway, while I would almost certainly come off second best in unarmed combat, as I point out to him, what about poison, a gun, a tank, a car? I could go on.

Rugby's Mike Tindall wins the tournament, giving weight to the 'new dad' theory of sporting conquest. If my extremely limited showbiz knowledge is correct, he has bred with a royal. With the golf and presentations over, the party escalates and it feels like being a Tory in the '80s, all Porsches, braying, champagne and cocaine (allegedly). I spot Square Man hugging a speaker and throwing his shoes at people. Time to go.

SATURDAY JULY 21ST

My close personal friend Tiger Woods is on a charge at The Open. Go on Tiger, lad. It's also the World Matchplay Darts from Blackpool, with Phil Taylor on commentary having won the tournament a staggering 16 times.

Perhaps to cleanse myself of the previous evening's debauchery, I make the big decision to go for a swim. It'll never catch on. I get back for second-half commentary of Chester's pre-season friendly at home to Bury, tuning in seconds after the Shakers score the only goal of the game. Live commentary of a National League North team's friendly, truly a time to be alive.

I catch the end of Lewis v Wilson at Blackpool, a comeback victory for Jackpot. Presumably he celebrates with a Meat Feast.

SUNDAY JULY 22ND

Golf on headphones, I flick through Twitter to discover that MvG is gone. I watch the darts in the bath, and the start of the German Grand Prix. Hamilton is on a charge from 14th, but I'm also up against The Open and the darts. Decisions, decisions. In the event, I retire to bed to watch darts and listen to the golf and the Grand Prix, a partially successful strategy. There's also the Tour de France and something called the Anniversary Games. Anniversary of what? The Olympics?

The Grand Prix is mildly eventful – Vettel goes out and Hamilton wins to regain the championship lead, later surviving an inquiry. Tiger briefly leads The Open then shits the bed, and Molinari wins. I sleep-watch the darts, eventually coming to in time to see Barney late doors. Go on Barney, lad. I watch a repeat of the afternoon session including brief highlights of de Zwaan beating MvG, a seismic victory from the lowest-ranked player in the tournament.

MONDAY JULY 23RD

Oh Monday, I'm dreaming about you. England take on South Africa in under-19 cricket. Audible shrug. I pick up The Boy and get back for the second half of England U-19 0-5 France U-19. France appear to be quite good at football, at all levels.

The Matchplay continues apace in Blackpool. Big John Henderson has match darts against Huybrechts, but takes an age to throw and his rhythm is gone, the Belgian victorious 13-12. We repair to the garden for cricket and shots, the former on the iPad, the latter against The Boy in the goal at the end of the garden. The iPad battery dies and I revert to talkSPORT2 for darts on the radio. My close personal friend James Wade is up against Wattimena, so we head indoors for the denouement on the big TV. Go on Wadey, lad.

TUESDAY JULY 24TH

I turn on the darts with Chisnall 7-2 down and watch him pull it back to 7-7. With commentary of Chester v Morecambe in my ear, he remarkably wins 11-8 from 7-1 down. Cullen dispatches Gurney. Jeffrey de Zwaan has three match darts against Lewis, whose head appears to have gone. Jackpot peppers the treble 20, but de Zwaan gets there 11-9 with a 94 finish including a double double; into the quarter-finals at the first attempt. Anderson v Barney is absolutely breath-taking, the Flying Scotsman dispatching the Dutch Master 11-9 in front of a rampant Blackpool crowd.

WEDNESDAY JULY 25TH

School's out for summer. We enjoy a family chippy in Portobello, which means that I miss Whitlock 11-7 Wade. I sleep-watch the next two games with an electric fan on. So hot. Cross is gone, and I head downstairs for Wright v Huybrechts. It's preceded by an idiotic dance by Wright, briefly interrupted by a weird bowing handshake. Ever the showman, the Blackpool hordes lap it up. An extremely strange man, but he gets the job done, 11-5.

By way of a nightcap, I have a touch of Oakland A's on my phone, a rain delay in the BT Sport game.

THURSDAY JULY 26TH

I wake up searching for the iPad, then order Google Home to "play talkSPORT2", where de Zwaan and Chisnall are locked at 5-5 in Blackpool. The Lowlander accelerates and comfortably wins 16-8 for a semi-final place. Not the Dutchman we expected.

Pictures restored, I'm not really concentrating on Cullen v Anderson when the latter hits a nine-darter in a neck-and-neck thriller. I take a side dish of European football with the last knockings of Aberdeen 1-1 Burnley, a full ten months before the Europa League final. Cullen with match darts is distracted by a fly on double 9! Anderson forces extra time and gets over the line in an immense match.

Trawling the MLS, I take in a bit of Orlando 0-2 New York City. I can't sleep so return to the MLS for the newly-dubbed El Traffico between LAFC and LA Galaxy. I turn it off with FC 1-0 up.

FRIDAY JULY 27TH

With little in the way of fanfare, it's the start of the snooker season, the unheralded Riga Masters. In the wake of the World Championship, I made the mistake of following the victorious Mark Williams on Twitter, a terrifying insight into serious drinking in caravan parks. Nevertheless, he goes to Riga as favourite.

I dip in and out of the action, including on the iPad at the dinner table. There are three of us in this relationship. Her Indoors swivels the pad 90 degrees in her favour, and I ask her why she wants to see Ali Carter v Ryan Day in the Riga Masters.

"Desperate", she hisses.

The snooker is soon relegated to a side dish as I strip down to my pants upstairs in front of the fan for Mensur v Webster. The rain has finally come and this is my Friday night. It's Furnace Friday in Blackpool and as Wayne Mardle says, "Mensur can sweat up, he's a big lad".

It's a turgid affair, described as "pushing custard uphill with a fork". I even check in on Hull v Hull Kingston Rovers for ten seconds. 0-4.

Whitlock v Wright is next, the Australian Wizard versus the David Brent of darts. I leave it at 11-3 to Snakebite and embark on a futile blood moon watch, returning for the final leg as Wright hits bullseye for 16-5. I watch the last 38 seconds of Hull 16-20 Hull Kingston Rovers.

It's so hot that I sit outside my front door and watch a repeat of El Traffico through the window. LAFC score a second and I head back indoors for 2-2. What a Friday night.

SATURDAY JULY 28TH

Her Indoors has taken The Boy to Shady Sharks in Queen's Park, leaving me to enjoy the Riga Masters in the bath, Neil Robertson locked at 1-1 with Liang Wenbo. Robertson with a century for 2-1, but back comes Liang to level it. Frame 5, Liang on a 147, breathless, not yet noon, but he inadvertently pots two reds at once to foil the effort. Fifteen reds, 14 blacks, all the colours for a 140 high break and the lead. Robertson hits back to force a decider. Deep into the decider a mobile phone goes off in the crowd with Wenbo at the table. It's scrappy, but Robertson holds his nerve for a great battling win.

In Formula One, Hamilton and Bottas nick pole position and second at the last gasp. I head out to see veteran surf band, The Barracudas, returning home to find Snakebite and Mensur locked at 10-10. The Gentle takes it 17-13 and is asked if he can win this tournament. "Never", says the big Austrian. I wake up to see Anderson overcome de Zwaan and we have our final.

SUNDAY JULY 29TH

An unscheduled visit to the RAF Museum, with Hungarian GP commentary on the drive home. We get back for the last ten laps on Sky. It's like dodgems out there, but Hamilton wins in Hungary for the sixth time. Elsewhere, Geraint Thomas becomes the first Welshman to win the Tour de France.

At the Riga Masters, I have no idea who is in the final. It's Neil Robertson v Jack Lisowski. The darts final is under way, but the U-19 final has gone to extra time with Italy and Portugal locked at 2-2. I sacrifice the snooker for now, and watch Italy 3-4 Portugal. Scenes.

In the snooker and darts, Robertson and Suljović are ahead, respectively. Blackpool is treated to the longest ever Matchplay final, an absolute ding-dong-do. Anderson needs a bullseye for the match... bounce out! The Scotsman finally takes it 21-19, a thriller in the post-Taylor era. What a tournament. What a sport. It's all over in Riga by 10pm, Robertson securing the first trophy of the season.

MONDAY JULY 30TH

It's a sport vacuum. I watch ten seconds of speedway. Fulham sign Mitrović on a permanent deal.

TUESDAY JULY 31ST

There is so little sport on the telly that I take The Boy camping in Dorset. The evening ends with a four-a-side kickabout in near total darkness played with handheld torches. Sport finds a way.

WEDNESDAY AUGUST 1ST

Stranded in deepest Dorset with limited phone signal and poor in-car radio reception, we head to the beach. I take a digital radio and listen to Test Match Special. Fun in the sun.

THURSDAY AUGUST 2ND

A planned trip to Corfe Castle is thrown into turmoil when the car doesn't start. I send The Boy ahead with some friends and await the RAC Man, attempting to follow the test match on my phone in the sweltering heat. Dave from the RAC knows the campsite well, and it appears that I am not the first or last London prick to run their car battery down by charging their phone with the radio on, doors open and hence internal lights on. He also knows his cricket and starts talking to me about spin, immediately putting me out of my depth.

Having done his business under the bonnet, he recommends that I turn the engine over for up to an hour. Citizens in my street are also partial to this. It's too hot to sit in the car, and I've already packed up the tent. As such, I lay in the minimal shade of the car and listen to TMS on the digital radio. It's an undignified business and a salutary lesson.

I eventually catch up with The Boy and we head to my old dear's, a shout of "Gone!" on the Studland ferry as another wicket tumbles. On the M3 home, we listen to the second leg of Burnley v Aberdeen, barely a fortnight since we listened to the first half of Brazil v Switzerland on the same stretch of road. Football never sleeps. In my rush to get home in time to watch some of the match, I reverse into a stationary lorry at a service station, and The Boy bursts into tears. The paperwork costs me a goal, but we get home in time for the last knockings of extra time in the garden. Burnley score a penalty to make it safe, 3-1, progressing on aggregate and avoiding an awkward discussion about the merits of Scottish football.

FRIDAY AUGUST 3RD

I awake to the news that the Oakland A's are in a postseason position, currently occupying the Wild Card slot. Let's go A's! I watch the cricket in the bath, the first action I have seen, yet I am familiar with the cadences of the test match as relayed by ye olde wireless in the preceding days. We revert to TMS en route to Watford Gap, arriving in time to see our host celebrating a wicket by performing laps of the kitchen island.

Astonishingly, it's the first day of the football season, and the Championship match between Reading and Derby is live on the same television that I saw Germany beat Sweden on a few short weeks ago. Even more astonishingly, The Watford Gap has no interest in watching it, and I am forced to the pub, thus missing a 2-1 win for Frank Lampard's Derby County. We get back for a nightcap of Red Sox v Yankees, the biggest rivalry in baseball. The same fixture is being played at The London Stadium next year and The Watford Gap will force a ticket on me.

SATURDAY AUGUST 4TH

Today's the day we fuck them up. It's only the first day of the National League North season, and Spennymoor Town at home is upon us. Whatever the predicament, the first day of the season is one of unique optimism. Freshly relegated, Chester have a new managerial duo at the helm, Bernard Morley and Anthony Johnson. The pair famously appeared in the Sky documentary Class Of '92, guiding Salford City to success thanks to the bulging wallets of Paul Scholes, Nicky Butt, and a brace of busy Nevilles. Having taken Salford to the promised land of the National League last season, the pair were roundly dismissed and have now rocked up at The Deva Stadium, a considerably different proposition, with the club owned by the fans as opposed to a phalanx of millionaire ex-footballers.

It's far too hot for football, but I bundle the family into the car and hit the A41. Serendipitously, the test match against India is reaching its conclusion and commentary switches to 5live for the dramatic denouement. It's absolutely gripping but, unfortunately, I miss England's winning wicket while arguing with The Boy about chewing gum. Stokes bowls, Cook catches. Safe hands.

Following a fractious meal at the famous Newcott Chippy, we arrive at The Deva marginally late for a prearranged book signing in the club shop. An orderly queue has formed, and I lurk at the counter, scrawling my autograph with the occasional "Up The Seals!" or personalised message.

It's a moment of great pride, but it does cut into my pre-match drinking schedule, and we take our seats in the main stand far too sober for such an auspicious occasion. The game can euphemistically be described as tight and Her Indoors spends the entire match complaining about being in direct sunlight. Had we gone behind the goal, she would have complained about having to stand up, but it would have been slightly cheaper. Chester hit the bar in the second half, but the bar is not the goal and the game finishes goalless. Some days later, Her Indoors will ask what the score was.

Bernard and Jonno appear to have brought their entire extended families with them and the Blues Bar post-match is full of Mancs acting like lottery winners in the splendour of The Deva, a palace of glittering delights compared to their previous places of work in Salford and Ramsbottom. The joint managers are having a pint outside in the sun, and they sign The Boy's programme, with Jonno admitting that we were rubbish but tried hard. Take a point, move on.

But we're not going home. By quirk of fixture, Chester are playing in the North West again on Monday night, so we plan to hover in North Wales in the interim. Simply pointing the car at the border, we dive into The Red Lion in Rhosesmor in time to see the opening of Sheffield United 1-2 Swansea City. The Boy, resplendent in Chester top, has a kickabout with a kid in a Barcelona shirt.

We check into a joyless conference hotel and head out for a meal, deep in enemy territory, The Boy defiantly still sporting his colours. There's a flashpoint when our waitress reveals herself to be a Wrexham fan and spits in our food. Either that, or she very sweetly encourages The Boy to "support your team". Scum.

SUNDAY AUGUST 5TH

I awake early and listen to a repeat of TMS, still digesting the 0-0 draw and its ramifications on the world of football. The English Football League is also up and running, but Channel 5 appear to have lost the rights. Instead, Colin Murray is fronting something called EFL On Quest, essentially highlights of the EFL on a channel called Quest. It's bewildering to watch, with no context to the results, and all of the pitches flooded with intrusive sunlight.

We fuck it off and head to Colwyn Bay, scene of the reformed Chester FC's first ever match. I listen to Aberdeen 1-1 Rangers then the Community Shield, lying on my stomach lost in football, with the tide eventually lapping at my feet. In Conway, I look in a pub and see Peter Crouch coming on for Stoke at Leeds in a game that they will lose 3-1. There are a few Stoke shirts dotted about, plus a kid in full Wigan kit. It's all too much to take in on a sweltering early August day. To add to the confusion, another TV is showing a repeat of an old West Ham v Arsenal game, having been left on after the Community Shield in which Man City beat Chelsea 2-0, a result that will live long in almost nobody's memory. I have actually been to a Community Shield game when it was still called the Charity Shield, and can only recall a decent hit from Mario Melchiot. Cursory research reveals Chelsea beat Man United 2-0 in 2000AD.

Back in the modern world, in an attempt to restore order, I buy a copy of The Non-League Paper. The vendor, a Man City fan, asks me who my team is and warns me that there are a lot of Wrexham around here. Fuck 'em. They'll never take me alive.

We check into a hotel on Llandudno bay. Viva Llandudno! As is customary, I immediately scroll through the television options. Joy of joys, the final of the Auckland Open is about to start on ITV4. Barney versus MvG, a pair of Dutch Masters in a muck sweat, half a world away, on a big screen in front of a comfy bed. Sadly, I have to make the ultimate sacrifice for a family stroll along the prom. I never do discover the winner of the Auckland Open. Yet somehow the world still turns.

MONDAY AUGUST 6TH

This is what it's all been about. Curzon Ashton away, an uncommon Monday night fixture. Situated in East Manchester, they play their home games on a Monday in order to avoid luring fans away from Manchester City's Champions League fixtures, thus preserving crucial revenue for the Abu Dhabi billionaires.

But first, another National Trust property, where The Boy is given a cursory grounding in pond dipping and impressively snags a newt at the first attempt. Rural byways eventually give way to the M56, which is suffering a massive tailback due to an incident. Thanks to years of experience, I have built time into the schedule for such events and we should be OK.

We arrive at Curzon Ashton in good time, part of a vast sports complex, with all manner of healthy activities taking place and people cycling everywhere. Bowling into the environs in search of refreshment, we run into the local press coming the other way, Dave Powell of The Chester Chronicle and Shane Pinnington of Dee 106.3. Big names. Big eaters. They point us in the direction of a nearby food complex, where we have an ill-tempered Chiquitos before trudging back to the ground. Big Al is already in place behind the goal, and someone else has some tins of cider in a bag. At this level of football, exactly the same people who weren't allowed to consume alcohol during the match last season are now allowed to consume alcohol during the match.

It's my first visit here and a measure of how far we've fallen, with the players clearly audible against the sub-thousand crowd. Pleasingly, we score a goal. And another!

Changing ends at half time, the city seems to simply end beyond the rudimentary terrace, giving way to untamed flora and fauna. As the sun sets, it's like the Serengeti, give or take a wildebeest. I manage to start a chant of "Yellows!" which spreads around the ground like moss, impressing The Boy no end. I overhear a story about one of our players taking an inordinate amount of cocaine. We score again and lock it down 3-0. We are top of the league, say we are top of the league! This comes as scant consolation when sat in static motorway traffic for over an hour, finally getting home at 3:15am.

TUESDAY AUGUST 7TH

Fatigued from life on the road, I ease into the day with Judd Trump in the bath. The evening brings Nottingham Forest v West Brom, which I watch upstairs with The Boy while trying to pack. The Tricky Trees take a second half lead, but The Baggies grab a late equaliser, providing a thrilling climax to an absorbing contest.

WEDNESDAY AUGUST 8TH

4:30am. Get in the car. Go. At one point we pass Brighton & Hove Albion's new ground. They can't be happy there, should have gone non-league when they had the chance.

Hours later we are on a ferry from Newhaven to Dieppe. Even more hours later, we are strolling round Le Mans. I look in a pub where a repeat of the Community Shield is in the 68th minute. A man utters the solitary word, "Chelsea".

THURSDAY AUGUST 9TH

The Lord's test match is under way, one of the defining moments of the entire sporting calendar. I was once in Lisbon for this auspicious occasion, and used up my entire monthly data plan to listen to the first over on TMS, Blofeld at the helm. It's a trickier business this time, with no radio reception in the car. I buy batteries for the portable digital radio, but it's to no avail. I'm in a news vacuum, the only snippet being rumours of rain.

Checking into a French holiday camp, I finally achieve resolution when it is confirmed that there has been no play. Shades of The Likely Lads. Meanwhile, the transfer deadline is approaching, with a late flurry of activity from Everton, but nothing yet from Spurs or Manchester United.

FRIDAY AUGUST 10TH

After much frustrating jiggery-pokery, I finally manage to get TMS via YouTube. There's been more rain at Lord's, but India are 15 for 3. We pop out to a nearby ghost town – when do the French eat? – and I expend my final data as India amass a handful of runs. We get back to hear them briefly grow a tail at 69-6, then enjoy the final wickets on the balcony replete with obligatory shouts of "Gone!", much to the bemusement of Speedo-clad passers-by. All out for barely 100.

A quick kickabout then we're into the first game of the Premier League, Manchester United v Leicester City. Coverage is prohibited, although I am briefly one of four people watching a live YouTube stream of a vaping man watching the game in a Man United tracksuit top with a branded pint glass. Not for me, Jeff. I finally resort to

live reports on talkSPORT as United unconvincingly win 2-1 to go
top of the nascent Premier League.

SATURDAY AUGUST 11TH

We continue driving south to a wedding, the reason we are here. It's
an outdoor ceremony, which I'm not sure is legally binding, despite or
perhaps because of the ukulele rendition of Froggy Went a-Courting. It's
followed by a woodland stroll, where we catch up with the cousin who
polluted The Boy's mind in the ways of Tottenham Hotspur. They're
actually playing right now, and we check in on their 2-1 win at Newcastle, going second in the league alphabetically. As for the cricket,
it's an analogue approach as the father of bride gives the test match
score in his speech.

And now the screaming starts. Chester are away at Blyth Spartans
following a promising start to the season. Resorting to following it
on Twitter between courses, the goals seem to come in batches, each
plunging me deeper into a pit of despair. Some whopper is banging
on about his BMW business while I am sinking into an abyss. 2-0,
3-0, 5, 6, what's happening? We make it 6-1, but it's not over yet. 7-1.
8-1. Eight bloody one! Useless, useless bastards. My day is genuinely
ruined and I go back to my tent to lie down, only re-joining the fold
when somebody generously delivers a rum and coke. I drink myself
into a stupor, to forget.

SUNDAY AUGUST 12TH

I am loath to miss a barbecue, but Bordeaux v Strasbourg awaits. Following a bracing dip, we make our excuses and hit the road, Her Indoors
at the wheel, me in a foul-tempered mess. We meet the exiled Chester
fan known as The Driver at a lake, with his wife. I make use of the
attendant burger van for a filthy merguez frites and pint of fizzy
muck before heading to the ground. It's the opening day of the Ligue
1 season, optimism abounds, and there's a decent atmosphere, with
another French match being shown on a big screen. It's unbelievably
hot, so we cower in the shade as The Driver collects the tickets before
another pint with a few Ultras of his acquaintance.

Safely in the stadium before kickoff, it's immediately the second-best
ground The Boy has been to, after Wembley. But not even Wembley can

compare to this build-up as we emerge from behind a massive banner, flares going off, smoke everywhere and an appalling din. Basically, everything you don't need with a brutal hangover. The hell doesn't stop during the match, with two blokes on raised platforms facing the crowd and bellowing into microphones in French for the entire 90 minutes. It's one of the least enjoyable football experiences I've ever had, and I've been to hundreds of Chester games. Her Indoors simply shuts down, going into screensaver mode. Unencumbered by alcohol poisoning, The Boy loves it, standing on his seat waving a Bordeaux flag in his replica shirt, bought for him by the incumbent manager's wife a few years ago. On the pitch, the home team have a man sent off early doors, and go down to a desultory 2-0 defeat. So much for early-season optimism.

It's a solid 90-minute drive to The Driver's new home. I have rendered myself incapable of operating heavy machinery so Her Indoors again takes the wheel, keeping a bead on his black Audi as he guides us in. We finally arrive at his ramshackle former garrison in the arse end of nowhere. Incongruously, we are able to watch yesterday's Match Of The Day. I manage three matches before the blackness comes.

MONDAY AUGUST 13TH

The Driver and I get up to date with Match Of The Day, then Match Of The Day 2 plus Channel 5 cricket in the other room. England secure an easy win over India to go 2-0 up in the series. Following some dreadful non-sporting activity in a nearby town, we return for a recording of EFL On Quest. Colin Murray holds it together, but Ian Holloway is bereft at the loss of Barry Chuckle, becoming genuinely emotional. By way of tribute, the crowd at Rotherham v Ipswich perform a moving rendition of 'To me, to you'. It's what he would have wanted.

TUESDAY AUGUST 14TH

We drive practically the entire length of France, arriving at Dieppe with hours to kill before our midnight crossing. Using mobile phone technology, I manage to ascertain that Celtic are out of Europe, yet again found wanting outside the cosy environs of the Scottish Premiership. We sling a pint down our necks and I take on The Boy in a final game of babyfoot. Won 10-0.

We are so far north that we can get English radio in the car. Sitting in a ferry queue for hours, I listen to garbled coverage of the Carabao Cup, the intermittent signal giving added jeopardy to the penalty shootouts.

WEDNESDAY AUGUST 15TH

Arriving in Newhaven at 4am, I get live updates of the Oakland A's victory over Seattle Mariners on my phone. We are not only closing in on the Wild Card, but have a possible tilt at the title. Of course, I've yet to actually watch a game this season, like a massive plastic.

Finally back in civilisation, it's the Super Cup, the traditional utterly forgettable early-season glorified friendly between the winners of the two primary European club competitions. There's added spice this year as it's between the two main Madrid clubs, Champions League winners Real, and Europa League winners Atlético. In Estonia. I'm still adjusting the HD when Diego Costa, the Elephant Man, scores after 52 seconds. It's been sullied, so we go for a curry instead, watching it on my phone of course. Pleasingly it goes to extra time, and we get home to see Atlético triumph 4-2. Does this signify a shift in power? Probably not. I watch a bit of Carabao Cup On Quest, and so to bed.

THURSDAY AUGUST 16TH

With little else going on, I get up to date with the Carabao Cup. It's a blur of penalty shootouts, quite literally given the Standard Definition Freeview. Her Indoors phones to say she's out for the evening, and I am instantly thrilled at the prospect of watching Sunderland v Sheffield Wednesday undisturbed. But first the draw, which has something of a chequered history. It's in the safe hands of Mick McCarthy and Chris Waddle; the South section first, then the North. Still car-lagged from France, I watch the second half in bed. 2-0 to Wednesday.

FRIDAY AUGUST 17TH

Following a turgid dinosaur show at Regent's Park with The Boy and friend, we get back in time for a bit of arrers in the shape of the Brisbane Masters, where Michael Smith is beasted by his namesake,

Raymond, a local hero for the night. Sacrificing Birmingham v Swansea, I get in the car, pick up one man and his dog, and drive to Watford Gap. Mets 2-4 Phillies.

SATURDAY AUGUST 18TH

This is it then. On a minibus to Trent Bridge with a bunch of whoppers to celebrate the 50th birthday of a man known only as Scargs, presumably due to his passing resemblance to former National Union of Mineworkers leader Arthur Scargill. Hundreds of pounds have been spent on tickets and we can't even get there on time, a combination of disorganisation and roadworks forcing us to walk the final mile to a match already under way. To say that I am fucked off is an understatement.

Finally taking our seats, we haven't missed a great deal and the torpor soon sets in. I use a pair of binoculars to scan the crowd. It is little exaggeration to say that one of the highlights is spotting a Mansfield flag. Bringing football flags to cricket is a strange custom. Conversely, you rarely see county cricket club flags at international football matches.

And that's lunch, at which point our group dissipates further, some to a pub from which they will not return. At one point, I am the only one watching the match out of a minibus of double figures. Why bother? That said, live cricket is all but unwatchable, hence its enormous reliance on alcohol abuse and alternative entertainment. Apropos of nothing, somebody asks, "How many caps did Phil Neville get?" 59? We're even forced to leave early to beat the mythical rush. As such, we hear the roar as Jimmy Anderson takes a final ball wicket to leave India on 307-6.

Back at Watford Gap, it's an absolute tear-up, even forgoing Match Of The Day. The entertainment culminates in the birthday boy performing a series of passable darts player impressions, each recognisable from throwing action and accompanying facial tics. He then displays a photograph of Anastasia Dobromyslova on his phone, describing her as his dream woman. By way of a finale, he describes in extreme detail a civil service darts semi-final he played in, still reeling from the defeat, which it transpires was in 2002.

A few stragglers play snooker and pool until the early hours. I tactically retire. We ride at noon, more or less.

SUNDAY AUGUST 19TH

Back on the bus to Trent Bridge, numbers depleted, albeit bolstered by the dog. Scargs the birthday boy nursing a pale ale. Chat turns to the weirdest place you've had a wank. Hundreds of thousands of pounds-worth of education and that is the best they've got.

Naturally, we go to a pub instead of the sporting event that we have bought expensive tickets for. We eventually take our seats and find ourselves in front of the cricketer Hayley Brown, who gives us some pretty decent gossip. On the field, England are floundering, losing wickets all over the shop. A quiz strikes up nearby, and there is much debate about players who have notched centuries from number ten. Apparently, somebody called Pat Simcox has done it. Not a clue. I don't like cricket.

The Premier League stops for no man and we duck into the Trent Bridge Inn to see a chunk of Brighton 3-1 Man United. Brighton can't have enjoyed that, should have gone non-league when they had the chance.

Back on the bus, it's a surviving triumvirate of my good self, Scargs and The Watford Gap. Reg the driver sticks on a bit of Del Shannon and delivers us without incident. We catch up with Match Of The Day then Match Of The Day 2, both semi-virgin. Despite having a Watford tattoo on his leg, The Watford Gap habitually avoids their scores so he can enjoy the ten-minute thrill of Match Of The Day highlights. It's a controversial strategy, but one that pays dividends tonight as he proceeds to kiss the screen during their 3-1 win at Burnley. I watch the A's losing to Houston Astros on my phone.

MONDAY AUGUST 20TH

Finally, homeward bound, having spent hundreds of pounds to drink gallons of lager and watch a few snippets of a largely atrocious England performance that I will inevitably forget, apart from the price. I don't really remember much about any cricket match I have ever attended, or even watched on TV. Yet listening to Monty clinging on at Cardiff while negotiating the Chiswick roundabout (me, not him) is firmly engraved into my sporting memory bank.

I attempt to listen to TMS on the M1, flicking between the unreliable digital radio and the white noise of 720 AM. I don't feel very well. Back in the real world, I pick up The Boy and his feral friend. Leaving them to run wild, I go upstairs and sleep through Sky Cricket, coming to for a bit of TMS in the garden. I then sleep through the first half of Palace 0-2 Liverpool, with Salah involved in a dodgy penalty and sending off.

TUESDAY AUGUST 21ST

I awake to the news that Oakland again go level at the top. Despite having attended two days of the test match, I entirely forget about the cricket until reminded by technology. With England chasing a historic total, I listen in the bath on my phone with a bit of background music. There's a familiar trundle of wickets as both openers are out inside 20 minutes.

I also forget that Melbourne Victory are away at APIA Leichhardt in the round of 16 of the FFA Cup, essentially the FA Cup of Australia. It's already half time and they're already a goal down. I watch the second half and one soon becomes two. A Kenny Athiu brace inside six minutes levels it, but with ten minutes to go, Leichhardt snatch victory from the jaws of Victory. Melbourne manager Kevin Muscat is no doubt spewing, although little does he know that he is the man responsible for my mild support of this Antipodean outfit. While in Melbourne covering the Aussie Millions poker tournament, the PR woman sorted me a ticket for the derby match via Muscat, then a player. Melbourne Victory and Melbourne Heart (now City) played out a 2-2 draw. Muscat was sent off for a horrific foul, but his generosity ensured that I would always keep an eye out for Victory on BT Sport.

Back to Trent Bridge and England continue to lose wickets. Giving it up as a lost cause, I start watching National League highlights outside, but this is curtailed when I discover that a shithouse hacker has stolen the best part of 750 quid from my PokerStars account. I smash up the table in rage, also slightly damaging the iPad.

Buttler and Stokes put up some resistance while I'm out of the house, but England limp into day five with one wicket remaining. Then we're into Swansea 2-2 Leeds in the Championship. Oli McBurnie with the opener for The Swans, I saw his first professional goal, notching on-loan for The Mighty Chester on a filthy day at Welling.

WEDNESDAY AUGUST 22ND

A's win. I go back to sleep and awake to Joe Root in my ear. This would suggest that England are no longer batting, and indeed I have slept through the 17 balls required for India to pick them off. Can I get a refund?

I'm so cross I go for a swim, killing time until Villa 2-2 Brentford. The baseball season is reaching the business end, and I manage to watch Texas Rangers 4-2 Oakland Athletics on something called Facebook Watch. It'll never catch on.

THURSDAY AUGUST 23RD

I awake to hear Tony Cascarino on talkSPORT talking about his brain tumour. While recuperating, he's been watching every game and looking to resume playing poker. One of the good guys, Cascarino once bought me a steak in The Vic casino on Edgware Road after I interviewed him. He is also responsible for one of the best sporting autobiographies ever written, which I received in the goodie bag of a pro-celebrity poker tournament that I actually won.

Over in France, our Bordeaux-supporting friend The Driver goes to Gent for a 0-0 draw. 22 hours in the car for that.

FRIDAY AUGUST 24TH

A's lose 6-4 to Minnesota Twins. The first baseball game I ever attended was The Twins at Oakland. As a guest of Electronic Arts, this meant sitting in a comfy corporate box with an endless supply of beer and hotdogs, enough to elicit a mild support that continues to this day. After the game, there was a minor altercation during which an Oakland fan exclaimed, "Fuck the Twins!" Oddly my fellow guest, a Daily Mirror journalist, somehow misheard this as "Fuck the twinge!" and was baffled as to the meaning of this unusual phrase. Even when it was explained to him, he still insisted he had heard correctly.

Back to the present, we find ourselves in a rudimentary curry house in Daventry, casually following Middlesbrough v West Brom. Still goalless, we get back to Her Indoors' brother's house and watch the end of the match on Sky Go. Middlesbrough score a last-minute winner that is clearly handball, thus invalidating the entire Championship and all football. Tony Pulis wears the club shop.

SATURDAY AUGUST 25TH

I enjoy a deep bath while tracking the developing chaos on the M6. It's not entirely recreational, as I need to get to Telford, or at least Wellington, where Telford United play. Fuck it, we'll take the A5, Watling Street all the way. What have the Romans ever done for us?

I round up The Boy and his Spurs-supporting cousin and bundle them into the car, Wolves v Man City on 5live. We catch the last 20 minutes in the Swan Hotel with a few auld fellas from Chester. Impressively, the newly-promoted Wolves hold the champions to a 1-1 draw. What bearing will this have on the season ahead? Some? None? Only time will tell.

In the ground, I am approached by a Chester fan of my acquaintance who shows me a selfie of him with John Portsmouth Football Club Westwood, who once shot me with a water pistol during Euro 2000. Another fan also claims, correctly, to have been at university with me. Spotting me with The Boy, another fan asks, "Is he ripped on Haribo?", a direct reference to my book, The Card, which some people have read. I've been standing here for decades and now suddenly everyone (four people) wants to speak to me because I wrote a book about how I used to get a lift to the match and now I don't get a lift to the match.

One person who thankfully doesn't speak to me is the Chester Zombie, previously renowned for emitting vile arse gas at Maidenhead United. He's got himself into a frenzy, as have several other supporters. Off the back of the 8-1 drubbing, we need a performance here. We get one, but sadly it's a mainly awful one. Gifting them two goals in the space of four minutes, a third in the second half seals it for the home team. Our late goal is scant consolation to the 535 travelling fans. Some of them turn on each other, and even the players' wives, shamefully. The bulk of the ire is reserved for the management team and I'm ashamed to say I was party to that goading.

The Boy's cousin has genuinely never seen anything like it, greeting the unrest with a combination of nervous laughter and genuine fear. I get the pair of them out of the stadium and we see the Chester Zombie hilariously complaining to a steward that he felt very let down by the experience.

On the radio, Robbie Savage sticks his neck out by predicting that both Manchester City and Liverpool will be involved in the title race. We listen to the Liverpool game in the car as they make heavy weather of beating Brighton 1-0. We get home for the last knockings on BT Sport. I later watch Match Of The Day on the TV while simultaneously catching up with the same programme on my phone.

SUNDAY AUGUST 26TH

Robbie Savage interviews Steven Gerrard ahead of the nascent manager's game at Motherwell. Frost/Nixon it is not. Apparently, Rangers have never been behind under Gerrard's stewardship. This record lasts all of three minutes, and it is already 1-1 by the time I immerse myself in hot water. It's an absolute ding-dong-do, with Motherwell scoring in injury time to make it 3-3.

This segues into the seemingly weekly Watford v Palace game, which The Hornets win 2-1, the most common score in football. The Belgian Grand Prix is under way, consisting of a first corner crash then a procession, Vettel from Hamilton. I once attended a Belgian Grand Prix as a competition prize. I can't recall a single thing about the race, other than the ear-splitting sound from the main stand. If there's one thing worse than watching a Grand Prix on TV, it's attending a Grand Prix in person.

I move rooms for Newcastle 1-2 Chelsea on the iPad, plus Bordeaux 2-1 Monaco on my phone. The Driver is in the crowd and astonishingly a Chester fan recognises him from my book and sends me a clip of him via Twitter.

Following another visit to the same Daventry curry house – different table – I settle in for Match Of The Day 2. Tragically this is sullied when I catch a glimpse of Fulham 4-2 Burnley on the news. Amateur night.

MONDAY AUGUST 27TH

I should be on my way to Chester v Hereford, but it is postponed because The Deva Stadium flooded the day after the 8-1 defeat at Blyth, causing major electrical damage. It never rains but it pours. Horrendously, this puts me at a loose end. In search of sporting salvation, I toy with BBC coverage of the Ireland v Afghanistan ODI on my phone. It doesn't take, so I have a look at the US Open tennis on Amazon Prime and promptly fall asleep. Heading home, we listen to Manchester United 0-3 Spurs in the car, getting back for the second half and a row with The Boy.

TUESDAY AUGUST 28TH

Oakland go 4-0 up against the Houston Astros, then promptly lose 11-4. What a sport.

I drop The Boy at QPR Soccer School for the day, a more professional outfit than Charlie Merson's mob and essentially cheap childcare. We reconvene for AFC Wimbledon v West Ham in the Carabao Cup, live from Kingsmeadow, where I once saw Chester City win a trophy. A second-minute goal gives The Wombles hope, but it is quickly dashed by a red card. Nevertheless, they get to half time with their lead intact, before succumbing to three late goals, crushed by the might of the Premier League.

I follow the other Carabao goals on the iPad and am intrigued to see that Swansea are playing Palace at the same time as Stevenage are playing Swansea U-21's in the EFL Trophy, aka the Checkatrade. Already a risible competition, this does little to reinforce its standing. Some thoughts there.

I catch up with the goal action on Quest then fall asleep with Oakland one down against those pesky Astros.

WEDNESDAY AUGUST 29TH

I avoid the baseball score so I can squeeze maximum value from the repeat and drop The Boy in the capable hands of QPR. The second Ireland v Afghanistan ODI is on the Red Button and I splitscreen it with Lions v Adelaide United in the FFA Cup. When somebody makes an 82nd-minute substitution, I realise that I am not entirely sure which team is playing in orange and which team isn't.

I watch the baseball repeat on my stoop, waiting for an Amazon delivery of some copies of my own book. Ireland get over the line in the cricket, although I miss the winning runs. A's win 4-3! The MLB has really got a hold of me, a near daily rollercoaster.

Jeans on for the first time in months, I head to the spartan upstairs room of a pub in East London where I am guest of honour at a meeting of the Chester FC Exiles, with butties laid on. There's a lot of admin to get through first, with the big take-away being that Burnley have pulled out of the darts league. I answer a few questions from the floor and, crucially, flog them some books.

In the downstairs bar, Forest are playing Newcastle (on the TV) in the Carabao. While buying a round I am fortunate enough to witness three goals live, all in injury time. First off, Newcastle equalise Forest's second-minute opener, then the home team twat in a brace to go through. As the commentator says, it's an "extraordinary end to a pretty ordinary game".

In the baseball, the A's lose in the 9th innings. Fuck it. I watch EFL On Quest on Quest+1. In the tennis, Murray is out and I've missed it. At 4am, Nadal beats Canada's Vasek Pospisil in the Arthur Ashe Stadium, live on Amazon Prime, a far from perfect viewing experience. Go on Rafa, lad.

THURSDAY AUGUST 30TH

It's the fourth test from the Rose Bowl in Southampton, which still doesn't sound like a proper test venue like Lord's or Headingley. As tradition dictates, I absorb the contest via TMS in bed, then Sky in the bath. England win the toss and choose to bat. Weather set fair. "You silly cunt!", I shout as Jennings goes for 0. Root now gone for 4, review lost. 36-4. Shambles.

I take the afternoon session in the garden, brown leaves on the lawn, a cold nip on my legs, desperately clinging on to the remnants of summer. I retrieve The Boy from the clutches of Queens Park Rangers and listen to 3pm commentary of Glasgow Rangers away at FC Ufa in the Europa League with a slender 1-0 lead from the first leg. They soon double this, but the home side equalise and then Rangers foolishly have two players sent off. Nevertheless, the nine men cling on to a 1-1 draw and they progress to whatever fucking stage it is now.

I listen to the interminable Champions League draw on talkSPORT, then watch the Carabao Cup draw on Sky Sports News. I'm all set for Burnley v Olympiacos, but am voted down by Her Indoors and The Boy who insist on using my big bastard telly to watch Captain Underpants. Reverting to iPad and headphones, I enjoy the 1-1 draw in blissful solitude. My body is here, but my mind is in Lancashire. Still thinking about that brick I had thrown at me in '88.

FRIDAY AUGUST 31ST

The A's lose 7-1 to the Mariners and are losing ground on both the title and the Wild Card. Of course, you don't look at league tables until at least 100 games in, but we are approaching end game. I leave The Boy in the capable hands of QPR and go to an outdoor gym, performing some half-hearted exercise for the duration of Setting Sons by The Jam.

All Mod Cons is cut short by TMS on the stroll home, where I get straight into the bath with Sky on the iPad, plus Sound Affects on the Bluetooth speaker. I get sucked into National League highlights on BT Sport and end up missing the Europa League draw. Chelsea will play BATE: audible shrug. Meanwhile, Ireland are all out cheaply versus Afghanistan and Usain Bolt makes his debut for Central Coast Mariners.

It's officially the last day of summer, with autumn approaching like the corners of my mind. England are very much in it as wickets tumble. On the last day of QPR Soccer School, The Boy picks up a medal for the crossbar challenge, and I see Tommy Cockles in the car park. India all out, England openers holding firm, I kill time with a repeat of the Europa League draw.

Friday night, big city, bright lights. I stay in and watch Leeds 0-0 Middlesbrough. But that's not all, there's also Wales Women 0-3 England Women, which sees 'The Lionesses' qualify for the World Cup, manager Phil Neville resplendent in Southgate-issue waistcoat. I also have a little dabble with Lyon 0-1 Nice, Balotelli subbed, Buffon boasting a feather-cut mohican. Of course, the interesting thing is that all three games feature a team in red against a team in white.

With the football done for the night, the US Open is barely warming up. Rafa is up against the Russian man, Karen Khachanov. Nadal goes 2-1 up in sets and the commentator says, "both men's souls laid bare in that tiebreaker". 3-1 to Rafa. Venus and Serena to come.

SATURDAY SEPTEMBER 1ST

We're into September, the embers of the summer beginning to settle before the horror of winter. Yet still the sport comes. It's the final training session with Queen's Park Sharks and Shouty Steve. Sadly, it is considered impolite to listen to Test Match Special while staring into the middle distance so I am forced to make small talk with other parents. Back home in the garden, I enjoy the tranquillity of solitude with a hybrid of 5live, TMS and Sky delivering the cricket plus Leicester 1-2 Liverpool. I briefly switch to the Italian Grand Prix qualifying to see Hamilton trumped by a Ferrari one-two, Räikkönen setting the fastest lap in F1 history.

All a footnote, of course. Cowering from the sun, I use the Mixlr app to listen to live commentary of Guiseley v Chester, a rerun of New Year's Day, albeit a division lower. It seems to be heading for 0-0, but a sickening Guiseley goal two minutes from time prompts Her Indoors' usual speech about Chester always conceding late goals. She's still talking when I set off round the garden, tossing The Boy into the air at news of our injury-time equaliser. We still require a goal-line clearance to secure the draw, but it's a foothold in this already traumatic season. Take a point, move on.

I have somehow managed to avoid the Premier League scores and make the baffling decision to accompany the family to Asda in order to miss Man City v Newcastle, thus ensuring a relatively virgin Match Of The Day, barring the extended foreplay of Liverpool v Leicester. Sitting on a shoe seat listening to TMS amid a wreckage of school clothing, I immediately regret this decision. The scheme is foiled anyway when I can't resist looking at a pub TV to see that it's currently 1-1 at City.

We drive around listening to cricket until The Boy falls asleep, thus liberating the TV. It's a rare opportunity to use it for something other than sport, and we watch the gut-wrenching film Manchester By The Sea, which is tempered by the lead protagonist bearing a passing resemblance to Chester winger, Craig Mahon. This takes me into the second game of Match Of The Day, having neatly bypassed the previously seen Liverpool v Leicester. A touch of Cricket On 5 on the iPad, the Yankees game on the phone and I'm back in sporting nirvana. I attempt EFL On Quest, but give up after two games. It'll keep.

SUNDAY SEPTEMBER 2ND

The A's are losing ground as October approaches. I order the Google Home Mini to play TMS and watch the last knockings of EFL On Quest on the ancient portable. TMS in the kitchen: "Gone!" TMS in the bath with Celtic v Rangers on the iPad. Brendan Rogers v Steven Gerrard, master and servant. Over half an hour in, it's barely an exaggeration to say that I haven't seen the Celtic keeper, such is the home side's dominance. They eventually make a breakthrough in the second half, a 1-0 win scarcely reflecting the one-sided occasion.

While Sky shows the Old Firm derby, also kicking off at high noon is the so-called Old Farm derby between Ipswich and Norwich. Starved of television coverage, I manage to catch the Ipswich opener on Radio Suffolk on the iPlayer Radio app. I am surprised to learn that Jonathan Walters is back at Portman Road, a player they signed from Chester after he impressed in a pair of FA Cup games against them, both of which I attended. Norwich hit back and it finishes 1-1. Take a point, move on.

This takes us into the meat of the Prem, where Arsenal go to Cardiff, still lacking an identity without Wenger, like The Stranglers without Hugh Cornwell. TMS on, I relocate to the garden, where I watch the start of the Grand Prix, Vettel in a spin after clipping Hamilton.

Back at Cardiff, I miss Lacazette's thunderbolt while trying to pick up my sun hat, but Arsenal eventually prevail 3-2. I watch the last four laps of the Grand Prix, as Hamilton wins to extend his championship lead. Back at the cricket, Kohli is caught and the series is in the balance. England win!

In the 4pm kickoff, Spurs are at Watford where they throw away a lead to lose 2-1. It's a double whammy – bad news for The Boy and good news for The Watford Gap, who will take great pleasure in reminding him of the result.

After fashioning a rudimentary barbecue, I play cricket with The Boy until we are driven in by the dark. I fire up Amazon Prime for a bit of Rafa with a side of Monaco 2-3 Marseille. Been there. Back at the US Open, Serena is taken to a deciding set, but wins through. In the MLB, it's Arizona Diamondbacks at LA Dodgers. Been there. I also have a soft spot for the Diamondbacks as they won the first World Series I followed, late on Channel 5, Jonny Gould in the studio, spitting redneck Randy Johnson on the mound. Gould once attempted to humiliate me while he was hosting an auction of sporting memorabilia and I hadn't strictly adhered to the dress code. Not sure what Johnson's doing now. Probably spitting.

Match Of The Day 2 comes and goes, and it's a walk-off win for the Dodgers, putting them top of the National League West. On the other side of the continent, Sloane Stephens cruises past Elise Mertens in the tennis. Back in the MLB, the A's win to stay in touch. I'm thinking of calling it a day when BT Sport goes live to the Angels at the Astros at 1am. There's a huge Japanese contingent in to see Angels pitcher Ohtani. Randomly, one of the Astros player is mic'd up, indulging in some low-level sledging at first base. Back in New York, del Potro is into the first set. Sadly, that's where I have to leave it. A solid 16-hour shift.

MONDAY SEPTEMBER 3RD

High noon. Alastair Cook has announced his retirement from international cricket, bringing the curtain down on a glittering career, arguably the highlight of which was shaking my hand while interrupting an interview with Matt Prior, who was promoting his new cycling team. True story.

It's international week so there is no Monday Night Football. What a bollocks. Instead, I join The Yankees at Oakland with the game in progress. It's feasibly a battle for the Wild Card home advantage. It's Labor Day in America so an early start, 9pm here. If you're going to support a baseball team, you should really pick one on the East Coast. A's win 6-3 and it's on for young and old.

In the tennis, Čilić beats someone, and Sharapova screams her way to defeat against a Spaniard.

TUESDAY SEPTEMBER 4TH

Slim pickings. News filters through from New York that Federer has gone out to the 55th seed, and Colin Kaepernick becomes the face of Nike's Just Do It campaign. Just do what, exactly?

I, meanwhile, have an appointment at Ipswich Kid's birthday party, thus missing the 4pm England Women's game. The party is at something called Puttshack, essentially indoor crazy golf with electronic scoreboards. I confidently predict that it will be closed within six months before being informed that the company is already worth millions.

Chelsea Dad joins me on the lagers and announces that he is off to the Ryder Cup in Paris as a birthday treat. There's talk of getting the gang back together for the forthcoming England games in the Nations League, although nobody seems to know exactly what that is. I vow never to find out.

Back home, not swerving the Checkatrade, I tune into BBC Three Counties Radio to hear MK Dons beat Peterborough on penalties after a 3-3 draw, hearing the last few. It really is none of my business and this is a desperate attempt at a sporting fix.

My close personal friend Tiger Woods is announced in the US Ryder Cup team, sparking the usual debate that occurs every time this happens. In New York, del Potro and Isner are going at it in the tennis where the heat is becoming problematic. "This is like playing tennis in a sauna," claims the commentator.

Serena is struggling in the first set, but makes "a simply sensational recovery". I think I might prefer women's tennis, not just for the obvious reasons, but because there's less of it. A men's game can take four hours. Who's got the time? Serena goes through, watched by Spike Lee who compares her to Muhammad Ali.

Rafa v Thiem is next and both players are instantly drenched in sweat. Ben Affleck looks on, probably still thinking about Batman v Superman. This is more endurance than tennis, and with 22 minutes on the clock, Thiem is serving for the set against the holder, taking it 6-0, only the fourth time Rafa has laid an egg in a major.

WEDNESDAY SEPTEMBER 5TH

A's lose, Astros win. That's not good. I get to 6:30pm without knowing the Nadal result. As the US Open is being streamed on Amazon Prime, there's no way of recording it and I can find no evidence of a catch-up service. Progress they call it. I don't even know the England Women's result. Amateurish.

I manage to find a replay of the Rafa game, which I watch during Havant & Waterlooville 2-1 Aldershot. Past 2am New York time, Rafa wins a dramatic fifth-set tiebreak. As the commentator proclaims, "sport is the best form of reality TV". Incidentally, the US Open is the only Grand Slam to have fifth-set tiebreaks and thank fuck they do, otherwise they could have been there until the break of dawn. Back live, Nishikori beats the giant Čilić in five, like Arya Stark (SPOILER ALERT) felling The Mountain in Game Of Thrones. I leave Djokovic getting into his stride and lie down until I'm unconscious.

THURSDAY SEPTEMBER 6TH

The MLB app informs me that The A's beat The Yankees overnight and it's tight at the top. Let's go Oakland! The Boy is back at school and there are conkers in Queen's Park. Shouty Steve is hosting a training session ahead of The Shady Sharks' first game, so I wear flip-flops to avoid helping out. At the end of the session, he gives each player an elaborate printout of instructions and field positions. It's the first and last time we look at it.

Actual football is breaking out all over the telly and Wales beat Ireland 4-1 in the Nations League, whatever that is. There's also a bit of England U-21 0-0 Netherlands U-21 and a touch of Germany 0-0 France. I still have no idea what the UEFA Nations League is.

Thoughts turn to different shaped balls as the NFL season is mere hours away, kicking off with Atlanta at Philadelphia, where the tailgate parties are already under way. The relatively brief season will take us into deep winter, climaxing in the Superbowl next year. Every year I think I'll get into it, and every year I flounder. I don't support a team, I don't really understand how the league system works and I only have a rudimentary grasp of the rules. Nevertheless, I can mindlessly sit through the odd game, particularly if I've stuck a bet on it.

Also in America, the men's doubles tennis semi-final is afoot, but I struggle to care. Bryan and Sock beat Cabal and Farah. No further questions.

FRIDAY SEPTEMBER 7TH

I wake up and drive to Portmeirion, a village on the west coast of Wales. I haven't taken leave of my senses; I am on my way to Festival No.6 to review it for a music magazine. It's a fucking long way, but the hours drift by accompanied by TMS drifting in and out, Alastair Cook's last test match.

On a whim, I take a detour to Bala Town FC and park outside the ground. I once lived nearby and regularly visited the town, yet never had any concept of the existence of the football club. A tidy ground. I then drive past the house where I watched the 1982 World Cup Final, quite possibly in black and white.

I eventually get to the festival, set up my tent, get arseholed and enjoy a sport-free night. It'll never catch on.

SATURDAY SEPTEMBER 8TH

News filters through that Shady Sharks have turned over Primrose Hill 3-1. Get in Sharks. Validation for Shouty Steve's methods.

I temporarily leave the festival and drive through a violent rainstorm to Chester, TMS struggling to be heard against the elements. I sign some more books, meet up with my older brother and stand next to Big Al on the Harry McNally Terrace. We're playing Bradford Park Avenue and we don't expect much. What we get is an eight-goal thriller with Chester eventually prevailing 5-3. Scenes. Up to 17th.

A touch of TMS takes us back into Wales, before I give up and listen to CDs of the groups we're going to see. England are actually playing Spain tonight at Wembley in the mysterious Nations League, not to be confused with the National League or indeed National League North. It was at the same festival two years ago that I watched Sam Allardyce's only England match on an iPad in the press room with weak wi-fi. An absolutely turgid affair, the iPad started buffering in injury time and I missed the only goal of the game and Big Sam's regime.

Not again. I simply set up my phone for goal alerts and take back control of my life. Boom. Rashford 1-0. Oh, Spain 1-1. Oh, 2-1 to Spain, game over. Painless. Some hours later, writhing in my canvas shack, I listen to 5live coverage of the US Open where there has been an incident involving Serena Williams.

SUNDAY SEPTEMBER 9TH

Wicket alerts all day. Djokovic wins the US Open overnight.

MONDAY SEPTEMBER 10TH

I wake up writhing and listen to a 5live interview with the daughter of Muhammad Ali. Tent down at first light, we are gone, punk rock

CDs in the mountains. Tiredness kills. Following a number of near misses, I drop my brother at Cheltenham and press on, TMS for company, Cook on 40 in his last ever England innings. Go on Alastair, lad. Closing in on a century, he finally gets there as I fill up outside Oxford. I get home in time to see him out for 147, almost tearful. There's also a landmark for Jimmy Anderson. Go on Jimmy, lad.

I pick up The Boy and give him to QPR for 90 minutes. I dip into Scotland 2-0 Albania and Portugal 1-0 Italy, but struggle to care. Tired and filthy, I have a late bath for Houston Astros at Detroit Tigers. This MLB has really got a hold on me.

TUESDAY SEPTEMBER 11TH

It's the last day of the last test of summer, which is trickling through my fingers. England win it, meaning the only test match they didn't win was the one I paid hundreds of pounds to attend. I don't like cricket.

I listen to commentary of Chester FC v Football Club United Of Manchester while watching England play Switzerland in a friendly at Leicester. We definitely chose the right Chester match to attend, as this one finishes goalless. Meanwhile, England scrape a 1-0 win, Rashford again, to avoid a record fourth consecutive defeat.

WEDNESDAY SEPTEMBER 12TH

A fifth straight win for the A's keeps the pressure on. Elsewhere, it's an early start for snooker's Shanghai Masters and I immediately fall asleep. Coming round, I catch up with EFL On Quest in the bath thanks to the QuestOD app. What a world.

I have to take The Boy for a hospital appointment, but Quest again comes to the rescue as I record Ronnie v Neil Robertson. I accidentally see Ronnie tweeting, but thankfully it is mainly about fitness. I watch it in the evening, 6-3 to Ronnie. Go on Ronnie.

I follow an A's game live as they go 10-0 up at Orioles in the third inning. Also in America, I watch DC United v Minnesota on Ladbrokes. I leave it with Rooney's side 1-0 down.

THURSDAY SEPTEMBER 13TH

The A's win 10-0 to move one game behind the Yankees in the Wild Card race. Uninvited, YouTube informs me that Williams is through in the snooker, and I am underwater in time for the decider between Wilson and Day. Wilson reels off a 135, missing the black that would have given him the highest break. True story. I keep an eye on Selby v Ding from the garden.

Shady Sharks have a training session, but The Boy is sick as a dog, spewing his ring everywhere. We get back for a recording of the snooker on Quest, but it cuts off. An amateurish mistake, I should have also recorded the next show. Or perhaps the onus lies with Freeview. Either way, I put my foot through the TV and send the bill to the BBC. Not really. Instead, I awake at 2:30 am to see a repeat as Ding and Selby go to a decider. The Jester from Leicester hits a wild one to let in Ding, who makes it safe at seven minutes to midnight local time in front of a partisan crowd.

This takes me straight into the NFL, Baltimore Ravens at Cincinnati Bengals live in so-called Thursday Night Football. Meanwhile, the Baltimore Orioles deal a blow to the A's post-season hopes with a 5-3 victory. Bengals win. Who cares? Go to bed, you tool.

FRIDAY SEPTEMBER 14TH

High noon underwater, Ronnie and Wilson locked at 4-4 in a first to ten semi. What a time to be alive. Ronnie cruises home without breaking sweat. Go on Ronnie.

I catch a bit of the Davis Cup in Westfield shopping centre. GB's Norrie goes two sets up against Uzbekistan and then loses 3-2. A disgrace.

Back home for the torpid second halves of Birmingham 1-1 WBA and St Mirren 0-0 Celtic. What a night.

SATURDAY SEPTEMBER 15TH

Shanghai Masters semi for breakfast, Ding v Hawkins. Not for me, I'm off to Boston. Lincolnshire, not Massachusetts. It's a convoluted route that entails a train to Peterborough where I am greeted by a phalanx of coppers, clearly wary of a fat man in a lurid blue smock. Turns out they are actually waiting for Pompey fans as Portsmouth are playing Posh. No sign of John Portsmouth Football Club Westwood and his infernal bell.

As arranged, The Hack and wife are waiting in the station car park. He drives me the relatively short distance to Boston using the old-fashioned method of looking at road signs. This works to an extent, but I eventually let Google Maps take the strain, delivering us smoothly to Boston Town. Unfortunately, we're playing Boston United.

We relocate to a pub and watch Spurs v Liverpool on Sky, although I'm not entirely convinced as to veracity of the feed. The only lager is Carling, which hugely amuses The Hack, a devout real aler. He has recently done a phone interview with Jimmy Tarbuck, who reversed the charges to the tune of £53. Strong anecdote.

We switch pubs at half time, relocating to a multiscreen hell-hole. As with any market town in England, it's full of blokes in replica shirts, mainly Liverpool, one Spurs, despite being walking distance from an actual football match. Liverpool win 2-1. Good for them.

After a sweaty chippy, we walk to the actual football match and endure one of the worst halves in living memory. Goalless at the break, I escape to a windowless bar with Sky Sports News on a flapping screen and rapidly pour lager into my head. The second half is a huge improvement and Chester nick it 2-0. At the end, a fan shakes my hand and says he loves my book and my column. Wait 'til he reads this crap.

Back at Posh, I dive into a hotel bar opposite the station for a snippet of Watford 0-2 Man United, pleasingly catching both goals. Back in London, on the train there is a discarded Millwall v Leeds programme. I leave it; none of my business.

Back home, I fall asleep during EFL On Quest, Match Of The Day but a pipe dream, albeit recorded. I awake at 4am and listen to the latest very important boxing match. What really went on there? I can't work out who is who in my befuddled state.

SUNDAY SEPTEMBER 16TH

Straight into EFL On Quest like nothing ever happened. Uninvited, YouTube informs me that Hawkins downs Ding in Shanghai. I attempt to ignore it. The A's have lost, as have the Yankees. It's tight at the top with the Astros still in contention. I watch a repeat of Diamondbacks v Astros in the bath; I thought I knew the result, but now I'm not so sure.

Today is Queen's Park Day, whereby the middle-class masses mince around the park, pay a fortune for glorified takeaways and endure low-grade entertainment. For this I am sacrificing Super Sunday. That said, I'm not sure of the 'super' credentials of Wolves 1-0 Burnley and Everton 1-3 West Ham.

A couple of hours out of the house has thrown the sporting schedule into chaos, the danger of deferment proving all too real. News filters through that Hamilton has won the Singapore GP and a glimpsed picture of Ronnie hints at victory in Shanghai. This is later confirmed – Go on Ronnie – amid a cacophony of live and recorded sport, including seemingly endless NFL. I'm struggling to get on top of it and give up with Cowboys leading at Giants.

MONDAY SEPTEMBER 17TH

Keith Deller on Twitter weighing in on Brexit. Guess the rest. I shook his hand at Ally Pally.

I settle in for the evening with 7:45pm commentary of the FA Youth Cup, Chester away at Marine. A player called Tom Ruffer comes on for us. His father Carl also played for Chester and I recall him once taking a swing at me at an end of season do. We win 6-0.

On the TV, it's Monday Night Football, with an 8pm kickoff that ends Southampton 2-2 Brighton in the south coast non-derby. I even have a dip into the speedway, Somerset v Poole Pirates in the first leg.

Late doors, we're into the original Monday Night Football, a largely unwatchable NFL game. Forget it.

TUESDAY SEPTEMBER 18TH

TalkSPORT scrape the barrel by playing the audio of a moron baiting Manchester United players at Watford Junction after Saturday's game. This will remain a topic of national importance until at least the next ad break.

I catch a snippet of a baffling Chinese Super League game on Sky and then we're into the U-19 European games, Inter 1-1 Spurs, both down to ten men. This is the beginning of wall-to-wall European football, with actual Inter v Spurs kicking off at the absurd time of 5:55pm, along with Barcelona v PSV, Messi's 42nd hat trick helping them to a 4-0 win.

Spurs go one up and I convince The Boy to put on his Spurs onesie for luck. So, of course, they concede a ridiculous equaliser and throw it away at the death. They have absolutely Spursed it up and The

Boy bursts into tears just as Chester are awarded a penalty against Kidderminster, something of a conflicting moment.

Her Indoors is out somewhere, so I have to take the wall of sport upstairs, Liverpool 3-2 PSG on the iPad, Chester 3-1 Kiddy in my ears, all accompanied by Dr Seuss on paper as The Boy is finally felled.

Back downstairs, Sky are competing by showing Stoke 1-0 Swansea on a wet Tuesday night. Former player Shaqiri shrewdly avoids the driving rain by coming on for Liverpool against PSG at Anfield.

I am ready to drop after the Euro highlights, but Facebook Watch is showing the Red Sox at the Yankees. I watch it in bed and fall asleep plugged into the phone. Her Indoors looms over my shoulder and asks if I have any preference as to the result. I can't be bothered to explain the Wild Card ramifications.

WEDNESDAY SEPTEMBER 19TH

Yankees win, Astros win, A's lose. It's looking like a Wild Card game away from home. I've barely had time to mull this over and we're straight into the Australian FA Cup, Avondale v Sydney, 10:30am kickoff our time. The holders Sydney go 2-0 up, but are pegged back as the home team forces extra-time, during which Sydney knock in another couple to win 4-2.

Sky again put the big guns up against the Champions League, showing QPR 2-0 Millwall. The Boy recognises a player from Soccer School. I go for all kinds of multiscreen, including the self-explanatory Champions League Goal Show. I am soon enjoying the tears of Ronaldo, who is sent off for giving someone a head massage. United win, City lose.

THURSDAY SEPTEMBER 20TH

I learn that my book, The Card, has been long-listed for the William Hill Sports Book Of The Year. Scenes.

Despite this fresh literary status, I still have to sit through an interminable Shady Sharks session, and so miss the only Chelsea goal of their Europa League tie. I get home to see Arsenal take the lead and then head out to fellow author Lily Allen's book launch party, courtesy of Chelsea Dad.

West Ham Dad is on the decks when I get there, but a lot of people are still at the Mercury Music Prize, so I attack the free bar and follow the baseball on my phone. Later on, I accost a man in an Oakland Athletics Billy Beane shirt, telling him we're winning 17-2. He doesn't seem to understand what I'm on about, he just likes Billy Beane, the accountant who inspired the Moneyball book and film, which I am yet to read or see. Weirdo.

FRIDAY SEPTEMBER 21ST

Not at my absolute best, I choose a family curry over Wigan v Bristol City. I watch the last knockings in bed, a rainy empty stadium. 1-0 to Wigan.

SATURDAY SEPTEMBER 22ND

Regent's Park for 8:30am, no way to live. Shady Sharks are up against Regent's Park Wizards, who turn up late with no proper kit, shambolic. We turn them over 3-0 and The Boy is made Man Of The Match again. I almost blub.

After an early goal, I sleep through the first half of Fulham 1-1 Watford plus Eastleigh 1-0 Dagenham, where there is much hilarity at a sign proclaiming 'Today's Special: Chips'. The BBC are still throwing their weight behind the early rounds of the FA Cup, albeit with primitive coverage. I have a look at Lymington 0-7 Torquay, somehow managing to miss every goal. Unfortunately they don't show replays.

Hauling myself out of the house, I have other business. For reasons unknown, Paddy Power have given me four VIP tickets to the Champions League Darts in Brighton. I meet up with Saints Dad and the lesser-spotted Port Vale/Arsenal Dad in a local Irish pub, which is showing a snide feed of the 3pm Premier League match between Liverpool and Southampton. We see Liverpool's opening goal in what will prove to be a 3-0 home win. Meanwhile, Chester are in the FA Cup against City Of Liverpool and my phone informs me of the opening goal in what will prove to be a 4-0 home win.

The 16:02 from Clapham Junction is cancelled due to a technical term that on closer inspection turns out to mean no driver. We do some serious drinking and get the next one, briefly chatting to a fellow darts fan who informs us that his mate is absent because he is doing a line of coke off the knee of a shitting man. This charming anecdote somehow sets the tone for the day.

It is absolutely pissing down with rain at Brighton and we barrel down the hill to the Brighton Centre, meeting up with the fourth man. The VIP area consists of little more than a free bar and Saints Dad throws himself at it with gusto, at one point returning with two paper pint pots, each containing a quadruple JD & coke. There are a lot of empty seats, presumably the reason for the freebies from Paddy Power, desperate to avoid the embarrassment of the place looking empty on the Beeb. They have also thrown in a complimentary meat item and a free £10 bet. I stick mine on Mensur 'The Gentle' Suljović to beat Peter 'Snakebite' Wright, thus netting a handsome profit of £12.50. Sadly, the promised £50k to be shared among the crowd in the event of a nine-darter doesn't materialise.

We are seated upstairs at the back, pretty much as far from the dartboard as it's possible to be. Of course, nobody goes to the darts to look at the dartboard as the action is relayed on giant screens. However, due to some experimental varifocal contact lenses, I can't even see that. At one point, I am reduced to watching the coverage on my phone at the bar, albeit at arm's length.

From my seat, what I can see is the gantry, where Paul 'The Asset' Nicholson and Alan Warriner-Little give their expert opinions to Caroline Barker, who once briefly met me at The Non-League Paper Awards. The chat seems animated, but once the cameras are off they all immediately avoid eye contact and go back to their phones. Before turning pro, Warriner actually appeared on Bullseye as a contestant, swept the prize board and then refused to gamble. Unbelievable.

The free bar has taken its toll on a few alleged VIPs, including a drunken prick behind us. At his feet are the usual placards that fans are invited to write witty messages on. However, in this instance somebody has chosen this as an unlikely medium by which to reignite the Madeleine McCann mystery, simply asking "Where's Maddie?". The drunken prick vocalises this concern, shouting "Where is she?", as if I somehow have undisclosed information. We get the fuck out of there, mercifully making the last train home. What a sport.

SUNDAY SEPTEMBER 23RD

Rotting in bed, EFL On Quest, a remarkable Villa goal in defeat, it eventually becomes a blur of increasingly shit teams. I hit the Red Button for NFL, where Cleveland Browns are celebrating their first win in 635 days. A player retires at half time.

Order is restored at 1pm with live coverage of the darts, where they still haven't located Maddie. West Ham 0-0 Chelsea is so dull that I agree to a Super Sunday family walk – 5live as a backstop, obviously – which takes us into Arsenal 2-0 Everton, some controversy over an offside goal. Guingamp v Bordeaux is under way, but it's all cut short by a family meal, a futile attempt to restore civility into a house swamped by sport.

I catch up with the darts, where van Gerwen misses match darts and Anderson nails 140 to stay alive, the Geordie Nicholson providing high-pitched commentary. Oh for Sid.

Snakebite defeats his nemesis MvG, but can't raise himself for the final, letting Gary Anderson in for an easy win. I watch yesterday's Match Of The Day and today's Match Of The Day 2, plus a Tiger Woods win that overshadows Justin Rose earning ten million pounds. A touch of late-night MLS sees LA Galaxy take on Seattle, with Zlatan netting a penalty to give him his 501st career goal, a decent haul.

MONDAY SEPTEMBER 24TH

Unannounced, we're into snooker's China Open. There really isn't enough snooker on TV these days. I enjoy a bath with John Higgins, the tomato-faced Caledonian. The FA Cup draw is delayed, but when the balls finally come out of the velvet bag, Chester are drawn away at Dunston United, apparently Gateshead's other club. Who knew? Gazza, for one; he grew up there.

The evening brings the FIFA Football Awards, presented by Idris Elba, who puts in a hugely misjudged performance. There is an obligatory World Cup montage. Too soon. I then inadvertently find myself welling up at the story of Lennart Thy, the German player who missed a Dutch league match to save the life of a leukaemia patient by donating blood. Bloody footballers.

Noel Gallagher makes a presentation and uses the occasion to have a dig at Manchester United, which makes him look small and parochial. I first met Gallagher at half time during England v France in Euro 2004, showing him a photo on my digital camera of someone who had been stabbed in the leg the night before.

I wake up for the last knockings of the Yankees 4-1 win at Tampa Bay Rays that confirms a Wild Card slot for the A's. Let's go A's. It's a sporting double header in Tampa Bay as in the NFL it's Pittsburgh 30-27 Tampa Bay. Where is Tampa Bay anyway?

TUESDAY SEPTEMBER 25TH

Ding in the bath. Shady Sharks training, two and a half hours of Shouty Steve talking overloads to seven-year-olds.

The Carabao Cup is back and a Derby equaliser at Old Trafford wakes me up, a decent free kick. Derby ahead now, but up pops Fellaini in injury time, scoring while apparently sporting a Paddy Power novelty wig, as distributed at the darts. Penalty shootouts are so commonplace these days that they're almost an anti-climax. That said, it's a high-quality contest until a calamitous effort by Phil Jones sees Frank Lampard's Derby progress.

Minutes later, I watch Hibs lose on pens to Aberdeen on my phone. This life. I then avoid the rest of the Carabao Cup scores in lieu of tomorrow night's highlights on Quest. It's a risky strategy, but the rewards validate the peril.

Ahead of the Ryder Cup, there's a celebrity match involving Condoleezza Rice and David Ginola and I don't know what's real anymore. Ten past midnight, the Yankees are at Tampa Bay again and swiftly go 7-0 up. Stick a fork in me, I'm done.

WEDNESDAY SEPTEMBER 26TH

The overnight baseball scores are in. The A's have lost, the Yankees and the Astros have both won. A Wild Card away game is looking the most likely outcome.

In China, Selby is getting into his stride. Liverpool are at home to Chelsea in the Carabao, and Hazard scores a sensational winner minutes after Sturridge hits the bar. 2-1 Chelsea, Liverpool gone.

I make it to the Carabao highlights intact. For the benefit of The Boy, I record the Spurs v Watford game, which for logistical reasons takes place at MK Dons, former MK star Dele Alli captain for the night. It's a ding-dong-do in which they share four goals equally, Spurs triumphing on penalties. Stick that up The Watford Gap.

THURSDAY SEPTEMBER 27TH

A's win, Yankees lose, two now the magic number for home-field advantage. There's some kind of meaningless Ryder Cup captain's game. Selby joylessly crushes another Chinese player. Vikings at Rams sends me to bed.

FRIDAY SEPTEMBER 28TH

I listen to the Non-League podcast because I'm on it, banging on about my award-nominated book. Serendipitously, the co-star of the book, The Driver, is back in the country, appropriately to pick up a car. Naturally, he intends to take in the accompanying Chester game, although why he chose to return for Chorley away is never fully explained.

It doesn't help that Her Indoors is in Budapest doing a self-guided walk, otherwise known as a walk. Unperturbed, I put together a plan that sees us hit a couple of local pubs, pick up The Boy from school then all head to Watford Gap. The Watford Gap – also a Budapest weekend widower – is already shouting at Leeds v Toronto, some kind of rugby league. The sporting fare marginally improves with the Ryder Cup highlights and late baseball. We even roll back the years with two stone-cold playoff final classics, Charlton v Sunderland and Man City v Gillingham. It's the first time I've seen the incredible Charlton v Sunderland game in detail, although I remember it being on during the early stage of courting Her Indoors. Tragically, I couldn't bring myself to ask if she minded if I stuck on the highlights and the moment passed. Never again. As for City v Gills, I've said it before and I'll say it again: Never Leave Early.

SATURDAY SEPTEMBER 29TH

Completing a triumvirate of embittered exiled Chester fans, The Hack rocks up and it's egg on toast all round. Minutes after leaving, my car appears to lose power. We briefly consider going back and taking The Hack's car instead. We press on and the car goes into limp mode, whereby I have to wrestle to get anything more than 50mph out of it. I also appear to have solved the energy crisis as the fuel meter claims that I have enough petrol for 100,000 miles. It's not that far to Bromsgrove, where we leave The Driver to take possession of his new car and follow us up in convoy. The hideously congested M6 makes this a chore, enabling us to listen to the entirety of Man Utd 3-1 West Ham. I suddenly spot that the analogue petrol indicator is deep into the red, and mercifully find a service station in deepest Lancashire on the descent into Chorley.

Big Al has all the tickets, and we have to leave one with a steward along with a rudimentary description of The Driver, whose phone is dead. Amazingly, we all make it in for kickoff and witness an enjoyable 0-0 that we really should have won. The game is interspersed by tales of The Battle Of Chorley from a few seasons ago, an incident of serious hooliganism that The Hack ranks as the worst he's ever seen, including multiple England tours. I wasn't there, and my only previous visit was for a pre-season friendly in 1990, a 2-0 defeat during which I committed a youthful indiscretion that earned me a nickname still in use today. In fact, one of the hard-line proponents of this slur is at the match, and takes a photo of me to commemorate the occasion.

There's a hint of trouble after the game, and we do ourselves no favours by losing the car, wandering round the tight backstreets until we stumble upon it and get the hell out of Dodge as fast as the car will limp. The journey back is a long, drawn-out process, and one second of Savage on 606 proves too much. Instead, we listen to commentary of Chelsea v Liverpool, with Sturridge hitting a sensational equaliser that the commentator drools over without ever describing how it was actually scored. It's not until Match Of The Day that we see it to be a long range screamer that seems to defy the laws of physics. And now, the baseball.

SUNDAY SEPTEMBER 30TH

The Watford Gap is up early to watch the NRL Grand Final, whatever that is. As such, I opt for The Ryder Cup in the kitchen with a touch of the Russian Grand Prix: Hamilton wins under team orders. There's also the small matter of the China Open final, Selby v Higgins. We're basically in different rooms shouting at different sports.

He eventually joins me for The Ryder Cup, which is almost too fast-paced to follow, hole after hole after hole. Stronger together, Europe bring it home amid emotional scenes. Selby beats Higgins in a decider past midnight China time, which is my cue to leave. Tracking down The Boy, I bundle him into the car and subject him to Cardiff 1-2 Burnley.

We get home and I am overjoyed to see The Watford Gap's NFL team, Miami Dolphins, 38 points down. And it absolutely makes my day that his MLB team, San Francisco Giants, are beaten 15-0 by the LA Dodgers.

Still it comes. I'm straight into the World Grand Prix of Darts, double to start. I take Match Of The Day 2 in bed. Enough.

MONDAY OCTOBER 1ST

Oakland Athletics slugger Khris Davis hits exactly .247 for the fourth straight season. You couldn't make it up. Elsewhere, Olympic sliding-down-a-mountain-on-a-tray person Amy Williams reveals that the 'sport' has effectively left her crippled, unable to walk up stairs and destined to spend the rest of her years gingerly easing herself around a bungalow, buffing her medals. Worth it. Over in Paris, a rogue golf ball has blinded a Ryder Cup spectator in one eye. Sake.

11:55am brings the European Masters snooker, a perfunctory win for Luca Brecel. I place The Boy in the capable hands of Queens Park Rangers and immerse myself in baseball, where unprecedented back-to-back tiebreakers will see the winners moving on and the losers facing the sudden-death Wild Card. Milwaukee Brewers 3-1 Chicago Cubs, Colorado 2-5 Dodgers.

This overlaps with Bournemouth 2-1 Palace and the darts, where Steve 'The Adonis' Beaton vanquishes the World Champion, Rob Cross. As the inimitable Sid Waddell once said of the be-permed Beaton, "He's not A-donis, he's THE-donis".

I still manage to squeeze in a bit of EFL On Quest, including Rachels Riley (Countdown) and Yankey (former England footballer) making the Carabao Cup draw. Further drama is to follow when studio guest Ian Holloway is stricken by food poisoning live on air and has to disappear to void his bowel while Colin Murray manfully struggles on solo.

It's been a solid opening to October, but I find myself sucked into Kansas City Chiefs at Denver Broncos. The Kansas quarter-back, Patrick Lavon Mahomes II, is kind of a big deal. The fourth quarter becomes a case of an irresistible force against an immovable object. Kansas finally overcome the bucking Broncos. I'm not in Kansas anymore. Or Denver. I'm in bed.

TUESDAY OCTOBER 2ND

Liang Wenbo versus sweary cockney Alfie Burden goes all the way to a seventh frame decider. It's a ding-dong-do, but Liang gets there 4-3 during Countdown, presumably neither party aware of the drama unfolding on the other screen.

In the park after school, a Spanish mum asks me what cricket is. It's harder to explain than you might think, and during the process I manage to drop my phone, scratching the screen, a permanent blemish on hours of future sport.

Back home for Hoffenheim v Man City, the home team score after 44 seconds, but City swiftly equalise and nick a winner at the death. Juventus take on Young Boys, Ronaldo watching on, suspended amid rape allegations. They seem to get by without him, crushing Young Boys with a Dybala hat trick.

The main event of the evening also finishes 3-0 as Chester dispatch Hereford, causing me to run round the garden and toss The Boy in the air, as convention dictates.

Manchester United versus Valencia is simply too torpid to watch, so I opt for Champions League Goals, plus darts, plus snippets of Ipswich 0-2 Middlesbrough, pleasingly catching both Championship goals. I even get a glimpse of the translucent Mark Selby, back from China.

Manchester United somehow failed to get to their own ground on time and so the game drags on to 10pm, whereupon I stumble upon a Carabao Cup penalty shootout, Southampton victorious at Goodison after a 1-1 draw. The action, or lack of it, at Old Trafford is draining. Whatever you think of them, United could traditionally be relied upon for entertainment, but under Mourinho it's like pulling teeth. I universally support all British teams in Europe, but would laugh if Valencia could nick it. It finally crawls to a goalless conclusion as boos ring around Old Trafford.

"And this one is going to the 12th!"

5:19am, MLB Wild Card, Colorado at Chicago Cubs, extra innings. Listen in sleep.

WEDNESDAY OCTOBER 3RD

I think I know the baseball score. I think Milwaukee won. Were Milwaukee even playing? Maybe I dreamt it. In an attempt to establish some kind of normality, I watch snooker in the bath: McGill 4-3 Carter. This eases me into another mammoth sporting day.

It's Judgment Day, or Judgment Night our time. Oakland Athletics go to New York Yankees for a one-game Wild Card shootout after a

162-game season, the most preposterous schedule in all sport. Losers go home, winners move on.

Elsewhere, Steve Bruce has been sacked a day after having a cabbage thrown at him. Mark Selby is looking to win consecutive tournaments on different continents, beating Mark Davis 4-2.

Football never stops, and I listen to commentary of Chester Youth 3-2 Wrexham Youth, including a brace from Tom Ruffer, some years after his father attacked me. I then sleep through the second half of Spurs 2-4 Barcelona and Napoli 1-0 Liverpool in the Champions League.

A bad night for English teams, but this at least leaves me fresh for the Wild Card game. Billy Beane can't watch. Yankees win 7-2. Oakland never in it. Fuck it all. What a waste of seven months.

THURSDAY OCTOBER 4TH

Allen v Muir in the snooker, a sedate pace, The Pistol firing rubber bullets. Muir chasing four snookers, but I can't leave it, the ghost of Alain Robidoux hanging over me (he's not even dead). Allen eventually gets over the line, but I'm now late for the school run. Straight to Shady Sharks training, Shouty Steve claims to have been at Wembley last night where Lionel Messi gave him some badges. It is possible that this isn't true.

I fall asleep during the Europa League, waking for Superchin Gurney 3-0 Anderson in the darts. In an ill-tempered conclusion, Gurney clearly tells his opponent to "piss off".

I catch up with Europa League highlights. Arsenal, Chelsea and Rangers win, Celtic lose. In the snooker, Selby is knocked out by Ryan Day and we're already into back-to-back baseball games. The first goes to extra innings, as there's no such thing as a draw. In America, there have to be winners and losers.

I'm now sucked into Thursday night NFL. Even a touch of live Japanese Grand Prix practice, Hamilton fastest. When am I supposed to sleep?

FRIDAY OCTOBER 5TH

Unannounced – to me at least – cricket is back and England are playing a warm-up against a Sri Lanka XI. Meanwhile in Australia, Bentleigh Greens are the first 'grass roots' team to make the semi-final of the

FFA Cup, the approximate equivalent of a non-league team making the FA Cup semi. And it's live! They lose 2-0 to Adelaide United as England win via the Duckworth-Lewis method, all accompanied by the new Bunnymen album.

Man has destroyed the planet, enabling me to sit in the sun-drenched garden to watch Lisowski 3-4 Hamilton. In Japan, a different Hamilton narrowly avoids a crash. I accidentally watch a UFC weigh-in and then it's endless baseball.

SATURDAY OCTOBER 6TH

Regent's Park, early doors, the BT Tower shrouded in mist, relaying the chilling message: GOOD MORNING LONDON. WE ARE AT WAR.

Not really, although Shady Sharks are up against Brent Cross, looking to avenge the previous thrashing. This seems less likely when our keeper concedes a howler. However, we force an equaliser, greeted ungraciously by major celebrations from the touchline dads and mums, one of whom is heavily pregnant. It finishes 1-1. Take a point, move on.

We're moving on to Bournemouth for the weekend and find ourselves driving past Twickenham, which is hosting Northampton v Leicester in some kind of rugby. It's like a Countryside Alliance march, coaches full of Barbour jackets spilling onto the streets of London.

While the egg is being chased around Twickers, we find ourselves stuck in traffic on the A338 listening to the first half of Dunston v Chester in the FA Cup. Due to a lack of commentators, impromptu commentary is provided by youth team coach Calum McIntyre, who does a sterling job. Unlike the team, who appear to be making an absolute pig's ear of it. We listen to the second half in the hotel as Chester go down 4-3 to a team that nobody outside of Gateshead had ever heard of before today. An absolute disgrace.

Round at my old dear's, a family meal has preposterously been scheduled during the tea-time game, Manchester United v Newcastle United. Fortunately, we are eating at a glass table, enabling me to secrete an iPad at my feet and keep an eye on the action, as do a brother and nephew. Dramatically, Newcastle score an early goal. And another! Mourinho surely hanging on by a thread. On 70 minutes, Man United pull a goal back. Six minutes later, they're level. And of course they win it in the 90th, Alexis Sànchez of all people. What a game. What a sport.

An interminable episode of Strictly Come Dancing is made bearable by watching MvG beat Snakebite, who again bottles it. Back in the hotel for the snooker and the baseball, I swivel the TV in my favour for Match Of The Day. I don't make the end as the blackness comes swiftly.

SUNDAY OCTOBER 7TH

Picking it up where I left off with the Match Of The Day repeat, I unsuc-cessfully attempt to buy a ticket for Glastonbury. I once watched the final of Euro 2008 there on a mini TV during Leonard Cohen, Torres with the winner for Spain against Germany.

There are three Premier League games today, but sadly I'm nowhere near a TV. On the beach for Fulham 1-5 Arsenal, I follow the commentary on headphones then nick a bit of wi-fi from a Harvester for a touch of BT Sport. We watch the last mile of the Bournemouth marathon, cheering various tortured runners towards the finish line. Not a sport, simply a feat of endurance and mindless-ness. Overnight there has been some kind of UFC brawl, garnering headlines to sell subscriptions for this pathetic, desperate non-sport.

I have a token look at Southampton 0-3 Chelsea, then we're in the car for the much-hyped game of the season, Liverpool v Man City. It's a tactical gamble that pays off as it's a turgid affair, the only incident of note coming when City's Mahrez balloons a penalty. We hear it live on the M3, again the scene of rarefied sporting drama.

We're back home to see Jimmy Robertson beat Joe Perry for the European Masters, followed by a barrage of NFL, MLB, National League highlights and Match Of The Day 2. Enough already. Now PSG are beating Lyon 5-0, four for Mbappé. I even stumble across the Youth Olympics on the Red Button. Then it's rugby league's so-called Million Pound Game, which finishes Toronto 2-4 London Broncos, saving a lot of teams a trip to Canada next season. On the same continent, DC United are winning 2-1, a brutal penalty from Rooney.

MONDAY OCTOBER 8TH

I torture myself with the FA Cup draw on talkSPORT2. Having dis-patched The Mighty Chester in the greatest moment in their history,

Dunston will play... Gateshead. You couldn't make it up. In the Youth Olympics, Venezuela are playing Brazil at basketball. Fuck that. I'm not an animal.

I drop The Boy at QPR Soccer School and catch up with the MLB then women's futsal. It's international week, hence no proper football. I briefly flirt with Glentoran in the Northern Ireland league, Sky scraping the barrel there. It's a festival of baseball, with both the Astros and the Dodgers moving on, with a brief distraction of Jamaica v USA in cricket.

There's blood everywhere as The Boy appears in our bed with a gushing nosebleed in the dead of night. I relocate to his bed with the iPad and fall asleep during game three, Red Sox at Yankees.

TUESDAY OCTOBER 9TH

Slim pickings. Red Sox at Yankees still hanging over me, the only matchup yet to be resolved. I catch the repeat while wrestling The Boy to bed. Sox go 10-0 up, and win 16-1. I see the last over of South Africa beating Zimbabwe in a T20 game. Then it's England Women 1-1 Australia Women on the big screen, live from Fulham. That's living alright.

WEDNESDAY OCTOBER 10TH

TalkSPORT2 have got the cricket. This is seismic. Nobody told me. Test Match Special replaced by adverts for Checkatrade, surely signalling the end of days. Mark Nicholas at the helm, the mercenary snaffled from Channel 5. First we are treated to Darren Gough's cultural tour of Sri Lanka, the doughty Yorkshireman revealing that he has seem some "big Buddhas". Michael Palin, eat your heart out.

I take an overground train to south London and fire up the talkSPORT app. Rain stops play. I drive a pair of ropey old slags (their words) to Sutton Coldfield to perform their comedy show. We drive past The Belfry en route to the Premier Inn, where I watch a bit of musical wall climbing in the Youth Olympics. The cricket is abandoned after 15 overs.

THURSDAY OCTOBER 11TH

I awake in the Premier Inn to watch a bit of Youth Olympic hockey. Back in civilisation, I drop The Boy at Shady Sharks training and go to Kilburn library and read a book about New Order, missing a 1-0 victory for The Boy's team.

Finally, there's some football on TV, Wales surviving for just over seven minutes before succumbing 4-1 at home to Spain in a friendly. Israel v Scotland is at least in the UEFA Nations League, about which I am still uncertain. Either way, Scotland lose 2-1 as I spend the evening flicking between the fortunes of two minor nations. On my phone, England U-21 beat Andorra U-21 7-0 to qualify for the Euros.

FRIDAY OCTOBER 12TH

News breaks that Usain Bolt has scored for Central Coast Mariners, a decent hit, playing up front with Ross McCormack. It won't last.

SATURDAY OCTOBER 13TH

England win the cricket on the Duckworth-Lewis method, whatever that is. A mere footnote, as I have other business in East London. With no game for Chester, I make the perverse decision to infiltrate the away end of deadly enemies Wrexham, who are playing at Dagenham & Redbridge. Her Indoors beseeches, "Don't go, they're animals".

But I'm on my way into the belly of the beast, shorts on, a sweltering October day. Non-League Day in fact, whereby supporters of all stripes are encouraged to patronise their local shithouse team in the absence of 'proper' football. It's as good an excuse as any, but I've also been dared to attend by a Wrexham acquaintance who is meeting me there.

Turning left out of Dagenham East, the Wrexham massive have commandeered The Pipe Major, with a flapping Welsh flag striking fear into my English heart. I press on regardless, head down, lest I be recognised by particularly eagle-eyed readers of The Non-League Paper. Nestled between a cockles & mussels stall and a pie & mash shop, The Eastbrook pub is unpretentious, give or take the signed photo of Frank Bruno and sundry West Ham paraphernalia. I christen the facilities and get myself a pint as Jones of Wrexham arrives with his son, one on Stella, one engrossed in Shoot magazine.

Kickoff looms and we stroll past the grammatically incorrect 'Pats Coaches' that has delivered these feral Welshmen to this unglamorous part of Essex. It's a turgid first half, but Wrexham score a screamer that forces me to sit on my hands amid a sea of elation. Minutes later I have to suppress laughter as they scuff in a comedy own goal to hit the break level. Sadly, they score a winner in the second half, but the real victory is getting out intact.

I head to the chippy for a nice bit of fish and spot another Wrexham fan of my acquaintance. Randomly, he was the only person to witness me crashing out of the 2006 World Series Of Poker Main Event in Las Vegas, within touching distance of the money. I join him for a pint in The Pipe Major, where he is with a Bolton Wanderers fan with an irrational hatred of Tranmere Rovers, and another Wrexham fan who works on the Mirror sports desk, still reeling from their premature announcement of Mourinho's departure. We have a couple of easy pints and nobody attacks each other.

Rugby league's Grand Final is hanging over me, not that I will remember who is in it or what happens. I make it home for the second half of Republic Of Ireland 0-0 Denmark. Tired and emotional, I watch EFL On Quest in bed, Ian Holloway now recovered from his gut rot. I wake up for a few innings of MLB.

SUNDAY OCTOBER 14TH

The Grand Final highlights are dropped in favour of the tennis. Djokovic wins. Annabel Croft and Greg Rusedski discuss the result, both presumably oblivious of brief encounters with me, one emerging from an adjacent studio at British Eurosport, the other surprising me in the toilets at the Mini Masters. Pure showbiz.

Unusually I opt for Asda instead of Romania v Serbia, my decision vindicated when I get back for injury time of a 0-0 draw. There is NFL at Wembley, something I've been bludgeoned into attending on two occasions. I have little or no recollection of what happened on the hallowed turf, but for San Francisco 49ers v Dallas Cowboys, we were sat next to a 49ers fan from Dallas who had flown to London on her own for the game. Much to our amusement she spent the entire game shouting, "Go git 'em, niners!" and "That's what I'm talking about!". At one point I turned to my associate, The Watford Gap, and informed him that that was what she was talking about, something he has never quite got over.

Instead of wasting money on a ticket, today I keep an eye on proceedings in splitscreen with Scotland 1-3 Portugal in a friendly. I finally catch up with the Grand Final. Wigan win, which will please The Watford Gap, who has the club emblem inked on his back. I give up on Poland v Italy. Who cares?

RIP Peter Brackley, the voice of Football Italia and Pro Evolution Soccer. I awake in the dead of night to watch MLB on my phone. The Red Sox level the series.

MONDAY OCTOBER 15TH

Mark Williams posts a photo of his pre-match meal: pie, chips and beans. What access. What an athlete. He is tweeting ahead of the English Open from Crawley, the perfect accompaniment to a dreary October day. Ronnie, the holder, compares himself to a greyhound or a racehorse being held back to ensure that he is eager and fresh. Usain Bolt has been drug tested after a friendly.

Ronnie is taking on the unheralded Kurt Maflin. The Rocket goes one down, but is immediately into his stride to level with a century. It's all over in minutes, and I have barely towelled myself off before he has won 4-1. In his post-match interview, Ronnie expresses a desire to become a Buddhist monk, replete with a graphical mock-up. What a sport.

We're straight into Williams v Dale, the all-Welsh encounter. Williams claims that after he won the World Championship, Barry Hearn made him wear a towel for his promised naked press conference. Apparently the original plan was to go bollocko, with only "two fingers" covering his modesty (penis).

I pause the big telly to negotiate a cycled school run. Chelsea Dad informs me of garden furniture being thrown in Seville, where the England football team are playing. Sri Lanka Dad questions why the England cricket team are touring there during the monsoon season.

I get back and un-pause the telly from its 38-minute hiatus, mercifully with the action intact. Williams goes 3-0 up with a second century, suffering no obvious ill effects from his rancid pie. Dale gets a frame on the board, but the World Champion clinches it 4-1 on a re-spotted black. Apparently there's been some tabloid front-page news about a tweet sent concerning Williams' wife and some lube. Pretty relaxed about the whole thing, Williams denies responsibility and says she can't handle her drink.

There's a filler section on Eurosport in which Ronnie and Andy Goldstein compete in some kind of athletics. Fuck that. Robertson is 2-1 down when the TV un-pauses itself, losing the action. A nightmare.

As announced by the earlier ad hoc furniture rearrangement, England are playing at the ground of Betis.

In a rare nod to civility, Her Indoors insists on eating at the table. As such, we hear Sterling's early goal on the DAB radio, running to Sky Go comfortably in time to see it. I've still technically missed it. The first England goal in Spain since 1987 and I was making a Redbush tea. The Boy stays up until half time and is rewarded by two further goals as England improbably hit the break 3-0 up. Pickford shits the bed in the second half, but gets away with it and we scrape a 3-2 win. It's lauded as a great victory, but I'm not feeling it, still broken by the World Cup and confused by the Nations League. I retire upstairs to the office bed and fall asleep during MLB. I don't even make it to NFL's Monday Night Football. So tired.

TUESDAY OCTOBER 16TH

The mild afterglow of England's historic victory is tempered by news that Chester striker Matty Hughes could be out for the season, a massive blow to our promotion hopes.

Ronnie is on Quest standing by his derogatory comments about the Crawley Leisure Centre, unglamorous home of the English Open. Apparently the snooker players are being abused by bowls players on their way to the tables. There are also reports of kids in flip-flops using the facilities. Back on the baize, news breaks of a 147 from an outer table. I dip in and out of the snooker, which is competing with Ireland 0-1 Wales, an MLB repeat and live commentary of Hartlepool Youth 2-4 Chester Youth.

It's a relentless schedule, then I'm into back-to-back MLB games. Sky apparently now have the NBA and are showing live back-to-back openers. Philadelphia lose at Boston Celtics, where a cheer goes up at news of a Red Sox grand slam. It's a world of sport. I go to sleep plugged into my phone, baseball on.

WEDNESDAY OCTOBER 17TH

TalkSPORT2 fill in the cricket-free hours by discussing the wisdom of holding the series in the monsoon season. Keep up lads.

Back in Crawley, Ronnie will not let up: "I don't know what this gaff is".

It's a leisure centre with an indoor bowling green. Selby and Williams are even filmed having a quick bowl as the story gathers momentum.

Ronnie is playing somebody called Taylor, a passable impressionist. Sadly his repertoire doesn't stretch to a competent snooker player and he is dicked 4-0, Ronnie finishing with his 15th career 147 as I rise to my feet and applaud in front of a 20-year-old portable TV. Ronnie later admits to "twitching all over the gaff" and claims that he is not playing well. Jimmy White simply laughs.

Wembley is not for sale now, so that was a waste of everybody's breath. 3:15pm brings the toss in Sri Lanka. England win and choose to bowl in what has been reduced to a 21-over game.

Selby is taking on Ben Woollaston, and unlike in Belgium he manages to stay awake. My phone chirrups with Sri Lanka wickets during the school run, and I get back to watch England cruise to victory as John Higgins wins his snooker match.

This takes me into a repeat of the seemingly endless Major League Baseball National League Championship Series game four. All over the world, men are striking balls with bits of wood. They're all going to die. After more than five hours, The Dodgers take game four with a walk-off win in the 13th inning. And that's the ball game...

THURSDAY OCTOBER 18TH

I have an appointment with talkSPORT. Not listening, but talking, live on the air, to an audience of millions about my award-nominated book, The Card. Piss it. I get there early and see Dean Saunders coming the other way. I know where I'm going, but ask him for directions anyway, just for the drama.

"Cheers Deano, you Wrexham prick", I don't say.

Commandeering a table in the canteen, I sit and I wait. After a while, a tall, glamorous woman appears and says hello. Accompanied by an entourage, I belatedly recognise her as Jodie Kidd, the only other person in the world to have been banned from the Mini Masters. She for cheating, me for drinking, both right here, right now in this perfunctory canteen. What are the chances? I think about saying something, but the moment passes.

As does my allotted time. I am supposed to be on air, but nobody has come to get me. Eventually an assistant producer appears and leads me to the studio. It's like Spinal Tap. I can hear my absence being announced as I burst in and stick the headphones on. It's an icebreaker at least. I'm on the flagship Hawksbee & Jacobs Show, although Jacobs has been temporarily replaced by Sam Delaney, who I briefly met once, in The Groucho Club with Noel Gallagher, and it wasn't even the 90s.

It's patently obvious that neither of them has read a word of the book, but I manage to hold my own and even elicit a few laughs. Chelsea Dad claims it to be the greatest thing he's ever heard.

Buoyed by this relative success, I meet up with The Evertonian and Bealesy and go to see The Bunnymen at Drury Lane. Despite – nay, because of – my visit to the home of sport, I have missed a day and a night of sport. You can't put a price on that.

FRIDAY OCTOBER 19TH

BBC Sport Twitter announces that the Red Sox are going to the World Series. Unfollow. Ronnie is still in Crawley, where he overcomes Luo Honghao despite inadvertently clipping a red. Later shown a replay, he swears on live TV, furious at not declaring a foul on himself.

Friday night appears to be Championship night, and Middlesbrough go to Sheffield Wednesday. It's a turgid first half, but Boro win 2-1. I manage an MLB replay, but am too tired for the live game.

There's a rule change in tennis, meaning they won't mindlessly play endless games in the final set until someone collapses or dies of boredom. About bleeding time.

SATURDAY OCTOBER 20TH

Straight into an ODI, where Sri Lanka have set a total. Closer to home, we're off to Regent's Park where Shady Sharks take on Belsize Park Rockets in the big one. The opposition are coached by a pair of cocky young pricks, at least one of whom has COACH written on the back of his tracksuit top. One of their players bears down on goal and I instinctively bellow, "Take him out!". Ant & Dec aren't impressed by this advice and one of them, a floppy-haired fucker, gets all up in my grill, pointing out that they're seven and even asking me if I am ill. I calmly point out that I was merely instructing our defender to take him out via the legal method of tackling, but they're not having it. I defuse the situation by wandering off and standing with the mothers, inwardly ecstatic at each of our goals in a 3-1 win.

Back home for the last knockings of Melbourne Victory 1-2 Melbourne City, the fixture that began my casual support of Victory back when City were still called Heart and yet to be absorbed by oil barons.

England win on Duckworth-Lewis. Good for him. The 12:30pm so-called lunchtime fixture sees miserable moaning Mourinho take his Manchester United to Stamford Bridge, scene of his previous glories. Chelsea take a first-half lead, United take a second-half lead, and then Chelsea equalise in the 96th minute. Scenes.

In the FA Cup, Gateshead go to Dunston and turn them over 4-0, making Chester's demise there even more embarrassing. In the snooker, Bingham beats Maguire, barely seen since Sheffield. The so-called tea-time game sees me in the garden for the first half as Liverpool go to Huddersfield and unmemorably win 1-0 thanks to a Mo Salah goal.

This sets me up for three hours of EFL On Quest plus Match Of The Day. A filthy cold wakes me in time to see the last strikeout as the Dodgers move on to the World Series.

SUNDAY OCTOBER 21ST

A touch of VAR-affected A-League then the snooker final in the bath. The sporting calendar has been thrown into chaos by an invitation to Sunday lunch at a neighbour's house. Unbelievably, I sacrifice

Everton v Palace for a free feed, instigating a largely unnecessary media lockdown – nobody else gives the tiniest shit.

I get home and immediately fall asleep during the snooker. I wake to see the presumably victorious Bingham being interviewed, but switch to Quest +1 anyway in an attempt to turn back time. Bingham still wins, beating Mark Davis, conqueror of Ronnie. However, the tournament will largely be remembered for Ronnie complaining that the Crawley Leisure Centre smelt of urine.

Banished from my own TV, I go upstairs for the end of Dallas 0-3 Sporting Kansas in MLS then the end of Dallas Cowboys 17-20 Washington Redskins in NFL, real drama as a retaken field goal attempt hits the post. I accidentally wake up Her Indoors by shouting at Lewis Hamilton attempting to overtake for the title in the US Grand Prix replay.

Sunday night is a bumper time for sport and I catch the last knockings of Montpellier 2-0 Bordeaux. Forced to watch Match Of The Day 2 on my phone, I see Everton scrape home 2-0. I retire with Kansas winning in the NFL.

MONDAY OCTOBER 22ND

A sporting vacuum. Nothing until the FA Cup draw, conducted by Dennis Wise and Dion Dublin, the latter instructed to give the balls a stir, thus altering the future and ultimately the course of history.

We're into Arsenal v Leicester, my fellow William Hill Sports Book Of The Year nominee Alan Smith on co-commentary, and an early half-apology for "industrial language".

It's an unfamiliar one-screen set-up, so I rectify this by watching Hamburg-based hipsters St Pauli nick a late one at Duisburg. Somebody has booked an Ocado delivery (I know) and in the time it takes me to deal with it, I miss Arsenal's second goal – Aubameyang – something that The Boy takes sadistic pleasure in. He scores another one three minutes later (Aubameyang, not The Boy) and they win 3-1, but it's been sullied. Monday Night Football (UK) is followed by Monday Night Football (US), but I don't have the heart for it.

TUESDAY OCTOBER 23RD

In the absence of school, QPR kindly provide unofficial childcare, enabling me to get back for the start of the fifth ODI, Sri Lanka rampant with the bat. There's also a touch of UEFA Youth League, Shakhtar v Man City, seemingly being played in a field. The combined weight of sport takes me under and I awake to see Sri Lanka go past 300 in what is a dead rubber. No idea what happened in the Ukrainian field.

Sri Lanka set a record score, leaving England chasing 367. I follow it in the garden, 4 for 3 not the best start. In the UEFA Youth League, Manchester United dispatch Juventus 4-1, with an apology for offensive language delivered both verbally and onscreen (for the deaf?).

I relieve QPR of The Boy and get back to find torrential rain at the cricket, England with one wicket left. The match is abandoned and England go down to a record Duckworth-Lewis method defeat. So that's something.

I need to regulate my sleep for the World Series, which starts tonight. I keep an eye on the two early Champions League kickoffs, then we're into the meat: Manchester United 0-1 Juventus on the big TV, Shakhtar 0-3 Man City on the laptop, Norwich 2-1 Aston Villa on iPad, Chester 2-1 Witton commentary on phone (Cheshire Senior Cup Preliminary Round).

It's a full moon for a boys' night in, and The Boy makes it to half time in his Spurs onesie. Following the Champions League games, I watch Champions League highlights then we go live to Fenway Park, Boston for The Fall Classic (not to be confused with The Classical by The Fall). Tea and toast and online poker gets me through and it's a slugfest. Jack White is in. Fuck Jack White. I make it to the seventh inning stretch with the Red Sox one ahead. A sport so boring that the entire stadium has an allocated stretch. The Red Sox kick on and take it 8-4. I've got 50p on The Dodgers.

WEDNESDAY OCTOBER 24TH

Five hours sleep. Plenty. Unannounced, the World Seniors snooker has sprung up on FreeSports, live from the Hull Bonus Arena. I manage to get it on my phone in time to see the death throes of John Parrott 1-3 Leo Fernández, the Evertonian resplendent in a pair of upside down Dennis Taylor glasses. Never forget he once gave me his Daily Mail on a tube. The match is refereed by the lesser-spotted Michaela Tabb, who I once interviewed in Las Vegas during The Mosconi Cup. She revealed that she had either seen or was going to see Celine Dion. Quote unused, so that's technically an exclusive.

Following a revealing interview on FreeSports, Dennis Taylor himself is up next, taking on Dechawat Poomjaeng. John Virgo seems to have become self-aware, referencing his own catchphrase: "Where's the cue ball going?". Taylor has not picked up a cue in earnest in a decade, and promptly loses 3-0. I head downstairs and install the TV Player app on Windows 10 so I can splitscreen the snooker on the big TV with Countdown. Joe Johnson 0-3 Igor Figueiredo, another former World Champion gone. Ronnie notwithstanding, why do snooker players go off the boil as they age? Golfers seem to chunter on for decades. Some thoughts there.

I pick up The Boy from the clutches of QPR, whose pleasingly named right back Angel Rangel had popped by earlier on to sign a team photo. Back home for a bit of the MLB replay, 12 hours on. Cliff Thorburn goes down 3-0 to Rodney Goggins. The Grinder on a 30-second shot clock, unthinkable. Jimmy also goes down 3-0, to Poomjaeng. I barely even saw him. Thorburn and White, both massive cocaine users in their day.

And we're into the Champions League, Spurs away at PSV Eind-hoven. Been there to watch an England game behind glass, a first and thankfully last. Spurs go 1-0 down, 2-1 up, then they really Spurs it up. Lloris, the goalkeeper, is sent off, and they concede the equaliser in the 87th minute. What a bollocks. The Boy feels sick, although that may be cake-related. With Liverpool cruising to a 4-0 victory over Crvena zvedza (Red Star) I go to my office for a lie down with Alan Green.

Meanwhile, at a poorly-lit Hull Bonus Arena, Hendry goes two down to Fernández, draws level, then loses a re-spot shootout. It may be the first time I've ever supported him. Dennis Taylor is actually commentating in the room, within earshot of the players, one of whom he incorrectly calls "Ferdinand".

I rouse myself for Champions League highlights plus EFL On Quest.

Then we're into the real drama as the William Hill Sports Book of the Year shortlist is announced at midnight, on Twitter, one book at a time, in alphabetical order. It's a guaranteed three grand, with a chance at the big 30k. With two minutes to go, I can hardly breathe. The first few come out and I'm still in it alphabetically. Then it seems to have gone, but there's confusion with the alphabetic ordering of joint authors. It's a flicker of hope, but all seven books are eventually named and I have written none of them. Fuck it all. Fuck baseball.

THURSDAY OCTOBER 25TH

QPR continue their half-term childcare soccer school and I head immediately to an outdoor gym to sweat out the rage with some gentle exercise. By the time I get home, Igor is emerging from the shadows and getting into his stride at the crepuscular Hull Bonus Arena. Tipped by Ronnie, Igor swats aside Aaron Canavan 3-0. It's the same scoreline on the other side of the world in women's football between Western Sydney Wanderers and Sydney FC, but I don't have the heart for it. The highlight is a huge inflatable McDonald's M.

I can travel across the sporting universe without getting out of my bath. There's a lull in play at Hull so they show an archived match between Thorburn and a clearly unwell Alex Higgins. It's too upsetting to watch. Once it's over, I return to Hull to see Ken Doherty become the first former World Champion to get through, trouncing Goggins 3-0. Doherty briefly met me once, the first time I ever interviewed Steve Davis.

There's a repeat of the MLB World Series on, but I have to leave it with bases loaded for the QPR pickup. I have a chat with Saints Dad about team selection for the Shady Sharks' forthcoming cup game against Darryl's Dragons. I get home to see the Red Sox 2-0 up in the series. 79.6% of teams to do that have won The Commissioner's Trophy, so my 50p on The Dodgers is basically in the wind.

Ken Doherty is also 2-0 up against the ubiquitous Poomjaeng, triumphing 3-0 to fill the awkward gap before the Europa League. The Boy has commandeered the big TV so I am reduced to watching Sporting 0-1 Arsenal on the iPad at the kitchen table while going around the grounds on my phone watching goals on demand. What a time to be alive. I eventually take back control for a four-screen extravaganza, including Chelsea 3-1 BATE with a Loftus-Cheek hat-trick.

Ken Doherty goes one better, defeating Igor 4-1 to lift the trophy. Then there's some unbeknown darts on ITV4 from Dortmund. No MLB tonight as the teams are on their way to LA for game three. There's NFL on, but I can't be arsed with NFL. And finally, Dion Dublin has been racially abused in Chesterfield. What a country.

FRIDAY OCTOBER 26TH

Having managed something approaching a night's sleep, I stay in bed for the acrimonious second half of Adelaide 1-1 Newcastle Jets on my phone, allied to highlights of Miami Dolphins losing at the Texans on the iPad, taking minor pleasure in the despair of The Watford Gap, who has the Dolphins' gaudy emblem inked onto his body for all time. There's an awkward 45 minutes until live darts from Germany so I soullessly crush candy in the bath, which is not as much fun as it sounds.

12:45pm: ITV4, 20,000 tickets sold, head girl Jacqui Oatley at the helm, Mase the Ace and Warriner-Little on standby, it's a feast of arrows. It's only interrupted for the QPR pickup, with The Boy walking away with a trophy for Player of the Week. Get in, son. The presentation is followed by a photoshoot during which the kids are encouraged to shout the technically incorrect phrase, "QPR are the best!". One kid shouts "worst", the Chelsea ballbag. The indoctrination continues with talk of cheap tickets and some mild encouragement to support our local team. That would be a logical move, but football has never been about logic.

With renewed vigour, we watch the Friday Night Championship game, QPR 1-0 Aston Villa, The Boy's close personal friend Angel Rangel putting in a shift. It's been a remarkable turnaround from manager Steve McLaren following an appalling start to the season. He will of course inevitably be sacked: destroy and exit.

In Dortmund, there's a huge shock in the darts when Tony West beats van Gerwen at the 12th time of asking. MvG seems genuinely stunned at being turfed out of a tournament that he habitually wins.

A swift relocation to LA, I stick the MLB on the big TV. The Dodgers go 1-0 up, but it's time for feather.

SATURDAY OCTOBER 27TH

Straight into Sydney FC v Western Sydney Wanderers. Something's happened in the baseball; I accidentally see something about seven hours and 18 innings. I'm glad I bailed, but have to activate a media lockdown for the replay, which is already into extra innings, a whole other game. Due to baseball's scoring system, it has still been sullied. If the Red Sox don't score in the top of the 18th then I know that The Dodgers win. Problems, and yet another reminder that all sport should be watched live.

Meanwhile, Western Sydney Wanderers are 2-0 down, have a goal overturned on VAR and then the manager sent off in rage. Then what looks like a penalty is not referred to VAR, so where the fuck are we with all of this?

The A-League is one of the last bastions of attacking football, as both teams simply go at it from the off. Another Western Sydney Wanderers goal is ruled out for offside and it's not their day. Sydney scorer Adam Le Fondre, once of Rochdale, is interviewed. What a career, from Spotland to the Sydney Cricket Ground for being reasonably competent at kicking an inflated sphere.

The MLB repeat is now the longest in World Series history. A second stretch coming up. A 14th inning stretch? You couldn't make it up. Timewise, it's now comparable to a day of test match cricket, but without the meals. Football Focus comes and goes as does most of Middlesbrough v Derby, yet still they play in LA, now past midnight local time in a game that began in sunshine. It's now the longest game since 1984. It's now longer than the entire 1939 series. Finally, we get to the bottom of the 18th and I know what's coming. A solo home run for the Dodgers, and they're back in the series at 2-1. More importantly, my 50p bet lives. 7hrs 20mins. We go again tonight.

There's a T20 against Sri Lanka, so I splitscreen it with some rugby league, England 18-16 New Zealand, This gives me flashbacks of The Watford Gap once forcing me to attend the same fixture at the London Stadium, my first and hopefully last live rugby league game. Hung over from a Killing Joke gig the night before, it was a hugely unpleasant experience, the only highlight coming when I bought a £2 pasty from one of our group for £3. Worth it. England 2-9 New Zealand, I think, followed by a drink in a shopping centre.

It's been a mammoth day of sport already, but this is all over-shadowed by listening to Chester 3-2 Alfreton. Up the fucking Seals! It's arguably the worst set of Premier League fixtures in living memory, so I have an acca to liven it up. Straight into the evening fare, it's Leeds v Forest, Leicester v West Ham, and Sri Lanka's innings. Glenn Hoddle has been taken ill while on BT Sport, each chirrup of my phone bringing possible bad news. Now there's been a helicopter crash at Leicester. Not good.

I half-heartedly watch Monaco 2-2 Dijon, Thierry Henry now in charge, apparently. A touch of EFL On Quest HD, and then some of Match Of The Day, Lineker holding himself together in difficult circumstances. An absolute hero as a player and a presenter.

I head upstairs for the LA double, Lakers at San Antonio, and Red Sox at Dodgers, who throw away a 4-0 lead to trail 3-1 in the best-of-seven series. Even with the clocks going back, it's 4am, a solid 19-hour shift at the coalface of sport. Feather.

SUNDAY OCTOBER 28TH

In the bath for Selby v Li Yuan. On it goes, Barry Hearn's attempt to make snooker a glorified screensaver instead of appointment-to-view sporting drama. I dry naturally on the bed while watching Simon Whitlock versus Tony West. We have been invited to lunch at Chelsea Dad's so I send the family ahead while The Wizard puts West to bed, a case of After The Lord Mayor's Show following his victory over MvG.

Chelsea Dad has Palace v Arsenal on his massive new 49" TV. A shame he couldn't have bought it in time for the World Cup semi. Forced to eat at the table like humans, frustratingly we can hear the football, but not see it, relying on random children for score updates. Chelsea are also rattling in four at Burnley without reply, something our host seems pretty relaxed about.

Finally, the men are seated for Man United v Everton, but not even the new sound bar can raise the atmosphere at Old Trafford. Pogba takes a 26-step penalty – saved and in. United eventually win 2-1, but it's a tiresome watch.

I get back home to speed-watch three recorded darts quarter-finals. Tragically, the recording runs out with James Wade locked at 7-7 with Gerwyn Price, the former rugby player turned angry darts slinger. Wade evidently wins as he's in the semi-final against home favourite Max Hopp. The large crowd gets behind the German, who fucks up three darts to beat Wade and make the final. There's poor etiquette from the German crowd, cheering Wade misses. Predictably, he gives it the large one when he wins.

I listen to the Mexican Grand Prix then take live pictures. Through the kitchen window, the Wembley arch is lit up in the colours of Leicester City, out of respect.

Sunday night brings an onslaught of American things and Selby is through 6-5 in the snooker. At the darts, with the last German player gone there's an exodus and the final is played in near silence, an atmosphere comparable to Old Trafford. Wade beats Whitlock for his first title in years, dedicating it to his two-week old son Arthur, demonstrating the alleged sporting phenomenon of nappy power.

Match Of The Day 2 is tinged with sadness as five are confirmed dead in the helicopter crash at Leicester, plus there are ongoing concerns over the health of Hoddle.

Technically an hour earlier due to the clocks changing, Game Five of the World Series is one of four major sporting events taking place in LA, including Galaxy losing and missing the playoffs. I manage five or six innings, but it's too risky to watch the replay so I attempt to press on. I find The Boy asleep in my bed so prop up the iPad in his, bucking awake to see the Red Sox lift the trophy. I'm glad it's out of my life.

MONDAY OCTOBER 29TH

Oh Monday, I'm dreaming about you. Mark Williams is up against it, and gone. Selby is hammering wildcard Ken Doherty 6-0, the latter fresh from victory in Hull on Thursday night. What a life.

Wembley is lit up ahead of Spurs v Manchester City, former Leicester player Mahrez paying tribute to the victims of the helicopter disaster, which include the chairman. The pitch is still scarred from the recent NFL activity, and looks preposterous. Clad in his Spurs onesie, The

Boy is asleep in 20 minutes. City score the only goal of the game shortly before Real Madrid sack Lopetegui.

I head upstairs to see New England Patriots win at Buffalo Bills, Tom Brady at it, all field goals until late on.

TUESDAY OCTOBER 30TH

I can't find any snooker, so opt for a repeat of Bordeaux 0-1 Nice. There's the added jeopardy of a score ticker alongside the action so I construct an impromptu frame to obscure it lest any results are sullied.

I manage a bit of Selby 6-4 Milkins and a touch of Ding as Burton v Forest gets under way in the Carabao Cup. Due to more congestion on the accursed M56, Chester kick off late, but score after two minutes en route to a 4-1 home victory over Ashton United, the other National League North team in Ashton, which seems unnecessary. Burton have a penalty. I predict it will go eight foot over the bar. Not far off, looked nervous. Nevertheless, they win a thriller 3-2, Nigel Clough turfing Forest out. I keep an eye on Strasbourg 2-0 Lille in the French League Cup. Fuck Strasbourg.

WEDNESDAY OCTOBER 31ST

Underwater for Ding v Stevens, I instinctively parrot "go on Matthew" in a Welsh accent whenever the Welshman is at the table. During the interval, I watch a repeat of Melbourne Victory 2-3 Perth Glory. Something of a gamble calling your club Victory, or indeed Glory.

I leave the snooker at a crucial stage to go trick-or-treating. We get back for Chelsea 3-2 Derby in the Carabao, but I miss Chelsea's third as I am at the door handing out marshmallows. NYC FC beat Philadelphia 3-1 at Yankee Stadium in the MLS playoffs, David Villa on target. Neil Lennon is hit by a coin in the goalless Hearts v Hibs derby, and there's a pitch invasion at West Ham as they're knocked out by Spurs. I round off the day, and indeed the month, with Carabao highlights on Quest HD, something of a game-changer.

THURSDAY NOVEMBER 1ST

Putting the No in November. Selby v Robertson in the snooker. The big guns. Robertson wins. Matthew Stevens also through. Go on Matthew.

We go for a curry while following the FA Youth Cup: Chester 2-1 Barnsley. Back home to listen to commentary of the rest of it, I am astonished to learn that Man City v Fulham is not on TV. If a tree falls in the forest and nobody hears it, does it make a sound?

Sickened and appalled, I fill the gap with double Auf Wiedersehen, Pet on Yesterday, then we're into American things. I find it hard to watch an entire regular season basketball game so have a bet on Milwaukee to win at Boston. Milwaukee are 7 and 0, in that they have won their first seven games of the season. This soon becomes 7 and 1 as my money disappears into the ether. Chasing my funds, I back DC United to beat Columbus in the MLS playoffs. The bet is over when it goes to extra time and it's eventually decided on penalties, with Rooney missing one, the tit. And this in the week when he revealed that his pre-match playlist includes Ed Sheeran, James Bay and Sons Of Mumford. They probably lost on purpose to avoid further punishment.

I lump on the San Francisco '49ers to win at Oakland Raiders in the Bay Area derby, played at The Coliseum, home of Oakland Athletics. With a big lead, I leave them to it, as another MLS game is about to start. For the sake of completion, I listen to repeat commentary of Man City 2-0 Fulham, De Bruyne injured.

FRIDAY NOVEMBER 2ND

While I fester in a pit of despair, Allen and Stevens have already put 12 frames on the board, 7-5 to The Pistol. Go on Matthew. It's not to be for the Welshman as Allen makes it through to the through to final. BBC2 is showing World Championship Gymnastics. Not for me, Clive. As it's Friday night, I push the boat out with an acca on Villa, PSG and Eintracht Frankfurt. To my astonishment, it comes in. Winning at life.

SATURDAY NOVEMBER 3RD

The fact that I am watching Chinese snooker and Australian football with my breakfast can mean only one thing: an early start. Shady Sharks are up against Darryl's Blue Dragons in the cup, and the rival parents become increasingly quiet as we knock in one, two, and three goals without reply, the third an impressively dispatched penalty. We then hang around to watch Queen's Park Sharks' premier outfit, The Dynamos, tear some poor saps apart with speed and skill way beyond that of our zombie shufflers.

Back home, I attempt to sleep then kidnap The Boy and drive him to Brackley Town Football Club, overtaking my younger brother on the way. We're accompanied by Bournemouth v Man United on 5live, arriving with minutes left. I unsuccessfully attempt to watch it on BT Sport on my phone, thus missing United's winner, 2-1. It turns out it was on in the club bar, where we are joined by The Watford Gap and his mate TT, who lives nearby and is making his non-league debut.

It's a tepid opening to the game and my younger brother says he "forgot how boring this was". It's a shit sandwich albeit enlivened by two incredible long-range goals by Chester's on-loan winger Dan Mooney, the second an injury time volley to snatch a dramatic 2-2 draw. Limbs.

On the way back, we watch the goal in McDonald's on the phone of a Chester Exile. Radio commentary of Arsenal 1-1 Liverpool sees us home where we watch the last knockings. Sadly, I have to go to a sport-free dinner party, thus missing the rare 7:45pm Saturday night game, Wolves 2-3 Spurs. I eventually make my excuses and get home for Match Of The Day. Because I've been out, I don't know some of the scores. However, because I've been out I am unable to stay awake to watch it. A cruel, cruel irony.

SUNDAY NOVEMBER 4TH

Shaking off the cobwebs, we head to Burnham Beeches, some sort of wooded area in Buckinghamshire, for a nice family day out. Nightmare. I secrete an AM radio device and manage to sneak updates on Wigan 1-2 Leeds, an absolutely crucial three points. They all are, whatever time of season it is (apart from at the end if you're stranded in mid-table).

We trough down a perfunctory pub lunch and the family sleep through Chelsea v Palace in the car. We get back for the last minutes of England v New Zealand in rugby league, again. I take to the day bed for the second half of the football and am woken by a

Palace equaliser. Enjoy it while you can, lads, you're going to lose 3-1. The Palace chairman takes consolation in the bosom of TV's Susanna Reid.

In the darts, the Dutch masters are at it again. I find a sporadic feed of ITV4+1 and watch Raymond van Barneveld beat Michael van Gerwen, Barney maintaining an Indian Sign over his lightbulb-headed compatriot. As so often happens when a player knocks out MvG, they seem spent for their next match and Barney succumbs 10-2 to the resurgent James Wade, finally living up to his given moniker, The Machine.

I watch an unsatisfactory repeat of Mark Allen beating Neil Robertson to lift the International Championship in Daqing. Back in Vienna, it's the final of the World Series Of Darts between James Wade and Michael Smith. In an astonishing climax, both players have chances to win it, Smith somehow busts 121 and Wade staggers over the line in a final leg shootout, winning 11-10 for his second title in two weeks following a barren five years. Scenes. They'll be dancing on the streets of Aldershot tonight.

I wash it down with a mash-up of Match Of The Day and Match Of The Day 2, then it's wall-to-wall MLS playoffs. I fall asleep at Yankee Stadium.

MONDAY NOVEMBER 5TH

Fireworks. The Rooney debate rumbles on. Having officially retired from international football, he has been invited for one last hurrah at Wembley in a friendly against the USA, where he now resides. Cue weeks of angry men shouting about it, writing about it, and generally filling air until we die. TalkSPORT's Jason 'The Fun Boy' Cundy, for one, is furious, calling it "an embarrassing joke".

Very much like that character in The Fast Show, I simply go along with whoever is speaking at the time. Does it devalue an international cap? Is it disrespectful? Is it, as has been suggested, a circus? Or is it just a man kicking a ball about? Ultimately, I neither know nor care. One day this will all be rubble.

I leave them to shout about it and immerse myself in hot water for NFL highlights, the palatable half-hour packages infinitely more accessible than the interminable live coverage. Drying naturally, I get straight into Jill Douglas who is presenting snooker's Champion of Champions on ITV4. There really isn't enough snooker on TV these days.

In a comic bid for fitness, I find myself at an outdoor gym, where I have a chat with an elderly Fulham fan. As I invariably do when speaking to a Fulham supporter, I tell her that I once saw Chester beat them 7-0 in a league game. Oddly, none of them ever seem to remember it.

Fulham are playing at Huddersfield tonight in what is already a relegation six-pointer, which I watch while keeping an eye on the snooker. Huddersfield win 1-0 with an own goal, the first time they have scored at home this season and they didn't even score it themselves. The game is so shit I consider turning it off. They're both doomed anyway.

I chase it down with Tennessee at Dallas, and then we're into the first test in Galle, which I take in the day bed, waking up with England 10 for 2 and again at 196 for 6.

TUESDAY NOVEMBER 6TH

I briefly rally for the cricket, but head back to bed for the final session. Foakes on 50 now. The crowd at the tiny ground in Galle is 98% England fans. I eventually drift off and wake up for a 1pm meeting between Ronnie and Bingham in the bath (me not them). Inexorably approaching a thousand career centuries, Ronnie notches one in the second frame. And another! Back-to-back centuries in the space of minutes. Even more astonishingly, he is yet to complain about either the venue, Coventry, snooker, or simply the world. Anyway, whither Cov Kit? Surely he's here, in Cov. Pleasingly, Ronnie wins before I set off for the school run, and I get back to see the end of Higgins 4-3 Day.

The country is plunged into blackness with only European football as a salve. In the absurd 5:55pm kickoffs, the team formerly known as Red Star beat Liverpool 2-0 and Monaco lose 4-0 at home to Bruges, not the greatest of starts for Thierry Henry.

At the more civilised time of 7:45pm, it's a twitchy affair at The Deva as Chester overcome Nuneaton 3-2 with another Mooney screamer. Remember the name: Dan Mooney!

This overlaps with the 8pm Champions League games. Spurs get some valuable points on the board by beating PSV 2-1 at Wembley, while in the same group Inter draw 1-1 with Barcelona. Surely this is The Group Of Death.

Simultaneously in Coventry, Ronnie dispatches Higgins 6-3, a solid day's work for The Rocket.

Champions League highlights ease me into a tactical pre-sleep with a non-sporting chaser of US midterms.

At 4:35am, Foakes is closing in on a century in Galle. A view of the fort prompts a sudden recollection. We were once on holiday in Galle when I caught a stray cricket ball from a kids' game, declaring the batsman out to much confusion. True story.

Foakes on 95 now with Anderson at the other end, England 330-9. Can he do it? The significance given to test centuries is hugely disproportionate to their value in securing victory. If someone gets 98 or 99 they've still made a sizeable contribution, but centuries are so prized that they compromise the approach to the game. Just get on with it. If you happen to go past a hundred, well fucking done, but don't hinge the entire innings on it. It's different in snooker – if you're approaching a century the frame is already won. But in cricket, we've still got a game on here lads, stop nurdling about in pursuit of an arbitrary number and get on with it. Anyway, Foakes gets his century on test debut then promptly skies one for 107, thus proving me right.

England then inflict carnage with the ball and at 6:30am Sri Lanka are 42 for 4. And that's lunch. Or is it breakfast?

WEDNESDAY NOVEMBER 7TH

I wake to find England batting via talkSPORT2 on the bedside Google Home Mini. I watch the last over on the iPad as they post a healthy lead.

In the bath, I make a rare foray into the Chinese Super League. I wouldn't normally bother, but Shanghai can win the league with victory. I join the action half an hour in with them 1-0 up. Then 2-0. They win 2-1, a result that will live as long in the memory as this water does in the bath.

Into the snooker, it's Mark Williams 1-4 Kyren Wilson, the World Champion suffering a China hangover. Trump dispatches Brecel by the same score to set up an intriguing evening session.

I watch the early Champions League games with The Boy. Juventus v Manchester United on the big screen, Manchester City v Shakhtar on the iPad, snooker on the laptop, admin on the phone.

It all kicks off with a ludicrous penalty awarded to Man City when Sterling clearly isn't fouled. If only there were some kind of video assistance. Meanwhile in Coventry, Kyren Wilson can watch the last half hour of the football as he hands out a 6-1 midterm thrashing to the misfiring Trump. I miss Ronaldo's opening goal while pissing about on my phone, but what follows is less predictable as United steal an historic 2-1 victory at Juve. I support all British teams in Europe and am baying at the screen, Mourinho cupping an ear now. This charmless man.

Back in Manchester, a Jesus hat-trick helps City to a biblical 6-0 win. I have to forgo the highlights in favour of double Walking Dead, so instead stay up all night watching 30 minutes of each match on BT Sport. This will hopefully take me into the cricket, but tiredness is creeping in. No such problems for Mark Williams who is tweeting from what appears to be a strip club, then a McDonald's. The glamour.

THURSDAY NOVEMBER 8TH

England post a huge total overnight and declare.

On ITV4 in the bath, Barry Hearn declares: "I've never had an original idea in my life". I interviewed him once, or more accurately he interviewed himself. Never used it.

The boys on the baize are Selby and Robertson. The Jester from Leicester pays a heartfelt tribute to the late Leicester City chairman, Vichai Srivaddhanaprabha. The Aussie takes a lengthy opener, but the second frame is much quicker and Selby is on the blue before I realise he's on a 147, which he duly dispatches. I feel cheated of the tension, but still honoured to have witnessed the climax live. You wake up thinking it's going to be just another day then suddenly you're witnessing sporting history.

The match goes to 3-3, but sadly I have to leave it to pick up The Boy. I see Sri Lanka Dad in the playground, looking tired, watching the whole series live apparently.

Due to being plunged into darkness and cold for the foreseeable future, The Shady Sharks now have a training session in a gym in

Kilburn. On the plus side, there is excellent free wi-fi, thus enabling me to watch BATE v Chelsea in the Europa League, Giroud with the opener, his first of the season, having somehow won the World Cup without mustering a shot on target. The dad of two of the kids at training is actually at the match, the midpoint of a Tuesday to Saturday tear-up. For some reason, he's no longer with the mother.

Saints Dad delivers us home and I catch up with recorded snooker: Robertson through, no prizes for Selby's 147. It's then a triple whammy of BT Sport: BATE 0-1 Chelsea, Arsenal 0-0 Sporting, Bordeaux 1-1 Zenit, The Driver texting from the latter.

In the snooker, Mark Allen beats Barry Hawkins and then Neil Robertson. Or if you like, The Pistol guns down The Hawk and The Thunder from Down Under. It's all balls.

I head upstairs for NFL, NBA and MLS. The Steelers manage an impressive 50+ points. Good for them. Sport never sleeps. Sadly, I have to, and extra time at Seattle v Portland is too much. I am woken in some confusion by news of a dead dog and a change of plan. I switch beds to see England beat Sri Lanka, plus the retirement of the last 20th-century cricketer.

FRIDAY NOVEMBER 9TH

South Africa v Australia in a repeat of the second ODI. It may be foul here, but it's always summer somewhere. There's also the Women's World T20 to contend with. Fuck that, I'm off to the home of darts, Ally Pally. Not to watch arrows, but to see New Order. Nobody expected that.

Meeting up with The Evertonian and sundry acquaintances, we go to a pub where we recognise the massive head of a Wimbledon fan we used to live with in Liverpool. He's here mob-handed ahead of AFC Wimbledon's FA Cup tie at Haringey Borough. Apparently, one of their mates hasn't missed a Wimbledon game since 1987. True faith. I briefly consider attempting to get a ticket for the cup-tie as the tout I've been harassing for a sensibly priced New Order ticket is yet to buckle.

He finally sees sense and it's a belting gig, Barney standing on the same stage on which The Power threw his final competitive dart after decades of dominance. AFC Wimbledon grab a 90th-minute winner at Haringey, and Her Indoors even manages to record the snooker. Sadly, I see the result on my phone. Regret.

SATURDAY NOVEMBER 10TH

Dropping the family with family in Middle England, I drive solo to Chester for the big one against Altrincham, 5live for company. As I negotiate the A41, Brighton score the first goal of a day pregnant with possibilities. What a bounce. Imagine you've woken up in Brighton at sparrow's fart, got yourself to another country for a 12:30pm kickoff and taken an early lead. Limbs. Sadly for them, they go on to lose 2-1 to Cardiff.

I sign some books in the Chester club shop then have a swift one in the Blues Bar. Unannounced, my older brother randomly turns up on the Harry McNally terrace en route to a school reunion. Chester conspire to lose 2-1 to Alty. We always fuck it up in the big games.

Seething, I inadvertently jump a red light, drop my brother off in town and head south, dipping in and out of commentary of Palace 0-1 Spurs. I drop in on The Watford Gap and sell a signed book to a friend of his. He'll never read it. This makes me late for dinner at Her Indoors' brother's house, but that makes it easier to stealth-watch snooker on my phone. It's been a tough two days and in an almost unprecedented show of weakness, I am in bed for Match Of The Day. I top it off with radio commentary of Tony Bellew getting sparked out. I can almost feel it.

SUNDAY NOVEMBER 11TH

After a solid 11 hours in the repair tank, I emerge downstairs for the noon kickoff between Liverpool and Fulham, sadly on non-HD BT Sport. Savages. I take my breakfast with a touch of Ronnie on the iPad, earning a horrified look from the lady of the house. Salah and Shaqiri earn Liverpool a perfunctory 2-0 win, then we're into the BBC's wonderful FA Cup coverage where they chase the goals around the grounds with the aid of a phalanx of windswept touchline reporters. Her Indoors even pauses for Guiseley 4-3 Cambridge, remembering the time she left her handbag in a pub there.

We manage half an hour of goalless action between Chelsea and Everton then we're into a pub lunch with stealth snooker on the phone via the pub wi-fi, and Premier League score updates from a nephew. It crawls to a goalless conclusion at Stamford Bridge and we appear to have dodged a bullet. However, we are now away from a screen for the Manchester derby. As such, pudding is wolfed down so we can be in the car for the 4:30pm kickoff. City maintain their place at the top of the league by swatting United aside 3-1, power now firmly established on the blue side of the city.

Back home, I hit the day bed for the final stages of the Champion Of Champions snooker final between Ronnie and Kyren Wilson. It's got it all: a reckless cross-double, a waistcoat infraction, but Wilson hauls Ronnie back to 9-9 for a final-frame decider. The Rocket takes it with yet another century, then manages a quick a dig at Barry Hearn, moaning about the grind of the Northern Ireland Open, which preposterously starts tomorrow.

It's a quick change of discipline for the Grand Slam of Darts where Michael van Gerwen is again beaten in the group stage. Lewis Hamilton wins in Brazil and on the same continent River Plate draw 2-2 with deadly rivals Boca Juniors in the first leg of the Copa Libertadores final – a little bit tasty by all accounts. A touch of NFL and MLS takes me to Match Of the Day 2, where they rightly enthuse about City's 44-pass goal. I round off a solid day with lengthy FA Cup highlights on the Red Button.

MONDAY NOVEMBER 12TH

I panic and book a train for the big one at York tomorrow. Very much like Ronnie, I struggle to get enthused about the Northern Ireland Open. I drop The Boy in the capable hands of Queens Park Rangers and watch Mark 'The Pistol' Allen losing in front of his home fans.

I pick up The Boy in time for the live FA Cup draw, always a thrill on a bleak November evening. Along with the Grand Slam of Darts, we're straight into Hampton and Richmond versus Oldham, National League South taking on the might of League Two. The home side go ahead with an early disputed penalty, but are cruelly denied their moment of glory by an 88th-minute equaliser. They don't even get a replay as Oldham nick it in the 95th minute. What a sport.

A day after competing in a major final in Coventry, Kyren Wilson is still playing at midnight in Northern Ireland. Meanwhile, Harry Redknapp is entering the jungle, so fortunately I won't see or hear anything from him for the next few weeks. Sometimes they say, 'why do you watch so much sport?' It might be meaningless, but if the alternative is watching morons eating spiders then count me out. I go to bed and listen to commentary of Sri Lanka Women v South Africa Women. That'll show them.

TUESDAY NOVEMBER 13TH

Joe Cole has retired. Retired from what? I record the snooker and head to York, a chance to go top of the National League North for The Mighty Chester. Due to the vagaries of train pricing, I get there five hours before kickoff. Shambles. I take myself on a real ale tour, eventually rocking up at Bootham Crescent, a classic old school ground, surrounded by terraced houses. It will probably be my last visit here as they eventually plan to knock it down. Progress, they call it.

It's a shit game, mildly enlivened when fellow author, the gargan-tuan Jon Parkin, comes on for York to requisite abuse. It finishes goalless, and I sit at York station, drinking on my own. On the train, I briefly speak to a York couple. They are absolutely livid, claiming that Parkin didn't the touch the ball once.

I get home in the early hours and watch one frame of Ronnie then some women's cricket. 4:30am brings the Sri Lanka test. No chance.

WEDNESDAY NOVEMBER 14TH

"Hey Google, play talkSPORT2." Overnight heroics from Tom Curran in Sri Lanka. Closer to home, Claudio Ranieri has taken over at Fulham, who are now 5,000/1 to win the Premier League. In the bath, I catch up with the Grand Slam of Darts plus a bit of live snooker. I resume the indoor sporting feast downstairs until I am eventually forced out of the house by parental responsibility, taking my son from school to football for the umpteenth time in his and my life.

It's a rare night out as I have been pressganged into a quiz team, ostensibly for my sporting knowledge. Hosted in Hammersmith Town Hall by Evan 'Tinsel Tits' Davis off of the telly, it's a presti-gious affair. I manage to recall that the Isner match at Wimbledon went on for 11 hours, and I suddenly remember that Alastair Cook has 33 England centuries, albeit too late. I guess that Schumacher has the most pole positions when it's actually Hamilton. Fuck it all. We come close, and indeed had we played our joker on the easy first round instead of sport, we would have won.

I get home for a bit of PokerStars Caribbean Adventure on Channel Four. Even a glimpse of the garish carpet makes me feel nauseous, bringing back sickening memories of the time I folded pocket Kings there. Pissed up on booze, I go to bed and listen to women's cricket.

THURSDAY NOVEMBER 15TH

Bumble on talkSPORT misses a great catch as he was "caught short". Sri Lanka have fought back overnight and I watch the final over of the day, which is also the first of England's second innings. It's the first time I've actually seen this test match. Carry on then.

Due to leaving the house last night, I'm playing catch-up with the darts and snooker. I even watch Ronnie in the garden, in mid-November. Go on Ronnie.

It is announced that VAR will be used in the Premier League next season. The Boy and his teammates leather a ball round a Kilburn gym as I watch England U-21s beat Italy on my phone.

Back home for actual England who are playing USA in the Rooneygate game. It's 2-0 at half time while in the darts, James Wade is ousted by the Bavarian stick insect Michael Unterbuchner, possibly looking even thinner than in January. From my vantage point in the kitchen, the Wembley Arch appears not to be illuminated. Perhaps the whole game has been faked. Rooney finally comes on and puts in a decent shift, failing to score in a comfortable 3-0 win.

I join Smith versus van Gerwen in progress; the Dutchman edges it 10-8. Croatia beat Spain 3-2 so England can now win their Nations League group.

Largely confused by the whole thing, I watch the first half of Seattle Jellyfish v Green Bay Packers and call it a night.

FRIDAY NOVEMBER 16TH

Joe Root has posted 124 overnight in Sri Lanka. Go on Joe, lad. I can't commit to the snooker and end up watching Brazil 1-0 Uruguay, which for some reason is played at Arsenal. In the Nations League, Germany are relegated and Wales are beaten. I find a bit of England Women's cricket, but keep missing Ronnie, his 974th century proving too quick for me. In the darts, fiery Welshman Gerwyn Price edges hirsute Antipodean wizard Simon Whitlock 16-15 in an ill-tempered affair.

And finally, Kop King Kenny kops a knighthood.

SATURDAY NOVEMBER 17TH

On a cold morning in The Regent's Park, I am transported to warmer climes via talkSPORT2 as I sit on a bench on my own and listen to the test match. Shady Sharks are up against Eagles United, an all-American outfit with players called Oscar and Wyatt, a big lad who I'm sure I saw making out with his girlfriend in a pickup truck. It's an ill-tempered affair and at one point an opposition parent comes onto the pitch to move the ball forward for a free kick. Astonishingly, the ref lets it go, presumably just wanting to get home after a heavy night at Turnmills. Pleasingly, the Sharks hold on for a 2-1 win. No surrender to the USA.

On the way home, I am texted a link to the Fartgate scandal, whereby Gary Anderson and Wesley Harms have each accused the other of dropping their guts at the oche. What a sport. If only Sid was still with us.

The sporting extravaganza continues apace as we head directly to the New Windmill Ground, home of Leamington FC. Situated in a field off the M40, it stretches the parameters of an out-of-town stadium. We get to the bar early and are joined by all manner of stragglers, including The Hack, The Watford Gap and Le Chat Noir, all characters from my previous book. One reader turns his back on them as he doesn't want to ruin the perfect image in his mind.

There's also a rare appearance from Her Indoors' brother and nephew, who promptly leave at half time to get to the O2 to watch tennis, an astonishing set of priorities. As such, they miss the only goal of the game, a largely undeserved winner for Leamington. Shithouse.

On the way home, I secure the guest list for Killing Joke at The Camden Roundhouse. I meet Ipswich fan Bealesy in The Enterprise, where we watched England beat Nigeria prior to the World Cup. This time it's rammed, wall-to-wall with punters craning their necks to see Ireland beat The All Blacks. A war dance.

SUNDAY NOVEMBER 18TH

England beat Sri Lanka overnight. I take the snooker on my phone, with the first frame briefly suspended when Ronnie detects a buzzing sound in the venue. Go on Ronnie. Not feeling my best, I retreat to my eyrie for a perfect storm of football, snooker and darts. England beat Croatia 2-1 to progress in the Nations League. Scenes. Whatever the merits of the Nations League, I'd rather we'd beaten them in the World Cup. I almost become tearful at the sight of Southgate hugging players. What could have been. I think I'm hungover.

In the Grand Slam of Darts, Price beats Suljović, and Anderson beats MvG, striking a psychological blow ahead of the pending World Championship. In the snooker, Trump and O'Sullivan are locked at 4-4, the flamboyant Bristol potter one of the few players who can match The Rocket on his day.

In need of fresh air, I go for a quick walk, briefly checking in to see Northern Ireland equalise against Austria. In an attempt to finally defeat this hangover, I put everything on delay and we head for a curry. Back for the snooker on Quest+1, I splitscreen with the darts final where there is an unseemly scene of pushing and shoving between Gerwyn Price and Gary Anderson, who may or may not have farted. Price looks and acts like a small-town thug. I would be astonished if he hasn't been told 'it's not worth it!' on multiple occasions in a variety of South Wales public houses. Despite the aggro, he wins the tournament, his first big one, and is roundly booed at the oche, as well as throughout the presentation, almost unprecedented scenes of disapproval from the darting public. Price seems almost to relish it. By his own admission, he's a rugby player taking money off the darting pros.

In the midst of this, Switzerland beat Belgium 5-2. Nobody expected that. In cricket, the women lose to the West Indies. In the snooker, it's a battle of flair between the pretender and master. Trump beats

Ronnie, who then has a dig about having to get up at 10am. He's got ten days off now.

MONDAY NOVEMBER 19TH

The world awakes to news of the end of the Barney era, or at least after 2020. Raymond van Barneveld announces that he will retire after the next World Championship. This means that next year's Premier League will be a farewell tour for the popular Dutchman. The more cynical will even point out that his early announcement will ensure his place in the competition on sympathy instead of merit.

Checking digital Ceefax, I am perturbed to see that I completely missed Hartlepool 1-3 Barnet yesterday. Maybe I'm losing my touch. By way of recompense, I attempt to watch live curling in the bath, but can't get into it (the curling, not the bath). News breaks that some Canadian curlers have been kicked out of the tournament for being extremely drunk. Gazza has been charged with sexual assault.

I watch National League highlights, pretending not to care that Chester are no longer involved. In the Nations League, it's Germany 2-2 Netherlands so Germany are relegated and Netherlands are in the finals. The Boy steals the iPad, thus saving me from the torpor of Denmark 0-0 Republic Of Ireland.

I don't always bother, but I have a look at Monday Night Football: Kansas City Chiefs at Los Angeles Rams in the LA Coliseum, shades of the '84 Olympics, Carl Lewis and all that. I start casually watching it, then become utterly entranced as almost every play seems to result in a score. Records are shattered by the minute. In 773 Monday Night Football matches, this is the highest scoring, and also the first time both teams have scored over 50. It finally ends 54-51 to the Rams, a scoreline I will almost immediately forget.

TUESDAY NOVEMBER 20TH

Out of respect, I watch a replay of the NFL. Some game. Tea-time brings Denmark U-21 1-5 England U-21 then we're straight in to a 7pm friendly between Albania and Wales. The iPad is swiped for Bake Off: The Professionals, forcing me to watch the remainder of the match on S4C, the Welsh language channel.

Brazil appear to be playing Cameroon at the home of MK Dons, understandably in front of a record crowd. Neymar goes off early with an actual injury and Brazil win 1-0.

In the UEFA Nations League, it's Scotland 3-2 Israel, which sees the Scots promoted in this baffling format. International football relegates the FA Cup to my phone, where I am disappointed to see Tranmere Rovers win 2-0 at Oxford City. Elsewhere in the cup, I squeeze in some penalty shootout commentary then go for a lie down. It feels like a quiet night, but I still managed five games.

WEDNESDAY NOVEMBER 21ST

Martin O'Neill and Roy Keane have parted company with Ireland following some of the worst football in their history. Footage emerges of Ronnie on talkSPORT moaning about snooker, sat in the same chair that I occupied for my 15 minutes of book chat. What an honour for him.

7:30pm brings commentary of Mansfield 2-0 Chester in the FA Youth Cup, thus sparing me a trip to Bournemouth in the next round that I inevitably would have attempted. As our game ends, Salford City score to set up a grandstand finish in their 7:45pm kickoff against Shrewsbury in the FA Cup. Even co-owner Paul Scholes is briefly spotted smiling, but the Shrews clinch a 3-1 win in injury time. Didier Drogba retires. Who knew he was still playing?

At 1:15am, LeBron is back at Cleveland for the first time as a Laker. I wait until LA go behind then get a fiver on with Betfair, who have generously given me a free £5 bet. The next hour or so is an absolute sweat as I cheer every point, buck at every rimshot, and generally reduce myself to a gibbering mess chasing a few quid that I'll probably never spend. In a thrilling finale, The Lakers finally get it done, 109-105. It's minus two degrees outside.

THURSDAY NOVEMBER 22ND

Thanksgiving? Thanksgiving for what? Fuck knows. What it does mean is that while America decimates its turkey population, there are three televised NFL games back-to-back. I leave Chicago at Detroit for Shady Sharks indoor training. Perhaps inspired by the Lakers' victory, I attempt a three-pointer with an under-inflated football, succeeding only in inflaming a residual drinking injury to my wrist.

Disgustingly, there's no football on TV. I settle for the women's cricket semi, where Australia thrash the West Indies amid tearful scenes. The Redskins are at the Cowboys in what nobody is calling the Wild West Derby. Meanwhile, England Women take on India Women and beat them in what is described as 'a walk in the park'. New Orleans Saints beat Atlanta Falcons, then it's headphones in for the third test.

FRIDAY NOVEMBER 23RD

Woken by a wicket, England appear to be posting a reasonable total. Harry Kane has agreed to accept £290,000 a week for the next five years. Very reasonable. We go straight to Butlin's, Minehead for the darts – ITV4's Player's Championship, where Jacqui Oatley is talking about the stink in Wolverhampton. A quickfire format, Klassen gone, Lewis through. Go on, Jackpot.

I head to Shepherd's Bush and meet Ipswich fan Bealesy in an alleged sports bar. They agree to put on Ipswich v West Brom albeit with no sound. We leave in disgust just as Bealesy's interview with Ipswich manager Paul Lambert begins. Finding a pub that's showing it correctly, I even rinse the wi-fi for a bit of darts on my phone, Cross in trouble versus Reyes. West Brom take the lead and we have to leave them to it to watch The Damned at the Shepherd's Bush Empire. Scenes. On the bus home, I learn that Gerwyn Price has gone.

I get back home for the 18th hole of a one-off head-to-head between Tiger Woods and Phil Mickelson, who are playing for $9million, winner takes all. It's a vulgar yet compelling spectacle, not least when they start giving each other ludicrous gimmes, some of them from metres away. I'm firmly of the belief that all putts should be completed, whatever the distance. You wouldn't award a footballer a goal simply because he faced a tap-in, as Ronnie Rosenthal will attest.

The match grinds on to a 21st hole, Tiger now taking a gimme. Go on Tiger, lad – a close personal friend on the basis that I once interviewed him for 20 minutes. They seem to be showboating as to who can allow the longest gimme, despite taking chunks out of the putting green as darkness descends and the livestream falters. Cynics would assume there's some kind of carve-up behind the scenes, but Mickelson eventually takes "every penny of nine million dollars".

SATURDAY NOVEMBER 24TH

I manage to sleep through an entire day's cricket, England on fire with the ball. I swerve a Shady Sharks friendly and am woken briefly with the news that The Boy has retired from all football forthwith. We're already into Rotherham v Sheffield United. While I slumber in the capital, thousands of Yorkshiremen are up and about, eating, drinking and swearing. I manage to get eyes on the iPad for Rotherham's second equaliser, coming in injury time. 2-2. Scenes.

The teams are in for Chester's inevitably doomed stab at the FA Trophy, away to Southport. It's a short trip to Merseyside for the faithful, but a step too far for me. Instead, I listen to the commentary in the bath while watching the darts. England appear to be beating Australia at rugby at Twickenham, should probably have a look. In the midst of this, Hamilton has secured pole in Abu Dhabi, giving me flashbacks of quiz failure. How can the F1 season still be going?

Goalless at half time, part of me wishes I was at Southport: the frozen feet, the steamed-up chippy, the loathsome journey. Instead, in solidarity with the 281 travelling supporters, I listen to the second half in the garden, staring at the Wembley arch, the ultimate destination for the Trophy finalists. It finishes 0-0. We go again at our place.

Meanwhile, 81,275 are at Twickenham for a famous England win. My outdoor vigil means that I have missed all other football results so I attempt to get to Match Of The Day intact via the 5:30pm hurdle of Spurs v Chelsea. Back to the darts, Lewis is gone, beaten by Ratajski, earlier conqueror of Gerwyn Price.

Chelsea in yellow, the Wembley pitch still scarred. Five minutes in, the day's Premier League results start scrolling across the screen. I look away and hit mute, hearing only the word "Liverpool", which adds to the mystery. In terms of chronology, it seems wrong watching this match without knowledge of what has gone on before, like skipping ahead a chapter.

I have a cursory look at Wales v South Africa on the iPad before I realise that Brentford v Middlesbrough is on. The only Championship score I know is Stoke 2-2 QPR, my phone deciding unprompted to offer goal updates, presumably geography-based.

The Boy returns to tell me it was Fulham 1-2 Southampton, as his mate was there, son of Saints Dad, presumably also there. The Boy also informs me that Shady Sharks lost 1-0 and drew 3-3. And, following further consideration, he has decided not to retire.

In the rugby, it's a clean sweep by the home nations. Further afield, Boca v River Plate has been delayed as the visiting coach has been attacked. In the darts, Wade is gone. Boca goes from 8pm to 9pm to 10:15 on a Saturday night.

EFL On Quest sees The Boy's mate Angel Rangel score for QPR, causing his manager Steve McLaren to ask "what's he doing that far up?". And another! There's an idiotic overlap with Match Of The Day. Still nothing from the Copa, rumours that Boca captain Perez starts after sustaining an eye injury in the bus attack. And Bunting beats Snakebite in Minehead. The Copa game is eventually called off. Match Of The Day reveals that Fulham actually beat Saints 3-2. Unreliable witness.

Midnight sees the T20 final between England Women and Australia Women. England win the toss and elect to bat badly. Australia easily reach the target. Fuck Australia. I tune into talkSPORT2 for the test.

SUNDAY NOVEMBER 25TH

After a brief sleep, I am up for the cricket plus Sydney FC 1-2 Melbourne Victory in the A-League. Go on Victory. Lapsing back into unconsciousness with talkSPORT2 for company, I am woken by the early kickoff between Aston Villa and Birmingham City, which I see to completion in the bath with a side of darts. The so-called Second City Derby is a lively affair, with Villa triumphing 4-2 and marching towards the playoff positions.

Meanwhile, in Abu Dhabi, Hülkenberg is trapped under a burning car. Not a Super Sunday for the German.

In the actual so-called Super Sunday, Arsenal win 2-1 at Bournemouth thanks to an own goal and an Aubameyang winner. On the bed surrounded by a world of sport, I look out of the window and see The Boy having an impromptu kickabout. In an attempt to re-join the human race, I actively try not to watch Wolves v Huddersfield. Instead I go to the shop, inadvertently finding some kind of rugby on the radio en route. Back for the second half of the football, it's actually a decent game, a rare 2-0 win for Huddersfield in their futile fight against relegation. In a slightly more high-profile fixture, the Boca game has been called off again.

With the main TV showing The Christmas Chronicles, I resort to my phone for van Gerwen 11-9 Anderson. Then the World Youth Final between 24-year-old Van den Bergh and 22-year-old Schindler. In a thrilling final, Daryl 'SuperChin' Gurney beats MvG on the bull.

Sunday night means American things. Lakers lose then we're into the MLS finals with Match Of The Day 2, where it is revealed that Arsenal manager Unai Emery is learning English by watching Peaky Blinders. I briefly forget about the MLS, by which time Atlanta are beating New York Red Bulls 3-0. I leave them to it.

MONDAY NOVEMBER 26TH

Sri Lanka v England rumbles on, Pushpakumara toying with my fiver. Gone! England win by 42 runs to secure the whitewash and slightly boost one of my numerous online betting accounts. Unable to go back to sleep due to the excitement, I'm straight into NFL highlights, the best way to watch it. Even if I've seen the game before I rarely remember the score, reabsorbing it like a demented goldfish.

I'm so distracted that I miss the FA Trophy draw: Chester are first out of the hat and will be at home to Solihull if they can get past Southport tomorrow. Practically at Wembley. In other draw news, the PDC World Championship draw includes two women. Women, playing darts. Whatever next?

Monday Night Football, that's what's next, of the soccer variety, not American egg-chasing. Burnley v Newcastle live from Turf Moor where, never forget, I once had a brick thrown near me. Kickoff is delayed by half an hour after the referee's assessor collapses, described as a medical emergency. I still manage to miss the first goal as Burnley's Ben Mee sticks it in his own net on four minutes. In a surprisingly entertaining encounter, Newcastle's Matt Ritchie is responsible for arguably the miss of the season. And Burnley's Joe Hart, perhaps realising his limitations as a goalkeeper, has an audacious stab at playing in midfield. It finishes 2-1 to Newcastle and the world continues to turn.

TUESDAY NOVEMBER 27TH

To BAFTA, for the William Hill Sports Book Of The Year ceremony. Picking up my editor on a street corner, we are bloodied but
unbowed. Longlisted, not shortlisted, it feels a bit like a third-place
playoff match, albeit with considerably more cheap white wine. We grab
a chat with occasionally depressed footballer Clarke Carlisle, one of
the judges, who tells me he fought long and hard for The Card to be
shortlisted, but it lost out to a book about darts. John Inverdale, the
host, introduces himself to me. He then proceeds to offend much of
the panel, which includes Nick Hornby, who once wrote a book about
casually supporting a local team that won everything, the diametric
opposite of my story.

Inverdale interviews the various nominees onstage, and the darts
writer peppers his chat with foul and abusive language. Finally, the
winner is revealed, and it's a split decision between a book about
boxing, and one about a child who swam the channel. Not a sport.

I drown my sorrows in a nearby pub with a William Hill employee
who is also a Chester fan. We find somewhere showing the Champions League, Man City grabbing a 2-2 draw at Lyon. We also follow
Chester's FA Trophy replay at home to Southport using mobile phone
technology. We lose 2-0 and will not play at Wembley this season.

WEDNESDAY NOVEMBER 28TH

Robbie Keane has retired now. I saw him equalise for Ireland against
Germany in the World Cup in Japan, so thanks for that, if not for
the weird goal celebrations. Some snooker has started but it's not
televised, so does it make a sound?

Not feeling at my absolute best, I attempt a bit of under-19s Champions League, Spurs 2-4 Inter, an omen perhaps? I leave Liverpool
U-19s drawing 1-1 at half time and will probably never learn the
result or remember the opposition.

The actual Champions League gets going early doors, but I barely
watch as Monaco lose again. Then we're into the main event, Tottenham v Inter on the big TV, with The Boy in a Spurs onesie for the
first half. They desperately need a win here and Christian Eriksen
comes off the bench to score the only goal of the game.

Further north, I keep an eye on Stoke 2-1 Derby, a wet Wednesday night as some kind of war breaks out with players being either stretchered off or sent off. Astonishingly, Villa and Forest play out a 5-5 draw. I watch PSG win 2-1 on the phone.

Across all of the BT Sport coverage, they appear to be contractually obliged to talk about the forthcoming Wilder v Fury fight on pay-per-view. I don't fucking care, I'm trying to watch the football. The only thing more cringeworthy is when Sky plug some drama show at the end of a big match. I'm not interested in Martin Tyler's Game Of Thrones.

News breaks that Paul Pogba has been dropped for bringing his hairstylist to the club hotel.

THURSDAY NOVEMBER 29TH

With no television coverage, I am reduced to watching Ronnie on the Betfair app. An absolute disgrace, it should be a national holiday whenever Ronnie plays.

Joe Allen has insisted that a Derby player did not bite him last night. Strong. It's Europa League night, aka The Emmerdale Cup, but I can't get a grip on it, flicking between Arsenal and Celtic in a Kilburn sports hall. We get home for a bit of Chelsea, but it's cut short for The Walking Dead. Compromise, they call it. I'll watch the repeat later anyway.

Thursday Night Football sees New Orleans go to Dallas Cowboys. In the MLS, New York Red Bulls are taking on Atlanta, who are 3-0 up from the first leg. New York have a lifeline denied when a goal is disallowed by VAR for being headed out of the keeper's hands – shades of Andy Gray for Everton against Watford in the 1984 FA Cup final. New York finally score in the final minute of injury time for a 1-0 win. Fat use.

In the invisible snooker, Mark Selby is beaten by wet-lipped Blackpool amateur, James Cahill. And the Copa Libertadores final between Boca and River Plate has now been moved to Madrid on the 9th December, presumably to make it harder to attack the bus.

FRIDAY NOVEMBER 30TH

On a whim, I decide to drive to Manchester to see Half Man Half Biscuit followed by The Mighty Chester at home to Darlington the next day. It simply doesn't get any better. Sadly, the English motorway system is unfit for purpose and I run into trouble in Stoke, swerving down Stanley Matthews Way to save the day.

It's a triumphant gig, during which Nigel Blackwell tells an extended and improbable anecdote about Glyn Pardoe and a bag of shuttle-cocks. Research reveals Pardoe to be the youngest player ever to appear for Man City. His career was ended by Martin Buchan, according to my United-supporting associate. Blackwell also reveals that he wrote Swerving The Checkatrade about a Rochdale-supporting friend, as Tranmere weren't even in the competition at the time. I get back to my grief hole for a repeat of the Copa first leg on FreeSports. I also catch up with the first half of Solihull Moors v Blackpool in the FA Cup, a very harsh disallowed goal for the home team, offside from a short corner.

SATURDAY DECEMBER 1ST

I wake up in the grief hole and immediately watch the second half of Solihull Moors v Blackpool on my phone. It finishes goalless. The magic of the cup. Following a rudimentary breakfast, I drive past the halls of residence where I watched much of the 1990 World Cup, including Roger Milla's heroics for Cameroon, sat on my own in the TV room as he caught the Colombia keeper in possession near the halfway line, the keeper of course being René Higuita of scorpion kick fame. I was also in the bar to see England 1-0 Egypt thanks to a 58th-minute header from Mark Wright. Little did I know at the time that he would have three spells as Chester manager and that I would briefly interview him pitch-side at Woking. True story.

From there, I drive directly to Prestwich while listening to The Fall. I park up by a Mark E Smith mural on the side of a chippy and gaze at it in wonder, tinged with inevitable sadness. I interviewed him once and he explained at length about the time he read the classified results on Final Score. He also claimed that he used to know people who would occasionally forgo Man City to watch Chester in the Welsh Cup as there was more chance of trouble.

Hopefully there'll be none of that today at home to Darlington, although I remember a Darlo fan in the 80s once strolling round the home end asking people for a fight. Due to the former league status of both clubs, today has been branded Retro Day, with fans encouraged to dig out their old shirts. Coincidentally, my first ever game was Chester v Darlo so I am right behind it, unearthing a triumvirate of retro shirts, at least one of which no longer fits. On the pitch, we have a debutant striker, Akwasi Asante, who notches a perfect hat trick – header, left foot, right foot – in a rousing 3-1 win. Scenes. Allied to the triumphant Biscuit gig, objectively this is one of the best weekends of my life. Crisis, what crisis?

On the way back, at Hilton Park Services, I am quizzed as to whether my shirt is Argentina or Huddersfield. Incorrect. I head to Watford Gap to stay with my Watford-supporting associate known as The Watford Gap. In the pub, I keep an eye on Wrexham 0-0 Newport in the FA Cup. In an unprecedented move, Wrexham manager Sam Ricketts has been barred from attending due to his pending move to Shrewsbury. Back at the house, I have to endure College Football (of the American variety) until the sweet release of Match Of The Day.

SUNDAY DECEMBER 2ND

Writhing in my pit, I listen to a replay of the boxing, Tyson Fury against someone. Improbably, it ends in a draw, a 33/1 shot. I am furious that I didn't put everything I own on it. Then we're into the Euro 2020 qualifying draw – the usual suspects – after which I manage to sleep through Chelsea 2-0 Fulham.

I emerge downstairs in time for the North London Derby, making the considered decision to watch it here, with a side of snooker. It's the correct move, as Arsenal beat Spurs 4-2 in a thriller and Ronnie comes back from 4-1 down to level it at 5-5.

Straight in the car, I listen to Liverpool v Everton on the M1, already plunged into blackness. With the game still goalless, I get home, bypass the family and run upstairs to watch the injury time. Everton keeper Jordan Pickford makes a howler, allowing Divock Origi to grab a dramatic winner. Limbs, Klopp on the pitch, audible singing of "your support is fucking shit".

I catch up with the UK Championship where Ronnie has beaten Ken Doherty 6-5.

"Grinding Cliff Thorburn reincarnated", says the commentator.

"Well, he's not dead", he corrects himself.

In his post-match interview, Ronnie compares himself to both a gladiator and the SAS. Go on Ronnie.

I catch up with Ding v Selt on the iPlayer, but it unfathomably stops at 5-5, harking back to the good old days when television coverage would simply end at the allotted time regardless of the action, requiring you to come back at 6pm to see what happened.

I hit up BT Sport for a touch of Ligue 1 as Bordeaux become the first team not to lose to PSG, managing an honourable 2-2 draw at home, The Driver inevitably there, a mere 90-minute drive each way from his rural base.

This takes me into Match Of The Day, and news that a banana skin has been thrown from the Spurs end at Aubameyang. The good old days.

MONDAY DECEMBER 3RD

Southampton dismiss Mark Hughes, who bookends the year with yet another sacking. It is only a matter of time before Robbie Savage recommends 'Sparky' for another job, still in awe of the time the older pro gave the callow youth player a lift from Manchester United to Wrexham in his Porsche. Did he make a man of him in an isolated lay-by? There's absolutely no suggestion that's the case.

At 1pm, I watch Ronnie in bed (me not him). It's also the UEFA Nations League draw with the recently retired Robbie Keane. He claims that the best goal he ever scored was in 2002 against Germany in Japan, which I fortuitously saw with my own eyes. England will play The Netherlands.

On the way back from the school run, I pop in on Saints Dad. He's pleased that Hughes is gone, but says that if they appoint Allardyce he will stop supporting the club. Seven bells brings the FA Cup draw, the bright yellow graphics piercing a bleak winter evening. Local non-rivals Tranmere or Southport will host Tottenham Hotspur, adding extra spice to the replay.

This takes us into the second round match between Guiseley and Fleetwood, with Joey Barton's team winning 2-1, all the goals coming in a five-minute spell. Pity anyone who thought they'd have a quick piss before half time.

Simultaneously, I have a touch of West Brom v Brentford in the Championship, a late home goal cancelled out by an injury time equaliser for 1-1. Presumably, numerous berks left early to beat the mythical traffic. This takes me into double snooker and for no apparent reason I watch a bit of Levante 3-0 Bilbao on the bet365 app. This is a low.

Luka Modrić wins the Ballon d'Or, and some tit asks a female player if she's going to start twerking, thus earning the outrage of social media for his allotted fifteen minutes until something else happens.

TUESDAY DECEMBER 4TH

1pm, Trump v King. Judd Trump looking increasingly like Half Man Half Biscuit's Nigel Blackwell, as confirmed by the singer himself, having previously alluded to his similarity to Jaap Stam.

I pause the iPlayer at 4-2 to take care of some car business and get back for the decider between former world champions Neil Robertson and reedy-voiced Caledonian Graeme Dott, the blonde Antipodean nicking it 6-5.

I then have to head to South East London for my annual appearance as a guest on the Scummy Mummies Christmas podcast. I watch a bit of Watford v Man City on my phone during the preamble, planning to catch up with it later. Sadly, the man of the house, an extremely casual Man City fan, casually informs me that they scraped it 2-1. In an attempt to calm down, I watch the snooker on their enormous television. At least I was successful in swerving the Checkatrade.

WEDNESDAY DECEMBER 5TH

Enjoying a restorative bacon sandwich outside a café at Forest Hill station, the generous wi-fi enables me to watch Ronnie O'Sullivan playing snooker on my phone. What a time to be alive. This privilege even continues on a Southeastern train, sat in a snooker bubble as the world goes by.

I get home for Williams v Maguire, which goes 4-0 then 4-5 then 5-5 as the school run looms, forcing me to record the deciding frame. I get back to watch Maguire clinch it, then catch up with last night's Premier League action, Watford unlucky not to get anything from the game.

Excitingly, there's a full set of midweek fixtures in the Premier League, with BT Sport showing Manchester United v Arsenal, former title contenders reduced to also-rans in a regional power shift. It's a decent 2-2 draw, marred only by an incongruous half-time interview with Tyson Fury. Meanwhile, the snooker continues on the laptop.

It's the first midweek Match Of The Day of the season, an impossibly illicit thrill. And for the first time in eight years – stats fans – every team scores a goal.

The snooker cannot be stopped, with Allen 6-5 Robertson then Ford 6-5 Lu taking us past midnight, the natural hour for these pallid vampires of the baize. The action in York overlaps with the first test in Adelaide as Australia take on India, two hefty cricketing powers by any metric. Australia tear into the tourists, taking four early wickets. And that's lunch. I find an Australian radio station and listen in bed.

THURSDAY DECEMBER 6TH

The Boy is claiming an earache. Pleading at my bedside, I give him the nod. It's difficult to prove, but fuck it, have a day off. On the plus side, this means the snooker is not interrupted for the godforsaken school run.

Between sessions we watch an episode of The Simpsons in which Homer watches baseball sober, finally realising how boring it is. He's right. I'm glad it's out of my life. I can't even remember who won the World Series. I might give it a miss next year, although The Watford Gap has procured tickets for Red Sox v Yankees in the MLB at the London Stadium next June (he'll probably pull out with a cricketing injury). That's who won it, the Red Sox. Playing a regular league game in another country is an abomination of a fixture for supporters, although unless they're on The Card I guess they can miss one out of a minimum of 162 games. What a sport.

I watch a bit of Trump in the bath, Judd not Donald. Gambling firms have agreed a voluntary ban on gambling adverts during live televised sport, thus dealing a huge blow to Ray Winstone's wallet: "Get on it!"

Trump and Ding are both heading out of York, presumably in a better state than my low-key exit last month. This leads into a solid evening of double snooker, with a bit of unscheduled Torino 2-0 Südtirol in the Coppa Italia on BT Sport.

RIP Pete Shelley of Buzzcocks.

What do I get? NFL's Thursday Night Football segues into Australia v India. Having smugly tracked down an Australian radio station, embarrassingly I realise it's on 5live Sports Extra anyway. Turn on, tune in, drift off.

FRIDAY DECEMBER 7TH

With the weekend almost upon us, I catch up with last week's EFL On Quest, an absolute boon to the schedules, with a very prompt catch-up service. Meanwhile, Ronnie kicks off with a century, moaning to the ref about something. Go on Ronnie.

The weekend starts here, and we're off to Staverton Hall, home of Her Indoors' brother. We manage to squeeze in the beginning and end of West Brom 2-2 Villa. The rural broadband makes it tricky to see Rodriguez's injury-time handball equaliser for West Brom, but the ref should probably have spotted it.

I order the nephew to make snooker come on the television, before retiring to bed for Australia v India.

SATURDAY DECEMBER 8TH

Birthday weekend. It's the big one, Stockport away. As has become tradition, all I want for my birthday is a slap-up corporate feed wherever The Mighty Chester are playing, followed by the obligatory three points. This means an early start, and we find ourselves traversing the Peak District at a ludicrous hour, majestic in its bleakness.

Rocking up at Edgeley Park at the allotted time, we bump into a gaggle of Chester associates, fresh from a heart-starter in a local pub. They have an adjacent table, and one of them generously sends over a bottle of Moët to mark the occasion. As we're a mere 17 days away from the 25th, it is of course a Christmas lunch, the curse of the Decemberist's birthday. I do at least get a cake, accompanied by a rousing chorus of Happy Birthday from the Chester table.

More excitingly, I spot Paul Wheeler, former Stockport and Chester striker, who I once saw score a hat trick at Mansfield. Getting him to sign my programme, I remind him of this historic feat and pleasingly he tells me he still has the match ball.

We're in the director's box, but there's a decent atmosphere from the 700 travelling fans. It should have been more, but the brain-dead fuckers of Greater Manchester Police put dozens of innocent supporters back on a train for no apparent reason. We take the lead through Asante, but Stockport equalise with a penalty. They then commit virtually the exact same offence and are not penalised, adding to the theory that home advantage simply means the ref doesn't give anything to the away team. It finishes 1-1 and we have a chat with joint managers Bernard and Jonno in the bar. I give them each a copy of The Card, signed to Effing and Jeffing – you decide.

We pick up a Chinese in Daventry and wolf it down with The Watford Gap and wife in a muted birthday celebration. I make the nephew fast forward Match Of The Day through the analysis and retire to bed. The blackness comes swiftly. Take a point, move on.

SUNDAY DECEMBER 9TH

I catch up with the snooker semi while the final is on, a high-risk strategy. Allen beats Bingham 6-5 and is already playing Ronnie in the final. Go on Ronnie. Into the final, Stephen Hendry calls Ronnie "Benjamin Button" in that he seems to be getting better as he gets older.

As I watch the snooker, various adults and children are in the kitchen pissing about with some spurious online personality test. Her Indoors interrupts the snooker to quiz me, with the answers revealing that I am a logician. No shit. We leave Ronnie 6-2 up and get in the car for the 4pm kickoff, Newcastle v Wolves. In order to add to the excitement, we pick a result each. The Boy goes for a home win, Her Indoors has away win and I take the draw. The fun simply never stops.

Predictably, they're both drooling within minutes as the baton passes from me to her and back to me. We get back in time to see Wolves grab a 94th-minute winner, with injury-time goals seemingly becoming more frequent by the day. Never leave early.

Ronnie beats Allen 9-6 to lift his seventh UK Championship. Go on Ronnie. I split the snooker final with the MLS final, Atlanta 2-0 Portland. This relegates the Copa Libertadores to my phone, River finally beating Boca 3-1 after extra time in the Bernabéu. Some game, I regret not giving it more attention.

The NFL cannot be stopped, with two games going to over-time. Can't they just call it a draw? Take a point, move on.

Australia clinging on against India now.

MONDAY DECEMBER 10TH

Snooker's Scottish Open begins. Sake. India win a twitch-up against Australia. Ronnie withdraws from the Scottish Open.

On Monday Night Football, it's Everton v Watford and it's live on Sky. It finishes 2-2, a 96th-minute equaliser now for Everton. They should just go straight to injury time. Watford deserve all they get for turning up in a shit green kit despite their traditional strip having no colour clash whatsoever. Pathetic. In a well-ordered society they would be docked three points.

I watch Bullseye in bed as my life ticks over.

TUESDAY DECEMBER 11TH

Actual birthday. Solid knock, bat in the air. No mess, no fuss, a local pub for a gaggle of friends, old and new. Sport never sleeps, and it's the final group games in the Champions League, both Spurs and Liverpool in danger of going out. Despite being within visible distance of Tottenham's temporary home, when the booking was made the pub staff made it clear from the outset that they would only be showing the Liverpool game. This suits us, as there are no Spurs fans and two Liverpool fans in our group, both from London of course. Elsewhere, Ipswich, Crystal Palace, Chelsea, Manchester United and Southampton are represented.

The match is shown on a variety of screens at ear-splitting volume. There's even an entire section of the pub populated exclusively by middle-aged Liverpool fans in full replica kits; scarves, flags, pissing down rolled-up programmes into each other's pockets. A taste of The Kop in North West London.

Following a sketchy campaign, Liverpool need to beat Napoli to progress. Spurs meanwhile have to get something at Barcelona and hope that Inter fail to beat PSV. My local barber has backed them at 66-1 to win the tournament, which seems ungenerous.

Liverpool take the lead through Salah, which raises the volume. The Evertonian turns up with a Dukla Prague away kit for me, an extremely generous gesture. I keep an eye on the Camp Nou on my phone, where Spurs are soon behind, a dismal European campaign surely ending in ignominy.

Alisson makes a late save to keep Liverpool in the tournament. Meanwhile, Spurs have miraculously equalised and PSV are somehow beating Inter. Final whistles all round, both English teams have squeaked through. It's a birthday miracle.

A select group decamp to the after-party at Chelsea Dad's Rave Shed. Shades of the World Cup.

WEDNESDAY DECEMBER 12TH

Foolishly I have agreed to drive comedy duo The Scummy Mummies to Cambridge as part of their Christmas tour. It's a sport vacuum, with the radio given over to Magic FM – all Christmas songs, all through December. Fuck Christmas.

I think it might be the first time I've been to Cambridge for non-football or Biscuit reasons. We're at the Cambridge Junction and at the urinal there's an advert for Half Man's gig next year. I take a photo of it and send it to The Watford Gap. On the way to a curry house after the show, I catch a tantalising glimpse of green on a distant screen through a pub window, something that matters to someone somewhere.

THURSDAY DECEMBER 13TH

The World Darts Championship has started and I'm stuck in a Premier Inn in Winchester, the second leg of this brief comedy jaunt. Christmas is the darts. The darts is Christmas. Imagine Christmas without the darts. You can't.

In the snooker it's Ding 4-3 Zhao, Ronnie on commentary despite pulling out of the tournament, a baffling set of priorities. While he's there, he may as well pot a ball or two. Go on Ronnie. I sleep through the cricket.

FRIDAY DECEMBER 14TH

Somehow I am still unaware of the last two days of football scores, and get back home for snooker and darts. It's the most wonderful time of the year, the darts stretching out between here and New Year, a crucial salve amid the Christmas madness. I'd happily watch every dart. However, there are teething problems when Ally Pally is briefly plunged into darkness. "Oi oi, stick 50p in the meter", somebody will inevitably shout.

In a crucial Championship match, West Brom win 2-1 at Sheffield United. Back at the darts, light has been restored and Gary Anderson makes it through, no farting reported. Starved of football, I have a little look at Livingston 5-0 Hearts. I don't even know where that is.

SATURDAY DECEMBER 15TH

Cricket in Australia is interrupted by football in Regent's Park as Shady Sharks take on Eagles United in bitterly cold conditions. The little shits cruise to a 5-0 lead before being pegged back to 5-3, then 6-3, 7-3, finally winning 7-4. Scenes.

Back in the warmth of home, I accidentally watch a bit of some hockey semi-final in which England lose 6-0 to Belgium. Garbage. Normal order is restored in the 12:30pm Sky kickoff as Manchester City beat Everton 3-1 with a side of darts and snooker.

There's no Chester match, so we listen to the last knocking of Spurs v Burnley on 5live in the kitchen, the Wembley arch a beacon in the distance. Approaching a goalless conclusion, Spurs relentlessly attack, but the visitors heroically hold firm. Injury time arrives, and we all know what happens in injury time, although you never really believe it will. Bang! Eriksen 1-0, 91st minute. Barking all round, The Boy tossed in the air, some poor saps inevitably hearing a roar from Wembley Way as they beat the rush. What a great memory they'll have of getting home slightly earlier than they otherwise might have.

In the snooker, Mark Allen – by his own admission, demonstrably hungover – comes back from 5-2 down to beat Daniel Wells 6-5. In between matches, Jimmy White talks us through his pre-match drinking strategy when he was at his prime. What a sport.

I head to a Christmas party at the home of a local Palace fan, meaning that I miss Match Of The Day. Fuck Christmas. I receive a text saying "a dark day for darts".

SUNDAY DECEMBER 16TH

As foolishly arranged, I get a train to South East London then drive a pair of crazed women to Bath in torrential rain. I am missing a genuine Super Sunday and break the news that I will be listening to the live commentary instead. This starts with Saints v Arsenal, an absolute thriller as the new manager, played by David Morrissey, secures a 3-2 victory, the clowns in the back of the car oblivious as to who's playing or what's happening.

Then we're into the big one, Liverpool v Man United, sadly interrupted at 1-1 by arriving at our destination. Mid-sentence with one of the gig organisers, I spot it on a pub TV and immediately dart in, 83 minutes on the clock, Liverpool 3-1 up now. 36 shots to 6 confirms an infographic, something I repeat out loud to nobody in particular. Mourinho surely hanging by a thread now.

Following the obligatory post-gig curry, I flick through the massive TV in the luxury hotel, which unusually has a full Sky Sports package. What a waste, the time I could have had if we'd got here earlier. Still oblivious to some of the results, I plough through individual half-hour Premier League highlights, with a touch of Australia v India in my ears. I awake at 5am: Wolves 2-0 Bournemouth.

MONDAY DECEMBER 17TH

I inflict talkSPORT on my passengers, some gibberish debate about Man City's Gabriel Jesus moving his mum in with him. It's too embarrassing to listen to in public and I switch off before the European draws, saving that minor thrill for later.

I get home for a darts catch-up, including a tearful MvG after having a pint thrown on him prior to his walk-on. A dark day for darts, indeed.

The FA Cup continues apace and I watch the replay between Southport and Tranmere on my phone. It's a bloodless 2-0 win for Rovers and Spurs will go to Prenton Park in the next round. Meanwhile, Derby grind out a goalless draw with Forest in what is probably called the Brian Clough derby. I sat near him at Burton Albion away once, and he gave me a dirty look. True story.

I flick between the football and a full live session of darts. Anastasia is thrashed by debutant Ryan Joyce, and Barney is shamefully beaten by Darius Labanauskas, woeful finishing all round. It's almost the end of an era for one of the greats. I saw him beat Taylor at the Tavern, and interviewed him once, an absolute gentleman and a close personal friend.

I catch up with yesterday's snooker, where Mark Allen has drunk his way to the Scottish Open title. I still haven't caught up with Match Of The Day. And mercifully I've missed the whole of Sports Personality Of The Year. No interest unless it's Ronnie.

TUESDAY DECEMBER 18TH

Something is afoot on Twitter. I hit the BBC Sport app for confirmation: Mourinho gone. A week before Christmas, it's an early gift for Manchester United supporters.

The relentless Christmas music continues as I drive a brace of idiots to The Stables theatre near Milton Keynes. I once saw Ian McCulloch do a solo show here. Big rednose. Tonight, I stay in the green room and use the excellent wi-fi to watch the FA Cup replay between Blackpool and Solihull Moors on my phone. It's an absolute ding-dong-do as the non-league team claw back an early two-goal deficit to take it to extra time, finally vanquished by a dodgy penalty. The magic of the cup.

I drop off two women at a golf resort in Hertfordshire in the early hours. I then drive home for a darts repeat plus highlights of Leicester 1-1 Man City in the Carabao Cup, followed by an appalling penalty shootout in which the Manchester team finally prevails.

WEDNESDAY DECEMBER 19TH

Solskjær is in at United as caretaker. Nobody expected that. Mourinho leaves Manchester's Lowry Hotel with the Corby trouser press unused. I watch a darts repeat in the bath then attend The Boy's Christmas concert, the reason I've had to curtail the tour. Fuck Christmas.

I head back to Hertfordshire and reconvene with The Scummy Mummies at Hanbury Manor, scene of Gazza's wedding to Sheryl. I drive them to Hertford and spend the bulk of their show in the White Hart pub so I can watch Arsenal v Spurs in the Carabao Cup. It is populated almost exclusively by Tottenham fans – the clue is in the name – who spend much of the game openly singing about "yiddos".

Son gives them an early lead and I nip out at half time to perform a menial task. Returning with ten minutes left, Spurs are now 2-0 up thanks to a deft lob/dink from Dele Alli, and that's how it ends. Sitting in a Skoda Yeti outside a provincial theatre, I receive confirmation of the semi-final draw from talkSPORT. Manchester City will play Burton Albion and Tottenham Hotspur will play Chelsea.

I finally get home to resume the same darts match I abandoned earlier in the day, plus Carabao Cup highlights, Dele Alli hit by a plastic bottle.

THURSDAY DECEMBER 20TH

A darts catch-up in the bath features a bizarre rant by James Wade following his aggressive physical intimidation of bemused opponent, Seigo Asada of Japan. After securing a narrow victory, Wade told Sky Sports, "I wanted to hurt him, I wanted to really hurt him in his face. That's for my son and also for the UK."

I go live to see Wade apologising profusely for his conduct, blaming the incident on an episode of hypomania, whatever that is. Elsewhere, Chuck Norris goes through on sudden death, and The Adonis is in action. Remember, he's not A-donis, he's THE-donis.

Sadly, I am wrenched away from the screen for a Christmas drink with a group of Liverpool fans known as Commodores, as in 'once, twice, three times a season'. They spend much of the evening forensically analysing the team and planning a trip to Bayern Munich. Nearby, a street vendor is peddling Premier League tat, the usual suspects now including Manchester City, whose traditional fanbase is beginning to shift.

I get home to see Mensur Suljović defeated, The Gentle gone before Christmas.

FRIDAY DECEMBER 21ST

Darts, darts, darts. It's what Christmas was made for. Big John Henderson through now. I briefly nip out to a nearby party, but return for West v North, the compass derby.

The arrows are complemented by Wolves 0-2 Liverpool, but the real action is to be had at Ally Pally. The hugely unpopular Gerwyn Price has a dart for 3-0, misses it and somehow conspires to lose against the unfancied Nathan Aspinall, aka The Asp. The hostile crowd can clearly be heard gleefully singing, "two nil, and you fucked it up!". The commentator describes it as "the night of the long tungsten". As for Price, he skulks off, incandescent with rage. He doesn't like it up him.

I finally catch up with Match Of The Day, Match Of The Day 2 and EFL On Quest. Phew.

SATURDAY DECEMBER 22ND

I forgo the Melbourne derby for the Shady Sharks and am rewarded by a 1-0 win and a 0-0 draw. I get back to see Melbourne City equalise for 1-1. Come on Victory.

We all pile into the car and listen to Arsenal 3-1 Burnley on the way to Bournemouth for an early Christmas lunch. I keep an eye on the darts under the table, SuperChin gone now.

Chester come from behind to beat Telford 2-1 in my headphones, but it's almost overshadowed by Crystal Palace winning 3-2 at Manchester City, including surely the goal of the season from Andros Townsend, an absurd volley. The 17:30 kickoff sees Solskjær take his new club to his old club and ends Cardiff 1-5 Manchester United.

Back at the palace, Gary Anderson survives a match dart at bullseye and MvG also goes through, putting Beergate behind him. I watch Match Of The Day with The Boy, who wisely takes himself to bed before Newcastle 0-0 Fulham.

SUNDAY DECEMBER 23RD

Back at my old dear's, I mainly concentrate on the darts. There are two Norwich-supporting kids present and one of them watches the entirety of Villa v Leeds on his phone, a crucial game at the top of the Championship. Villa go 2-0 up, to much jubilation, but somehow conspire to lose 3-2 to the obligatory 95th-minute goal, Leeds thus leapfrogging Norwich and going top of the league. Scenes.

We attempt to leave, but Everton v Spurs is an absolute ding-dong-do and I can't tear myself away from it. It eventually finishes 6-2 to Spurs, an absolutely freak result. The final whistle signals our departure and at Burley Services on the A31, we spot a man in a Spurs shirt, presumably elated.

I floor it to get back for the darts, but miss the first game. Stockport's rising star Nathan Aspinall goes through, as does World Champion Rob Cross, and the whole thing is temporarily put back in its box for Christmas.

On Match Of The Day 2, Spurs manager Pochettino dedicates the 2-6 victory to his wife on their 26th anniversary. It is of course a coincidence. Sport is closing down for Christmas, although the NFL seems to be playing round the clock.

MONDAY DECEMBER 24TH

Keith Deller's birthday.

TUESDAY DECEMBER 25TH

I've said it before and I'll say it again. If you watch sport, every day is Christmas Day except for Christmas Day itself, which is garbage because there's no sport to watch. Despite living in London for over two decades, this is the first time we've been here for the big day. Saints Dad and family take pity on us, inviting us for lunch. Also present are his parents, and his dad explains how for geographical reasons he has variously supported Ilkeston, Derby, Leicester, Southampton, Forest Green and Cheltenham. He also relates the tale of his son missing Southampton's winning goal in the 1976 FA Cup final as he had to go for the piss he had been holding in for the entire day.

In some pain, I listen to Australia v India in bed.

WEDNESDAY DECEMBER 26TH

Now that shit's out of the way, the real action resumes with a swathe of sporting events, kicking off with a bit of early A-League from down under. There's a touch of Fulham 1-1 Wolves on Sky One, and I split Final Score with Sheffield United 3-1 Derby, plus commentary of Southport 3-0 Chester, our traditional post-Christmas slump beginning in earnest.

The big story of the day isn't televised, Leicester 2-1 Man City, the latter's title defence on the ropes. The feast of live football continues with Brighton 1-1 Arsenal then Watford 1-2 Chelsea overlapping into EFL On Quest, Match Of The Day, in bed for cricket. This life.

THURSDAY DECEMBER 27TH

I wake up to talkSPORT, where Alan Brazil and Dean Saunders are deriding Stuart Pearce for holidaying in North Korea. Saunders presents the fact that Pearce likes punk rock as somehow deviant. Like a confused uncle, Brazil mentions something about "pogoing to Johnny and the Maulers", but then admits that he doesn't mind The Stranglers, who Pearce claims to have seen one or two hundred times. However, the puce-faced former Ipswich striker says he has no time for current punk pretenders, Idles. Glad that's sorted out.

At 12:30pm, I start betting on the darts, on my feet barking for the sake of a couple of quid, the nature of the sport making it a financial rollercoaster. In a rare trip into the outside world, I raid the spartan shelves of Sainsbury's and get back for the 7pm session plus Southampton 1-2 West Ham, which marks the halfway point of the Premier League season.

At the palace, Gary Anderson takes on Chris Dobey in an absolute thriller, only missing Sid to ratchet the tension further. It's so close that I watch some of it through one eye, Anderson eventually prevailing 4-3.

MvG takes on Adrian Lewis, a man who seems permanently surprised to be playing in a World Championship darts match live on television. My future close personal friend Bob Mortimer tweets, "Come on Adrian, you soft dozy bastard", but it's to no avail. He throws a few 180s but not much else and the Stoke Slinger is rolled over 4-1.

And so to bed to tour the world of cricket on 5live Sports Extra.

FRIDAY DECEMBER 28TH

We're in no man's land, but I maintain a semblance of normality by watching darts in the bath. Aspinall beats Devon Petersen in a tiebreak and I take the next match in the garden, a minor benefit of global warming in the handful of decades before the end of human civilisation as we know it.

Wade has match darts, but is beaten by debutant Joyce. At least he doesn't threaten anyone's face. It is rapidly becoming the year of the underdog, although Dave 'Chizzy' Chisnall makes it through. Now a fixture on the circuit, it's a far cry from his early years in the BDO when his parents' car once broke down on the way to watch him at Lakeside.

Despite being 2-0 up, Rob Cross mouths "rubbish" as he leaves the stage, a stage he has never lost on. Until now, as little-known Luke Humphries rattles off the next four sets to end his reign.

"The World Champ gracious in defeat", observes Wayne Mardle.

Southgate and Kane on the honours list.

SATURDAY DECEMBER 29TH

I go west, to Hereford, via Cheltenham, where I pick up my older brother. We have a pint in the Ronnie Radford Bar then watch Chester get comfortably beaten 2-0 in a dismal game, the stadium scarcely changed since Radford hit arguably the most famous FA Cup goal. It wasn't even the winner; remember Ricky George?

Back in the car for the classified results, old-school style, a fellow fan of my acquaintance points out that, "it wouldn't be Chester if it wasn't shit".

The commentary game is Liverpool v Arsenal, with the Gunners having the temerity to take the lead, the first visiting team to do so at Anfield in a year. It's a big mistake as Liverpool reply by leathering in five without reply including a Firmino hat-trick. We get back to Cheltenham to watch the second half on my phone, with the darts on talkSPORT2 and then YouTube.

We spend the evening at a listening party for The Doors' eponymous first album on vinyl, which I then win in a quiz while keeping an eye on Match Of The Day on my phone. Spending the night on a floor, I find a darts repeat on sketchy wi-fi. We have our semi-finalists.

SUNDAY DECEMBER 30TH

TalkSPORT are straight into the Arsenal post-mortem, Aubameyang with five touches apparently. Wi-fi restored, I grab the last ten minutes of Barrow 3-2 Salford in the National League. We then hit 'Spoons for a late breakfast and I keep an eye on the goalless first half of Palace v Chelsea. I take the second half in the car – a dismal 1-0 win for Chelsea – as I head home, refuelling in the same petrol station where I heard Alastair Cook's last stand in the summer. I get home for the second half of Southampton 1-3 Man City, then fall asleep as a Pogba-inspired Man United roll over Bournemouth 4-1.

At the palace, Michael Smith beats Aspinall in a thriller and MvG brutally dismantles Anderson to set up the final.

This takes me into the last Match Of The Day 2 of a momentous year. Can't face the NFL.

MONDAY DECEMBER 31ST

As tradition dictates, we yet again spend New Year's Eve at Watford Gap with the same people. As midnight breaks, The Watford Gap excitedly proclaims 2019 to be World Cup year. He's clearly confused, we've just had World Cup year, and splendid it was. Does he mean the Women's World Cup? Guaranteed a semi at least. Apparently, he's banging on about the Cricket World Cup. I'll take it, by which I mean I'll watch almost every match. Some day you will find me, caught beneath the landslide, in a champagne super over live on Sky.

But I suppose I'd better call it a year.

Early start tomorrow, at home to Southport, bound to be goals.

Back for the darts final.

We go again.

When the fun stops, stop.

ACKNOWLEDGEMENTS

Her Indoors for once shrieking,
"You live your life behind a wall of sport!"

The Boy for his patience and words of wisdom.

John Logie Baird for television, mankind's greatest achievement.

Tim Berners-Lee for the internet; it'll never catch on.

Steve Jobs for the iPad, and for making it splash-proof.

Steve Davis for generously giving his time,
and being an absolute legend.

The Watford Gap for letting me ponce his Sky Go account.

Amazon for flogging me a projector so I can now
literally watch a wall of sport.